Dr Marijcke Jongbloed  as a medical doctor, w and champion of wildli written extensively on the United Arab Emirat the environment in the UAE was recognised with civil honours in both the UAE and Holland. She now lives in France.

FAT LEGS DON'T MATTER

'My animals, my life'

MARIJCKE JONGBLOED

Sponsored by

TALENT CAPITAL
Empowering Potential

MOSAIQUEPRESS

Published by
MOSAÏQUE PRESS
Registered office:
70 Priory Road
Kenilworth, Warwickshire CV8 1LQ
www.mosaïquepress.co.uk

Printed in the UK

ISBN 978-1-906852-14-6

When something as magical as this happens between man and animal, Native Americans say, 'We have walked together in the shadow of a rainbow.'

– *Tom Sears*

CONTENTS

FOREWORD

This is a story about conservation, well before it became such an attractive theme.

Instant friends upon meeting more than fifteen years ago, Marijcke and I travelled together on several occasions. Amongst other things she organised art exhibitions to fund raise for the Arabian Leopard Trust.

In this strange world of different values there were times when I watched her serenely accepting impossible frustrations when others would have been moved to anger.

Looking back now, remembering the disbelieving attitude of those around her and the present proof of thirty-three young leopard cubs in a well-established Breeding Centre, I can only smile.

Many people talk about conservation but what counts is translating vague thoughts into concrete actions.

Books, bartering and even battles are all fair means to protect this fragile planet. Here is an example.

Spencer Hodge
15 March 2010

ACKNOWLEDGEMENTS

I took my time writing the stories for this book. The story about Adrian, the dog who smelled like alyssum, was the first, written shortly after his death in 1999. At first I wanted the book to be only a tribute to the animals, but friends who read the stories encouraged me to add more information about life in the Emirates and the events that made the years there so interesting. I want to thank those friends for their help: my writing partner PK Allen, my neighbour Lyn Hicks, my friend Jenny Copius-Peereboom, and last but not least Heidi Struiksma, who also has offered sponsorship to make this book a reality.

Of course my life would never have been so full and interesting without my friends in the Emirates, too many to mention all by name – above all the two men of that period that helped so much with the care of the animals: my partner of some years, Claus Müller, and my houseman Nambi Masanakomar. I would never have been able to enjoy my animal household so much without them. And although we drifted apart, I want to acknowledge Christian Gross, who was a wonderful friend and partner in many adventures. His role in creating and developing the breeding centre and the zoo cannot be appreciated enough.

I also thank Spencer Hodge for writing the foreword for this book. His paintings of the big cats are the most beautiful I have ever seen. We share a passion for those wonderful animals. I was very excited when he made a painting of the Arabian leopard, which featured on UAE stamps and telephone cards, thereby raising public awareness of that rare desert cat.

Wendy Scarborow gave me permission to use her lovely leopard drawing for the front cover of this book. Thank you, Wendy!

Chuck Grieve, publisher of my previous memoir, *Morning Comes and Also the Night*, offered to publish the re-issue of this book so that we could get back into print after the first publisher went into liquidation. I am grateful that he took on this task and helped me to keep the book available.

To Amal and Heidi I owe thanks for their financial support for this book. May they prosper in the years to come.

But above all I am grateful for having known at close quarters the animals that trusted me and gave me their love. They enriched my life and made it worth while. As James Herriot said: "It was the greatest good fortune not only to be fascinated by animals, but to know about them."

1

A LONG JOURNEY

As we entered the courtyard, my heart was beating fast with excitement. He was here, rescued, saved from the torture he had suffered for so long. I would be able to look him straight into the eyes and say: 'I kept my promise!'

He was sitting on top of the night box in the custom-built cage in a corner of the large courtyard, looking very relaxed. My friend Gerard softly called: 'Arnold!' and he jumped down and came to the wire of the cage. He rubbed his flank against the wire and rolled on his back, exposing his vulnerable underside. His paw rested against the wire and when Gerard started to tickle the pads underneath his foot, he growled softly, a sound of utter contentment. What a difference from the last time I had seen him, when he was lying curled up in the middle of a small low cage trying to get as far away as he could from the rowdy crowd that taunted him.

I thought of him by his official name "Nimrod Felix" – the happy hunter. The Arabic word for leopard is *nimr* and the *felix* indicated he came from Arabia Felix, the other name for Yemen. But Arnold was the nickname that Gerard had come up with when he first saw him, because he was reminded of the Arnold of Austrian-American fame.

Not that this Arnold was physically impressive. For a leopard he was very small. Even for an Arabian leopard, usually half the size of an African one, he was small. He had had a bad start in life. The cage in which he had spent the first year of his life was only a metre high, a metre wide and two metres long. Even the larger cage in which I had seen him a year later had not been spacious enough to escape the cruel prods of the sharp rod, with which his keeper tried to make him roar. After all, people had paid money to see him and wanted to hear him too. His tail had fractures in two or three places where it had been pulled hard to make him vicious. Nearby, the desiccated head of another leopard had been stuck on a high pole, with a sign underneath that said: "The female had to be killed because she was so dangerous. Please pay some money because it is very expensive to feed him."

The remains of what he had been fed in his entire life littered the floor of the cage. It had never been cleaned. Flies and maggots crawled all over the place. The leopard's eyes were inflamed and teary where the flies had infected them. The wire floor of the cage had no cover so that the metal cut into the leopard's feet whenever he moved. No wonder he curled up tightly, covered his face with his tail and retreated from the world. This is how I had first seen him in a small courtyard behind the Queen of Sheba hotel in Sana'a in Yemen, over a year before. It was then that I made my promise to get him out, no matter how difficult it would be.

Now he was here and it was amazing to see how just a few days of tranquillity and affection had restored the trust and good nature of this wild animal.

The story that led to the beginning of the Arabian Leopard Breeding programme in the United Arab Emirates started ten years earlier in the oasis city of Al Ain. I had chosen an expatriate life as an antidote against the bad weather and over-population of my home country, Holland, where I had a practice as a general practitioner in Amsterdam.

I had always been intrigued by the desert. I had never been in a sandy desert and longed to see the sculpted contours of a high sand dune and the green promise of a palm oasis in the middle of the wilderness. There would be the immense silence that had impressed me when I had visited a rocky desert elsewhere. It had satisfied a great need in my heart. I imagined that life, reduced to its bare minimum, would have more purity, more truth in a place like that. It would be hot, but having been born and raised in the tropics, I thought I could cope with that. When an opportunity presented itself to work in an Arabian hospital, I took it eagerly.

So I started the long journey from Europe to Arabia, and from medicine to natural history.

2

STARTING OVER

We were almost late getting to the airport. My father, who took me there, was so nervous about the impending farewell that he got lost in the streets of Amsterdam – a city he had known from childhood. Even though I had travelled many times before, this trip affected him more, as I was leaving to start a new life in the Middle East.

The young woman behind the KLM desk stretched out an impatient hand for my ticket and passport.

'Here, pap' I said to my father, 'please hold the cat.' Still rattled from our errant navigation of Amsterdam, he took the cat basket and perched it precariously on top of the suitcases. The basket was an almost round, hardtop affair, built to protect its feline cargo from G-force shocks. Without corners, it would roll – which is exactly what it did when pappie forgot to hold onto it as he turned to welcome my friends Ida and Chris, who had come to see me off. It toppled from the pile and rolled – quite a way in fact, with four of us in pursuit – before coming to a stop upside down. The cat suffered in silence but when we picked up the basket it became apparent that her fear had found another outlet. You could see nostrils twitching and foreheads furrowing on the normally implacable Schiphol travellers as they gave us a wide berth.

As I was still busy with the check-in, Chris said: 'You have enough to worry about. I'll handle this.'

Ida, his girlfriend, went along to hold the cat while Chris mopped up the noisome mess. Better friends one cannot ask for!

The cat, aptly named Catastrophe, was allowed to travel in the cabin with me. During the first take-off, she sat on my lap and anxiously gripped my wrist with her teeth, just enough to register her anxiety but not break the skin. After a few minutes she relaxed and settled down comfortably. In the row in front of me sat a lady with a small dog on her lap. The animals acknowledged each other with some interested glances, but that was all. It was 1983 – bad things on airplanes had not happened yet and business class passengers still had privileges, as did their pets. During the second take-off in Vienna Catastrophe was eating *paté-de-foie-gras* as if she were a seasoned traveller.

It was late at night when we arrived in Dubai, where I would be picked up by a representative of Whittaker, the American company I was going to work for. A visa document was waiting for me at a special desk. However, when I presented it at the passport checking counter, we ran into difficulties. The Whittaker administrators had got my nationality wrong on the visa request, mixing up my birth country (Indonesia) and nationality (Dutch). The passport officials determined that my passport was not Indonesian and I could not be permitted to enter. Fortunately the Whittaker representative was present at the airport and he was soon contacted. It took him the better part of two hours to organise a temporary visa. Finally we were allowed through. The hotel where we would be spending whatever little was left of the night was immediately across from the airport.

As soon as I reached my room, I let the cat out of her box and took the ready-to-use litter from my suitcase. By this time it was 11 hours since Catastrophe's accident at Schiphol airport. She had been a model of good behaviour throughout the flight. Now her relief was palpable. As Catastrophe scratched in the litter box, I stretched out on the bed hoping to get a few hours of sleep before morning when we were to travel by bus to our final destination. Alas, it was not to be. Catastrophe, who had been silent throughout the long day, started to meow as she explored the room. She meowed at the ragged carpet. She meowed from under the coffee table. She stood meowing at the door. She kept it up all night, and then through breakfast. .

'She's been quiet up to now,' I explained to no-one in particular. A couple of young Indians stopped to look in the cage. 'Pretty cat,' said one. Pretty or not, she was still meowing when we boarded the bus that was taking all the new arrivals to our destination, the desert city of Al Ain. Then she meowed for the next two hours of our trip.

I do not remember much of this trip except being tense with embarrassment. I could tell I was surrounded by a growing body of ex-cat lovers. So I watched the landscape with grim determination. Low sand dunes undulated into the distance on both sides of the road. Tufts of sedge and round saltbushes grew in profusion in the shallow valleys. Here and there stunted trees stood, widely apart. Some goats and camels were taking advantage of what little shade they cast. 'It is much greener than I had imagined a desert to be,' was all I could think. By the time we reached the hospital where we were going to work, my fellow passengers were thoroughly fed up with the cat's meows. We still had to sit through an hour of welcoming lectures and instruction, with Catastrophe keeping up her concert in the back of the room.

When I finally was dropped at the apartment that had been allotted to me, it turned out that the central air-conditioning was not working. Since it was the end of May, the temperature outside was close to 40°C and it was hot and stuffy inside. I was frazzled with lack of sleep, concern about the cat, embarrassment by her behaviour and now this heat! Catastrophe meowed some more. By this time her voice was getting quite hoarse. I put on all the fans and opened the fridge to get a cold drink. Catastrophe immediately jumped into the fridge and settled down on the vegetable shelf. Finally the meowing stopped.

At first I could not believe my ears. What bliss, this silence. I looked at the cat as she lay panting in the fridge. Poor thing, travelling is not really fun!

I hauled a mattress in front of the fridge and lay down with a book in front of the open door. That is where we spent the next few days while the air conditioning was being repaired.

I had earned the epithet "cat lady" long before I had arrived. When I was negotiating with my future employer I had insisted that they pay for the transport of my three cats.

'We don't pay for pets,' they said.

'Why not,' I countered. 'Other families can take their children. These pets are my family. And at least you don't have to pay school fees for them!'

Their sense of humour seemed to be in good working order, for in the end they did pay.

On the fourth day, still in my orientation week, the other two cats Cato and Catryn arrived by freight plane in Abu Dhabi. Arrival time was around midnight. I took a local bus to get to the airport, using the hands-and-feet language that I had perfected during jobs in other foreign countries. The Arabic I had learned some years before did not help me very much, because driver and passengers all came from the Indian sub-continent, where Urdu was the language of the streets. I arrived at the airport several hours before the cats arrived for the plane was late. It was a Martinair freight plane and as I sat waiting the ground staff kept me informed of the plane's progress.

'It is now landing at Bahrain,' said one young man, 'and there it will stay for forty-five minutes'. Two hours later it was still in Bahrain.

Finally, around 4am I was told to proceed to the huge godown where the cats would be delivered to me. A tractor, dwarfed by the size of the huge building, entered the large sliding doors, pulling two very long flatloaders behind it. At the very end of the second flatloader, more than ten meters behind the tractor, stood the two small cat cages. Despite my fatigue I had to smile at this ridiculous sight. Nobody wanted to touch the two cages till the veterinary inspector had looked at the cats. I wondered why we had to have a vet's check. No one had bothered to examine Catastrophe a week earlier. But then, she was a business class passenger and the new arrivals came as freight! The vet came after some time, rubbing sleep out of his eyes. From a distance he cast one look at the two sleek furry balls, ignored my papers and said offhand: 'Very good cats, you can go now.'

With a cage in each hand I went to look for a taxi to take me back to Al Ain. In the first light of dawn we drove through the desert landscape to my new apartment. The cats were obviously happy to see each other. Catastrophe was eight years younger than the two sisters and had been with us for only a year or so. Catryn liked to play with her, but Cato always remained aloof. Since all three were used to living in an apartment, they settled in quickly, spending the cool hours of the early morning sitting on three chairs on the balcony to watch the traffic going around the roundabout at which we lived.

With the "family" together I was ready to start my new job in the hospital.

3

SOME FATEFUL MEETINGS

As soon as the temperature started to decrease in the early fall, I went jogging in order to get into shape to play tennis. The safest place to do this was the nurses' compound behind the hospital, since there would be no outsiders watching and there was not much traffic. On one of the first afternoons I spotted what looked like a yellow tennis ball lying just off the road. I walked over to pick it up and discovered that it was the fruit of a plant with the most intricately shaped leaves. As I bent down for a closer look I saw a small tuft of flowering grass nearby. The inflorescence was incredible: tiny but lovely, with a maroon lip, delicately fringed white "ears" and bright orange anthers.

I did not realise it at that moment, but finding the flowering grass *Panicum turgidum* determined the way my life would be for the next twenty years. It fired my interest in desert flora so that jogging and tennis were soon forgotten and replaced by crawling around on all fours to take macro-photographs of interesting desert plants.

I found out that there was a Natural History Group that organised lectures and desert outings. During one of the first lectures that I attended a young man from an oil company showed slides of some desert plants and told us about the various adaptations they had developed to cope with the double problem of heat and drought. For example, many desert plants had firm, almost leathery leaves that were covered by white hairs. The leathery surface prevented evaporation while the white hairs served the dual purpose of reflecting sunlight and retaining moisture. Large thorns prevented browsing by camels or worse, grazing by goats. And the seeds of practically every plant were programmed to stay dormant for many years when there were no rains, and even to ignore short showers that might occur during droughts.

After the lecture I approached the speaker.

'It would be great if you could look at the local flora,' he said. 'I am based in Abu Dhabi and don't often have time to explore this area or the mountains. Take photographs and samples, and I'll give you the address of people who can help you with identifications. So little is know of this part of the world, you might even make new discoveries.'

Some days later I went to have a look at the library that was kept for the Natural History Group at the offices of the local zoo. I was shown to the book collection by one of the curators. It did not take me long to discover that the library did not have much that interested me. There was one small book with about 30 plants that were found in Oman, simply described and illustrated by drawings. Most of these plants could also be found in our region, so this small booklet became my first guide to the wild flora of the desert.

When I went to thank the curator for having let me use the library, he accompanied me to the door. On the steps outside lay a small pile of hay. The curator kicked at it and said with disgust: 'Look at this rubbish. How can I feed that to my animals?'

Then he told me about the concept of "tendering" that governed much of the commercial life in the Emirates. Contractors put in sealed bids for certain contracts (in this case delivering hay to the zoo throughout the year) and usually the lowest bid was accepted without paying much attention to the quality of the product that was being offered. Often the last bidder was a friend of one of the administrators, who had been told (against regulations) what the other quotes were, so that he had a chance to underbid. The administrator would receive a nice kick-back and all would be happy, except for the person who had to work with the substandard product.

'Where are you from?' I asked the curator.

'I am from Canada', he said, 'I arrived just a month ago and I am already regretting it. This zoo is a mess.'

'In what way?' I wanted to know.

'No one around here has any idea about the proper construction of animal enclosures or about animal husbandry. The director kept animals as a hobby and therefore was considered to be an expert!'

I was impressed that he seemed to care so deeply for the animals. I liked him for getting angry about the bad quality of a bunch of hay. I became interested in this man who soon became my companion on my discovery trips into the desert. His name was Claus Curt (he was of German origin), which I shortened to CC.

****

It was around this time that I read an article in the newspaper about the presence of caracals in the region. It was written by an expatriate who had lived in the area for quite a long time. It listed all sightings and road-kills of this interesting medium-sized wild cat that had been recorded in the last decade or so. I noticed that there was one specific road-kill I had heard of that was not mentioned, so I decided to contact the author. I left a message with the newspaper and a few days later I received a call from Gerard. That first time we talked for two hours on the phone. The next weekend he came up from Dubai and we spent a whole day talking.

At one point he said: 'There are even leopards in these mountains.''

I was extremely interested.

'How can that be? The mountains look so forbidding and barren! It seems unlikely that anything larger than reptiles, small birds and rodents can live there.'

'That is true now,' said Gerard, 'but there used to be gazelles, which were the main prey for the leopards. However, they have long since been shot by local hunters and the larger predators like leopards and caracals have to kill feral goats to stay alive. There are plenty of those around but of course in principle they belong to someone. So the killing does not make the animals popular with the owners. Threatened by both starvation and bullets, the leopards have become very shy and secretive. No one knows exactly how many are still around.'

Later Gerard told me that I was the first Western person to believe his claim of the existence of leopards. He became a close friend over the years and we shared many animal adventures and interesting activities, until a strange set of circumstances turned him into one of my bitterest enemies.

* * * *

Another meeting with far-reaching consequences was that with the archaeologist of the Al Ain museum. Walid was a pleasant Iraqi from Tikrit, who had fled the oppressive regime in Iraq like so many of his sensible compatriots. He called me one day to tell me that he had found a whale skeleton washed up on one of the beaches of the Gulf. Did I want to come along when he went to collect it? Of course I jumped at the chance to see more of the country on an interesting quest. I took my camera along and we set out with a large truck to collect the whale bones for the museum. For several hours we drove through an endless "sea" of undulating sand dunes which turned from rust brown to yellow to glittering white as we approached the coast.

The Gulf, when we came to it, stretched like a sheet of transparent blue cellophane to the horizon. Tiny ripples lapped the beach, posing as waves. On the flat expanse of the beach the whale bones stood out in an impressive pile. But Walid cried out in dismay: 'Oh, what a shame. All the cervical bones are missing.'

Obviously other people had been impressed by the bleached bones and taken some souvenirs. We collected what was left and as we drove back to Al Ain, I suggested: 'Would you like me to write a short article for the English language newspaper, to see if anyone has found those missing bones?'

A WHALE OF A PROBLEM
By Marijcke Jongbloed

"In the middle of April, a small plane was landing on the airstrip near Jebel Dhanna. As he was coming down, the pilot saw something floating in the water near the coast. It looked like an upturned boat with men clinging onto the hull.

As soon as he landed, the pilot notified the authorities. A rescue team went out. However, to their surprise they found not a wrecked boat, but a whale being devoured by sharks. A rare find in Gulf waters. The whale was not identified at the time, but its skeleton washed up on the beach near the Golf Club area.

Someone told the archaeologist of the Al Ain Museum, Dr Walid Al Tikriti, about the episode in June. He expressed keen interest, because the museum is making plans to develop a Natural History Collection, and the whale would be a great addition to the dugong skeleton that he already had.

He rushed to the spot to investigate and, to his delight, the skeleton was quite complete. The nine-foot-long lower jawbones (if that was what they were) were especially impressive. He arranged with the local authorities to collect the skeleton after Ramadan. Since it lay in an area of the beach that is restricted to the public, he did not think it necessary to hide or guard the bones.

Unfortunately, that turned out to be a mistake. Early this month, a small expedition went down to collect the skeleton. When Dr Al Tikriti arrived at the scene, it turned out that several of the bones were missing: the two magnificent jawbones; a whole section of what looked like the cervical vertebrae, seven in all; and another six to eight vertebrae from another part of the spine.

This is really quite a disaster, for it is a difficult job to reconstruct an animal like this, but if parts are missing it is almost impossible. Even if one of the jawbones was still there, the other one could be copied, but now all we have is part of one. We do have a picture of the section of cervical vertebrae (see drawing), but even from that it would be hard to judge the actual size and shape of the missing bones. It would be so much better to have the real thing!

Needless to say, the museum and the Emirates Natural History Group would be delighted to retrieve some or all of the missing pieces. We have posted a notice at the Golf Club and we hope that it – and this article – may bring some results. As we said in the notice: future generations will be grateful – and so will we!**"**

(Reprinted from the Khaleej Times, 24 July 1984)

Whale skeleton on the beach of Jebel Dhana

'That would be marvellous,' said Walid. 'I took some pictures which show the missing bones, maybe you can use that as an illustration'

The article had two effects. One was that we recovered the missing bones. They had been taken by members of the Abu Dhabi Natural History Group and were duly donated to Walid, who was happy with his complete skeleton.

The other was a call from the newspaper editor: 'I liked the article about the whale bones. We need articles like that for the paper. Can you write anything more about the environment or natural history?'

I don't know what possessed me as a relative newcomer to think that I could, but I promised I would try. The series of articles that resulted were partly based on the trips I made every weekend with CC, the zoo curator. The newspaper editor liked the anecdotal trip reports and offered me a weekly column in his paper, and for the next three years I spent most of my spare time writing. Having to note down what we discovered every week forced me to look closely at everything in order to be able to describe it and to develop a strict discipline to produce the articles on time.

CC taught me where to look for things (under rocks for bugs and lizards, in moist nooks and crannies for ferns and other tiny plants) and how to observe what I saw. For the first time in my life I really used my eyes. Even birds that had been just blobs in the sky now became recognisable, by their flight pattern, their behaviour and – with the aid of binoculars – by their plumage.

Within six years after I had arrived in the Emirates my first book was published: *The Living Desert*. It was a collection of the weekly columns. But that still lay in the future during those early days in which I roamed the sands and the *wadis* and fell in love with CC.

4

LIFE WITH CC

Surprising myself, I fell for CC. He was not at all my type. Whereas till now most of my boyfriends had been younger, more or less unconventional and rather good looking, this man was ten years older than I, he had what the French so charmingly call *l'embonpoint* (a well-rounded paunch) and his thick, grey hair did not hide the fact that his head was very flat at the back. Added to that he was the most conservative chauvinist I had met in a long time. Not the man of my dreams. But then, I was not exactly slim myself and I had just turned forty. Our lack of physical attractions did not hamper the development of our relationship. More importantly, we seemed to have a lot of common interests.

A few days after our first meeting on the steps of the zoo office building we made a date to have a meal downtown after a Natural History Group meeting. Soon we were spending most evenings together. Evenings turned into nights and we became lovers.

One evening as we were sitting in a restaurant I looked at him across the table and realised that this was the man I wanted to grow old with. I was not head over heels in love (as he seemed to be) but I felt comfortable and safe with him. There were times when I was away from him, at work, when the thought of him would set my body tingling with remembered and anticipated passion.

I had a feeling ours was going to be an out-of-the-ordinary relationship when one day he came home from work, saying: 'I brought you some presents. This morning the banana brigade (this is what we called the municipality workers who were always clothed in yellow overalls) descended upon the zoo and started spraying with insecticide. I was horrified that the poison would harm my animals, so I ran after them, shouting protests. They looked at me as if I were the man from the moon.' He chuckled as he remembered the expression on their faces. 'I am sure they were thinking: *What is that man getting excited about? We are breathing the stuff and we are* OK. You know, these guys wear no protection at all. But it really is poison, look at what I found afterwards.' With that he handed me a dead butterfly, a Lime swallowtail. I admired the beautiful wings and felt a pang of pity as I saw the tongue curled sideways out of its mouth.

'You said presents, plural. What else have you got?'

He pulled a large matchbox from his pocket and carefully slid it open. A large, live scorpion stirred inside. He had found it before the spraying had started. I was scared of the scorpion, but CC taught me what one can do in order to study it (or any other insect or spider) closely or take good photographs without being hurt. First he put the matchbox with the scorpion into the fridge, and then a big rock in the freezing compartment.

'Does that not hurt the scorpion?' I asked.

'No, not if you only do it for a few minutes, but it slows it down so much that it will sit still for quite a long time until it warms up again.'

In fact the poor thing looked quite dead when we put it on the ice-cold rock. Sitting on the cold rock prolonged its inactivity for a while. It gave me a chance to focus the camera and be ready for the scorpion to come back to life and start moving, which it soon did. In this way I managed to get some impressive pictures. The method works only for exothermic creatures, such as insects, arachnids and reptiles that match their body temperature to the surrounding temperature.

Because we were living in a Muslim country we had to take

precautions to hide our love affair. CC would go to his apartment after work to shower and shave before taking a taxi to my place. He had to be back at his place before 6am when the zoo bus would pick him up from his house, so in the very early morning he would get up, climb the stairs to the roof of my apartment building and go down by one of the other staircases in the building in order to confuse any possible watchers.

In those days expatriates were watched constantly by the CID and files were kept on every person. Some couples that I knew at work had been given the message to get married or be deported, so many chose the easy way of marrying according to Shariah law. This involved a simple ceremony with the imam from a mosque. One vital part of the ceremony was that the husband-to-be had to provide an amount of money for his future wife so that she would have some resources if they should ever divorce. One of my friends provided 1500 dirham (about 300 US dollars) for his wife and the imam almost fell over with surprise when she accepted this pittance.

While the Shariah law ceremony made local relationships legal, it did not count for anything anywhere else. Therefore if at a later time the couple wanted to separate there was no need for a difficult divorce. It could also be done if the male of the couple was still married back home, since men were allowed up to four wives. This would have applied to us, because a few weeks into our relationship CC told me something that shattered me. It was after a party as we were driving home. Out of the blue he said:

'I think I should tell you that I am still married.'

'What do you mean, you are married?'

'Just that. I have a wife in Canada.'

'And why is she not here?'

'She did not want to come. We have not had a close relationship for a long time. In fact I had been sleeping on the couch for three years.'

I could not believe my ears. I would never have started anything with a married man but by now I was so hooked that I found it impossible to break off the affair. Even if his marriage had been unhappy, it did not change the fact that he was not free and our relationship could be threatened at any time. Being utterly conservative he definitely did not like the idea of the Shariah law marriage, not even if it gave me some protection in a hostile land. I did not force the issue, but when our pillow talk turned to having children I put my foot down. Although I had yearned for children in the past, I was not ready to be an illegal single mother in my forties.

Animals were to be my "ersatz" children.

5

TORTOISES

A colleague at work was due to leave the country and asked if I was interested to have his two tortoises. I had never kept reptiles so I was eager to try it. I gave them a closed night box but in the daytime they roamed freely around the study, which had a tile floor that could be cleaned easily. The cats showed only mild interest in their new housemates. CC immediately recognised them as having originated in his zoo. They were West African spur-thighed tortoises (*Geochelonida sulcata*), a giant tortoise that can grow almost as large as their better known cousins on the Galapagos islands. Mine were still quite small, still fitting in one cupped hand.

CC told me: 'In the zoo there are a few specimens that are quite old and over one meter in length. The females lay their eggs in burrows that they dig in firm sand. The burrows in their paddock are really deep and large. Remember Ahmad, the small keeper, that we talked to the other day? He can crouch-walk down into them.'

In the desert climate that was so similar to that of their native region, the tortoises thrived without much interference from the zoo management. Every spring hundreds of little tortoises hatched and climbed out of the burrows. Still tiny enough to crawl through the mesh of the fences, they roamed far and wide through the zoo and even reached the roads surrounding the zoo. No wonder some of them made it to the local markets to be sold, and others were taken home by those who found them to become pets. Soon after he arrived at the zoo CC organised round-ups of the baby tortoises and kept them in more secure enclosures to raise them. The long-living reptiles multiplied rapidly and by the time CC left the zoo years later the number of tortoises had risen astronomically.

In the wild these tortoises are endangered, because decades of famine due to war and drought in the West-African countries from which they originate have decimated their numbers. Being so large and relatively easy to catch, they are a major source of protein for starving tribes. As they become fertile only when they are about six years old and have reached the size of a small dog, few survive long enough to reach fertility and consequently they are dying out rapidly.

The two I kept were soon joined by three smaller ones which I found in the *suq*. Whenever I sat working at the table in the study I could hear them grunting and sighing. Gradually I realised that they had a certain repertoire of sounds. One type of grunt was always used when one came across another. Another type of whistling sigh was an expression of surprise or fear (a meeting with a cat). A series of small grunts accompanied the satisfaction of finding food. When I told CC about my observation, he laughed.

'There is no way tortoises can communicate through sounds, they don't have a voice box,' he told me.

'I'm sure of it,' I countered, 'Maybe you can't hear it because of your streptomycin ears.'

CC was deaf to low frequency sounds due to years of taking malaria prophylaxis during his early years in Africa. Deaf or not, he insisted that it was impossible for tortoises to produce sounds. Then I came across an article written by Peter Dickinson, the curator who used to work at the Al Ain zoo before CC. This man had observed the same phenomenon and devoted a scientific article to it.

'Look at this', I said, 'Maybe now you'll believe me!'

Grudgingly CC admitted that I was right. He could not stand to be wrong about anything and would only change his mind when presented with overwhelming proof. I was gradually finding out that he was a difficult man to live with. However, the fun times made up for the difficult moments and I was enjoying having someone around to do things with. And then there were the nights…

I did not want to keep the tortoises forever, so I contacted a zoo in Europe that I thought might be interested. They were. At that time I did not know how to legally transport endangered species of animals into Europe. Getting them out of the Emirates would not be a problem, but at Schiphol airport I would have to smuggle them. Even though it felt wrong for me as a nature lover to do such a thing, I decided the end justified the means. The tortoises would serve a better purpose and have a better life in a European zoo.

When the time came to travel home on vacation I prepared a shoebox to fit in my carry-on bag. At Dubai airport this had to pass through the X-ray machine. Immediately I was taken aside by a female customs officer who reprimanded me:

'You should not have done that,' she said, shaking her head as she opened the shoebox.

Oh, oh, I thought, *I wonder what the penalty is for smuggling tortoises.* The lady officer picked up one of the small animals and peered at it closely through her thick lenses. 'Did you not know that X-rays can harm them? They seem to be all right now, but please don't do that again.' She put the tortoise back, closed the box and waved me on.

It was late afternoon when we arrived at Schiphol airport. This time I decided on a different strategy. I had put on a pair of jeans with huge pockets and the tortoises would have to spend half an hour in there. They were still small enough for this and a wide jacket hid the bulges on my thighs (which were already rather large anyway). Pushing my cart laden with suitcases I approached customs.

Suddenly I felt something warm spread over my thigh.

Oh dear, I thought, *the tortoises don't like my pockets.*

Once one had started the others followed suit, even those in the other pocket. With dark patches spreading over the front of my jeans, I leaned into the cart as if it were very heavy and tried to look nonchalant. To my great relief no one stopped me.

I was now officially a wildlife smuggler.

6

UPHEAVAL

Life in the Emirates in the mid-eighties was interesting and exciting. The inland town of Al Ain was anything but cosmopolitan. For good shopping you had to go to the coastal cities. But the local markets (suqs) were overflowing with fresh produce that was often not known to me. I learned to prepare and eat ochra (lady fingers) and sigalees (slip lobsters) and had wonderfully spicy one-dollar meals in small Indian cafeterias.

On our days off CC and I roamed the wadis, gravel plains and mountains searching for wild flora and fauna. I wrote my articles and gave "flora" talks to the Natural History Group.

Since CC was never off on a weekend, I decided to do shifts in the emergency room in order to have a weekday off. Everyone else wanted to have weekends off, so that was no problem. Things were going so well at work that I had been offered the post of chief of the department. I considered it but I was not really interested. True, it provided better pay, but it carried a lot of responsibility and I would not be able to have weekdays off.

Out of the blue that easy life was shattered.

A lady patient, traditionally dressed in full length *abaya* and face-covering *burqa*, was unhappy about the way I had treated her. She was addicted to large numbers of sleeping pills and pain killers that she had cadged from other doctors. I explained that she was feeling rotten because of the seventy-six pills that she had taken in the previous three days and I proposed that we should try another treatment. She refused and became quite agitated: 'I want those pills and I only got six pills before the weekend so what you say is nonsense.'

I wanted to give her some time to calm down, so I said that I would check with the pharmacy about the medicine that she had received from my colleagues. When I came back from having learned that she had indeed had seventy-six pills, the lady was jumping up and down in rage, yelling: 'You checked whether what I said was right, that means you think I am lying. (*Yes, dear, I do*). I will get my husband to kick you out of the country!'

As she swept out in a whirl of black cloth, I imagined I could see smoke and smell sulphur. She went to the medical director's office to complain about me. The Emirati liaison officer was there as a translator. When I was called in, he told me: 'You used bad language.' (*This is news to me.*) 'You said *yella*.' (*I most certainly did not.*) 'You should not look up her clothes, she is a very important people.' That at least made me smile.

The director, a very slick administrator who had most certainly come floating to the top because of lack of weight, said: 'You should give her what she wants.'

I replied: 'You can do that too, and then her death of an overdose will be on your head, not mine. I did not study medicine to kill people'.

Bad move.

It turned out that her husband was the second most powerful man in the Emirate.

That evening over dinner at a local hotel I told CC what had happened. He gave me total support, agreeing that one could not compromise where the ethics in medicine are concerned. The next day I was called to the hospital director's office and told I would be "terminated" (the lovely local term for being fired and deported!) in three months.

I did not want to leave. I was happy with the place and with my relationship. First I tried to fight the company's decision, but I got nowhere. A visit to the Minister of Health was also futile. It was also very degrading. I had to state my case in a huge room with dozens of men sitting along the walls in the ornate "Louis Farouk" chairs that are so beloved by the Arabs. Everyone was talking and it was difficult to make myself understood. The minister cut me short and said: 'We need people of your integrity but there is nothing I can do for you.'

It was obvious he had been informed about the situation beforehand and did not want to incur the wrath of his superior.

Worse was to come.

At first what happened next seemed an answer to prayers. Via a local friend I managed to find employment in a clinic owned by the head of the CID. The pay was lousy but at least I would have a visa and a powerful sponsor. I would still have to leave the country for a few days but then I could come back.

So I found a cheap apartment and moved my belongings and cats there. CC would live there and look after them till I got back. Two days before my scheduled departure I went to the CID office to pick up the new visa that I had been promised. The sponsor was not "in his seat" and I was told that he had gone on an extended vacation. No one knew about my visa. I was in a panic. How could he have left me stranded like this? Wherever I turned I got polite smiles and non-committal answers to my questions.

Finally the local acquaintance who had put me in touch with my would-be sponsor, told me that I had been declared *persona non grata* in all of Abu Dhabi Emirate. Not even the CID chief could override that decree. The patient's husband apparently was not someone whose decision could be thwarted.

It was around this time that I really learned to appreciate democracy. Until then it had just been a word, but now that I was the target of the tyranny of powerful people – in fact, one powerful man – it became an important and valuable concept.

The three months of suspense were over. I felt like a deflated balloon. It was a lonely departure. For some reason there was no one to see me off.

Still, I did not stop fighting just yet. I came back on a visit visa, and applied for a job in a hospital just across the border in Oman. I was invited to Muscat for an interview and exam, both of which went well. However, I did not get the job. The Dutch ambassador had already warned me that only English people were ever employed in Oman in those days. Apart from Shell employees no Dutch person had ever had a job in Oman.

Then my luck turned. I found a job in a clinic in Dubai, 160km away from Al Ain. It even paid more than my previous job. CC and I would have to have a LAT (living-apart-together) relationship, but that was better than none.

I moved out of the rented apartment and put my belongings and the cats in CC's apartment while I went back to Europe to wait until the Dubai visa came through. It was to be a long wait, for the Abu Dhabi ban was still on and caused problems even in Dubai. During this time I stayed with my friends of cat-cleaning fame Chris and Ida in Amsterdam, sleeping on a mattress on the floor of their study, totally broke. I had often dreamed about being a lady of leisure, but now that I was, I found out that this is no fun if you have no money to do things and go places.

After five months the long-awaited phone call came. The papers were ready and I could start work immediately. During the three months probation time I did various house sitting jobs for expats in Dubai, while the cats remained with CC in Al Ain.

As soon as I knew that my job was secure, I found and moved into a nice house on the beach and settled in with the three cats.

It was a year I could have done without but at the same time I was still convinced that I had done the right thing. Now that it was over I was looking forward to life in the big city. It was going to be quite different from the previous period in Al Ain.

7

ZOO ANIMALS

While I was struggling with the authorities about my "termination" and living in the cheap rented apartment in Al Ain, CC had his own problems at the zoo. His boss was originally an Austrian architect who had been asked to build the Al Ain zoo because he had once had a private collection of wild animals in Dubai and therefore was considered to be a zoo expert. He was anything but a zoo expert, although he could not be faulted where his love for animals was concerned.

'Listen to this,' CC said to me one day, 'I asked old Otto today why he only has a few fingers left on each hand. You know why? He keeps putting his hands into cages with wild animals, trying to pet them! The idiot!'

CC always told me that even a hand-reared wild animal remains a wild animal and should be considered dangerous, certainly when they are predators.

CC did not like the design of most cages and enclosures, finding errors that often endangered the health and even the life of the animals. The high fences of the ungulate enclosures were kept upright, as usual, with wire stays strung from the posts to a fixation point in the ground a couple of meters away.

'The trouble is,' said CC, 'that the fences have been put very close to the road, so they had no room for the stays on the outside. They then decided to put the stays on the inside of the fence. Small ungulates are skittish by nature. For their survival they depend on their quick reaction to danger and their speed. Whenever there is a panic in the herd, the animals race away and eventually reach a fence. Then they start running along the fence, and are decapitated by the stays.'

Sometimes it was the mother of a newborn baby who was killed. When that happened, the small gazelle had to be bottle fed at frequent intervals. There were no keepers that stayed overnight in the zoo - in fact initially there were no keepers that could be trusted with such a responsibility at any time. Not one of them knew anything about the animals they worked with and therefore they did not understand their specific needs. CC would take the baby gazelle home and thus we were joined at the dinner table by a dainty little ungulate that would nuzzle CC's sleeves whenever it felt like a little something. He even got up at night for extra feeds. I learned to prepare feeding bottles. Insisting on proper sterilisation of bottle and nipple CC said: 'Animal babies are much more vulnerable than human babies. They get sick very quickly and are difficult to treat when they are small.'

One day CC came home from the zoo looking absolutely shattered. I offered him a beer from my hoarded monthly quota of alcoholic drinks. It did almost nothing to relieve his tension and distress.

After a while he told me what had happened.

In the early morning he had received word from the customs authorities that a shipment of gazelles had landed at the airport.

'The director may have been notified, but forgot to tell me.' CC complained. 'I did not get to the airport till noon and then I discovered that they had not bothered to put the crate in the shade.'

As soon as he arrived at the airport he had the crate moved to an air-conditioned godown while he set out to do the paperwork. The long drive back on the truck that had no air conditioning stressed the animals even more. When CC was finally able to open the crate, of the twenty or so gazelles, only one was still alive. They were Speke's gazelles (*Gazella spekei*), a rare species both in captivity and in the wild.

'I have never felt so terrible in my entire life,' he said, his face drawn with fatigue and stress, 'Imagine how the poor things must have suffered. Dying of heatstroke is painful, and they must have been terrified in their long confinement.' My heart went out to him, but there was nothing I could say or do to help.

Later that evening I asked Claus to tell me about this gazelle. His knowledge of wildlife was encyclopedic.

'For a gazelle it is quite large, reaching to my thigh, and with foot-long horns. Its most interesting feature is its nose. Just above the nostrils on the bridge of the nose the skin is folded into two to five wrinkles. When the gazelle is excited these folds are inflated with air to form a sac the size of a tennis ball. This creates a resonance chamber for amplifying its call. It has a characteristic loud sneeze that sounds like a gunshot and can be heard over great distances.'

'Why is it so rare?'

'It comes from Somalia, and you know there has been civil war there for years. Very few are left, after having been shot, mainly for food, because the people in these war areas are starving. These gazelles don't reproduce quickly. Females usually have one young after a pregnancy of about half a year. Their life span in captivity can be up to twelve years, but in the wild few reach that age, since so many predators have it in for them: the big cats, hyenas, African hunting dogs and even pythons.'

The one surviving Speke's gazelle lived in the zoo for a long time. Claus never managed to get any other, to his chagrin, for of course one cannot do a breeding program with one gazelle.

CC worked hard at teaching the keepers (almost all from the Indian sub-continent) how to take care of young and sick animals. He was a stickler for detail, but fair and the men showed their respect by calling him Mueller-khan. In spite of his strictness he was well liked because he travelled in their bus and was always interested in their families. Years later, when I visited the zoo after his departure, keepers would come up to me to ask about him.

One keeper got his first hands-on experience when five leopard cubs had to be hand-reared. Two of them died in the first few days, but feeding and caring for the remaining three was still quite a job. I did not really know what was involved until I hand-reared three wildcat kittens some years later. CC and I used to go to the zoo after dinner to watch their last feeding session of the day. The keeper was sitting in the corridor of the cat house, surrounded by mewing little leopards. One after the other they drank greedily from their bottles, sitting on their haunches and clutching the bottles with their front paws. You could see their round bellies swell like balloons as the bottle emptied. Then it would be play time. They would jump and tumble over each other and us, slapping their chunky paws at noses and tails, race along the corridor and back and get into mock fights. All young cats are nice to watch but leopards are more interesting than many. They are incredibly curious and courageous, trying anything and taking great risks at times.

When the young leopards had grown up they were put into one of the ugly old cages in the zoo. The cages were ugly because the animals had to be protected from the public with extra wire and protective hedges that created distance. The hordes of people that visited the zoo every day seemed to have only one thought in mind: *How can we get this animal to howl or growl in pain/fear/frustration?*

'You know,' said CC, 'the gorilla at this zoo is the only one I have ever known that spits at people – only because people are always spitting at him.'

Another day he came back from work and said: 'Today I saw a teacher handing stones to her pupils so they could throw them at a baby giraffe.'

The zoo animals soon learned to stay out of range and were almost completely inactive during the day. Only in the cooler hours of the evening, when the public had left, did they come out of their corners and behave more or less normally. Often CC would take me around after hours in the zoo jeep, driving slowly through the lanes in the dying light. The zoo had a back section with huge enclosures where the animals lived almost as freely as in the wild. Here were the herds of various species of gazelles, the zebras, the large antelopes and the lions.

On one such night I saw a very young, pure white llama frolic by itself in the light of a full moon. The sand and the pale-barked eucalyptus trees were painted silver by the moonlight and the shadows underneath the trees were pitch black. Against this back-drop the long-legged woolly animal looked like a ballerina in the spotlights of a stage. The exuberance of the animal in the peace and quiet of the cool evening made it an unforgettable moment.

As we drove around CC told me about a funny thing that had happened that day at the zoo. Halfway through the morning a rickety old pick-up truck had appeared and three scruffy looking bedu tumbled out of the front cabin. On the back of the truck was a large wooden crate, tightly nailed shut. The gatekeeper talked with the men and then came to fetch CC.

'Mueller-khan', he said, 'these men have very dangerous animal. Come look.'

CC contemplated the crate that was large enough to hold a small pony. He tried to quiz the men.

'What animal? Like cat?' He was always hoping to be presented with an Arabian leopard! 'Where catching? Mountains? How catching?' Even while talking bedu English, he did not manage to get answers to his questions.

He climbed into the back of the truck and peered through a crack between planks. It was dark inside and very quiet.

'Get me tools', he barked at one of his own men.

'Be careful, Mueller-khan', they said, obviously quite scared, 'animal very bad, very bad.'

CC dislodged one of the top planks. Now he could see inside properly. At first he thought the crate was empty. Then he made out a small shape in the far corner of the crate. He could not believe his eyes. It was a hedgehog.

So much for the courage of the noble braves!

Still chuckling about the incident we got out of the car at the leopard cage and pushed through the hedge to get close to the bars of the cage. One of the young hand-reared males was particularly fond of CC. He would come up to the bars, stand on his hind legs while putting his front legs through the bars to give CC a hug. He was still small enough for CC to trust him. The leopard liked me well enough to play hide and seek with me but I never got a hug.

8

NAMBI

The beach house that I had rented in Dubai backed on to a row of houses that had a view of the sea. You could hear the sea and be on the beach proper in just a few steps. It was roomy and very empty as I had practically no furniture. Fortunately secondhand shops were everywhere and I found usable – if ugly – chairs and tables.

Dubai in the mid-eighties was an interesting town with people from all over the world. At work I enjoyed meeting the various nationalities. I would talk to people from the Basque area of France, from Fiji, from Newfoundland, from Sri Lanka and from Zanzibar in one day's work. The staff at the clinic came from the UK, Iraq, India, Australia, South Africa, Hungary, Scotland, the USA, Ireland, Serbia, Sri Lanka, Holland and the Emirates. Every day I learned new things about these different countries – mainly because all their festive occasions were used as an excuse for a celebration at the clinic! I learned about the feasts of Diwali and

St Lucia, I learned more about cricket than I ever wanted to know and I tried to fast (and failed miserably) along with the Muslims during Ramadan.

The only friend I had in those early days in Dubai was Gerard, the guy who was so interested in local animals. He had had many different jobs since he had arrived in Dubai some ten years earlier. Recently, he had been working on a survey of wild mammals for one of the sheikhs of the Emirate of Dubai. When it was finished he presented the results of the survey to the sheikh who turned out to be not in the least interested. Frustrated that his work had been for nothing, Gerard decided to turn the report into a book. At this point my weekly columns for the local English-language newspaper had also been turned into a book that was being published by a local company. We turned the occasion into a double feature and celebrated the birth of our first books together.

Gerard lived in a wonderful little cottage tucked away amidst half a dozen other houses. Once, when we visited him, I said to Claus: 'I wonder why Gerard's house has such a large garden. It is so much larger than any of the gardens in this neighbourhood.'

When we asked him about it, he said: 'My garden used only to go up to there,' and he pointed at a few meters of low wall just in front of the door. 'All the rest was a dead end public road with no other houses. So I erected a wall between two neighbouring houses that had their garden walls along the road and tore down my garden wall.'

'And that gave you no trouble with the municipality?'

'No, actually they thought it was a clever idea.'

In the garden there were several cages, some for birds and one for a breeding pair of wildcats that had been established during his wildlife survey. It was the only captive breeding pair of these endangered cats in the world and therefore quite important. The garage had been turned into a cage where he kept some red foxes. He had two large German shepherd dogs, a group of flamingoes and a small gazelle that all used the garden together. It was like a miniature paradise. Until one day, while Gerard was out, the dogs went on a rampage and killed all the animals that were not in a cage. What had caused them to revert to their natural instinct so suddenly remained a mystery.

Whenever CC and I visited Gerard, we used to say: 'Wouldn't it be wonderful to have a little house like this?'

The likelihood of that happening was not great. The cottages in the neighbourhood all belonged to the large real estate company of the sheikh of Dubai and the rent was incredibly low, compared to other houses in the area. The waiting list for these houses was miles long.

After the publication of our books, Gerard decided to return to his home country to continue his education. He intended to become a vet, but since he had to earn his keep and tuition while studying, it would be a long haul. Because of his good connections with the sheikh, he was able to convince the Ruler's office to let me rent the house after his departure. I was elated, all the more so because I had just been given notice to leave the beach house. All the buildings in that street were due to be torn down to make room for bigger and more expensive villas.

Gerard also asked me if I would like to take care of the wildcats and a family of marmosets.

'The marmosets are not well,' he told me, 'but they will improve if you feed them properly, which includes giving them these.'

He fished a cloth bag out of the fridge and opened it. I peered in and saw a mass of crawling brown worms. He took out a few and showed them to me. They were mealworms and it gave me the shivers just to look at them. How would I ever be able to handle them? However, the prospect of taking care of four lovely little monkeys made me say: 'It'll be a pleasure!'

In the middle of the summer I moved into Rd 333/69 F142, a prosaic address, but a wonderful haven for me. When I moved my stuff into the garden, I found Gerard busy painting my living room. What an extraordinary friend – I had never yet moved into a house where the person who was leaving did the redecorating!

With the house, the wildcats and the marmosets I also inherited an Indian houseboy named Nambi.

Nambi lived in a tiny room off the garage and would be working for me full-time. I was a bit concerned that it would be a chore having someone around all the time, especially someone whom I could barely understand. Nambi's English was rudimentary and his pronunciation unique, while my Urdu was non-existent. In time it became easier to communicate and Nambi proved to be a wonderful co-worker.

True, his housecleaning skills were not very well developed. He did not see dust above eye-level and since he was barely one and a half meter tall, dust and cobwebs remained a feature of my home.

However, he loved the animals and took good care of them and the garden also thrived, with me providing flowers and Nambi making sure I had vegetables and fruits. He came from a small village in Tamil Nadu, a few hundred kilometres inland from Madras. He had a wife, two sons and two daughters there. His dream was to go back with enough money to start a chicken farm.

Like so many people from the Indian subcontinent, he was gentle, kind and attentive to my needs. He figured out quickly that I liked to have water by my bedside at night and tea on the terrace outside for breakfast – and I never had to ask for these. Sometimes when I came home exhausted after a long day at the clinic, there would be a wonderful curry steaming on the stove. At the important Hindu feast of Diwali, he always brought me a box of the finest marzipan sweets. I knew these to be very expensive and he spent a large part of his small wages to pay for these, in spite of my protests. He always shared the gifts he received from friends and when he went home on vacation, he'd come back laden with gifts for all his friends, including me. Some were quite horrible, but of course I had to keep them all. I still have a shelf in my cupboard where tin vases vie for space with bamboo ornaments, glass ballerinas and wooden elephants.

Not only did he share his own possessions with others, sometimes mine were shared as well. Many times I would search high and low for a garden tool or kitchen utensil, before I realised that probably Nambi had lent it to a neighbour or a friend. He even gave the use of my house to one of his homeless friends while I was away on holiday. When I came home unexpectedly, I found a sleeping mattress next to a radio and an alarm clock on the floor of the living room, while the house smelt very strongly of pungent curries. The man sleeping soundly on the mattress was a stranger to me. He did not even wake up when I carried my suitcase inside and started unpacking. When Nambi came home a little later, I asked him: 'Who is that man sleeping in the front room?'

'Oh, madam, he my priend.'

'And why is he staying here?'

'He no house and your house empty!'

Of course, a logical explanation.

I had very ambivalent feelings about it. On the one hand I did not like the easy sharing of my living space, but on the other hand I felt humbled by Nambi's generosity. I had so much while others had so little. Nambi's own room was hardly larger than a cupboard – no second person would have fitted in. So all I said was: 'Nambi, maybe he can sleep with another friend now. I do not mind sharing, but please ask me first. And please, no curry cooking here!' Eating his curries was one thing – having the house smell of curry quite another.

In the end Nambi was the man I shared a house with longer than with anyone else, and the period of nineteen years that I rented number F172 was the longest time in my life I spent at one address.

9

MY FAMILY OF MARMOSETS

The marmosets that I had inherited from Gerard already had a long history. The old pair had been used as laboratory animals in Germany, before being sold to an animal dealer from Dubai. The local pet shop had sold them to a young sheikha who wanted them as pets. She had no idea how to take care of them and obviously was not able or willing to learn. When they became ill she took them to the vet, who diagnosed rickets, a disease to which these small monkeys are very prone. He told her to make sure the little creatures had proper food and enough sunshine and vitamin D. She ignored his advice, kept the pair in a dark room and fed them cat biscuits.

In spite of their poor condition they had mated and a litter of three babies was born. But the babies did not thrive and one of them died. Gerard, who was a friend of the sheikha's brother, had tried to persuade her to either feed them properly or give them to him. When the baby marmoset died he took it to the vet and they X-rayed it. They were horrified to see that the tiny creature had dozens of fractures in its fine bones. Eventually, when the marmosets were so weak that they hardly moved any more, the sheikha got tired of them and allowed Gerard to take them home. He put them in a birdcage in front of the bedroom window where they would have regular sunshine and started a fresh fruit and protein diet.

A few weeks later Gerard was due to leave and the marmosets became mine. There were two adults and two half-grown young ones that I called Jip and Janneke, after the characters in a well-known children's book of my youth. The young marmosets looked like punks because their fur was in bad shape and stuck out at all angles. When one of the babies tried to pull himself up to a standing position, holding onto the vertical bars of the cage, his hands slid down the bars. He could not raise himself, due to weakness or pain. The female had a fracture of her spine that caused her to have a humpback and her tail had so many fractures that it was no longer straight but resembled a corkscrew. The male who had not had to bear offspring fared a bit better.

CC taught me what to feed them. With their daily salad of lettuce, apples, oranges, bananas, raisins, hard-boiled egg, tomatoes, vitamin drops and calcium powder they became stronger by the day. The best part of the meal for them was the helping of live mealworms. For me it was the worst part, because I had to dig the crawling insects from the pouch, but the enthusiasm with which the treat was received helped me to overcome my loathing.

After a while it became difficult to buy mealworms in the quantity I needed, so I started breeding them myself. Of course it was CC who encouraged me to do that. He started me off with a healthy lot that I bought in a pet shop in Holland during my leave.

'This is what you do. You put the mealworms in a plastic container with lots of bran and some carrots, cut lengthwise. The bran is food and the carrots provide them with moisture. Then you take another container and cut the bottom out of it and replace it with mosquito netting. That is the box into which you must put the pupae that will become the beetles that will give you the eggs. The eggs will drop through the mosquito netting into a third container with bran placed underneath and in time you will have new mealworms.'

Sure enough, the mealworms ate and ate until they were really fat and then they pupated. Of course, only a portion of the mealworms made it to pupation, because the majority was fed to the marmosets. The soft, white pupae had to be taken out of the crawling mass of mealworms and set aside in their separate box. After a couple of weeks small brown bugs hatched. These bugs were given bread crusts and small bones as food and carrots for moisture. They mated and laid eggs, and the eggs dropped through the mosquito netting into the lower box. As predicted, I soon had a regular supply of mealworms.

The mealworms and the bugs produced a lot of droppings and the whole lot had to be sieved every few days. The droppings were spread in the garden as fertiliser. It was not difficult to breed the mealworms but caring for them took time and it was not a particularly nice job. In time it all became part of my daily routine and I did not mind handling the worms any more.

Whenever we watched the marmosets scramble for their share of mealworms, CC would say: 'They must be tasty, because monkeys are really quite finicky in their choice of food. See how mad they go over these worms!'

Eventually I came to believe that, too, and I could understand why there were restaurants in Europe that served mealworms and other insects as gourmet food. I never did taste them myself, though.

Next to mealworms, raisins were the marmosets' favourite snack. I could not give them many, because they would be too fattening, but once in a while I would get out the box and all the monkeys would gather near the door of their cage. Their little hands tickled in mine as they groped for the coveted fruit. The box had a picture of life-size raisins on it. One of the marmosets was too impatient for me to open the box, so he made a grab for the raisins on the picture. It was very interesting to find out that they could recognise two-dimensional images. They showed this talent again when I put up a new calendar in the kitchen. The cover had a life size portrait of a cat. Immediately the whole group came as close as they could get to the picture and sat huddled together discussing the finer features of this new housemate. In fact, the picture was so good, that one of the wildcats that I hand-reared around this time also recognised it and wanted to start a fight with it!

As the marmosets grew stronger and livelier, they needed more space. After a while we built a larger indoor night house in the kitchen and connected it to an outside "aviary" by means of a chicken wire tube that ran the length of the kitchen and passed through the hole of the exhaust fan (from which the fan had been removed). Underneath the chicken wire tube I mounted a "shit-shelf", for the monkeys were not house-trained. Outside they had trees to climb and ropes to swing on. It was right in front of the kitchen window, so whenever I stood washing the dishes curious marmosets jumped up and down right in front of me, twisting their heads for a better view.

Marmosets are a small species of monkey from South America. There are many different species of marmosets and the closely related tamarins. The ones I had were Common marmosets (*Callithrix jacchus*), also called *oustiti*. They had lovely intelligent faces, with long white plumes on their ears. Their soft hair was black at the base, tan in the middle and white at the tip. It smelled wonderfully, like fresh hay. Unlike other monkeys they had small claws instead of nails. Their tails were over a foot long but non-prehensile. Along with gibbons they are the only species of primate that usually mate for life and are monogamous. The female can have more than two babies, but usually only two survive since she can only suckle two. The male is very involved with raising the young, carrying them everywhere and teaching them the tricks of marmoset life. Often older siblings also play a role in taking care of young babies.

My marmosets were constantly on the move and very vociferous. They gave a running commentary on everything that happened in the kitchen and garden, interacted with the cats and quarrelled amongst each other. Their high-pitched cries could be heard all over the neighbourhood, but fortunately no one complained. Occasionally pandemonium would break out, with all the monkeys chattering excitedly in fear. Once this happened when I had left a brown terrycloth towel bunched up on the kitchen counter. It was easy to see that this must have reminded them of a furry predator of some kind. Another time their fear was elicited when I came into the kitchen wearing a long necklace of green and brown wooden discs. It took me a while to realise that the necklace resembled a snake, which must have been one of their deadliest enemies.

Not that any of these marmosets had ever encountered a snake or another predator. The fear was inborn. Strangely enough, they had no fear of the cats. They tried to touch them whenever they passed by their night box and even swung on their tails if one happened to sit on top of their outside aviary. Once one of them jumped out of the door as I was filling the water bowl and hitched a ride on Catryn's back. Friendly Catryn did not mind, though she looked over her shoulder a bit nervously.

The little monkeys managed to escape numerous times, taking refuge in the huge mesquite tree that cast its shadow over the back garden. Running with raised tails among the large horizontal branches of the tree and jumping to ever higher levels, they were obviously having a ball. However, since it was usually just one that escaped and the others were still in their cage, the escapee soon came back and wanted to be let in again.

Once the old pair started to feel better, they resumed mating and soon we had another lot of babies. It was an incredible sight to see the tiny faces peeping out from the fur on their father's chest or back, and later to see them venture out on their own. Soon we had six, then eight in the group.

One litter did not make it. The first baby was born in the early morning and transferred immediately onto the father, while the old female was struggling with the second birth. When an hour had passed without results I went into the aviary to have a better look and found that it was a breech birth that was not progressing. I called the vet, who came immediately. First we shooed the curious young ones into the night cage and closed the access to the aviary. The old male did not want to leave the side of his mate. Both monkeys shrieked in fear as the vet grabbed the female. The male was so concerned that he overcame his fear and jumped on top of the vet's head and slapped his forehead with a tiny hand. It was an incredible feat of courage – a twenty-centimetre monkey attacking a human, 1.90m tall!

We carried the old female inside and away from the very excited clan. I took her from the vet, feeling her tense body struggle in my grip. Very gently the vet started to manipulate the protruding bottom of the little baby. As soon as the mother felt that we were trying to relieve her of her pain, she relaxed totally and became almost limp in my hands. That helped the delivery and in an instant the baby was born, no longer alive, of course. The female was given a shot of oxytocine to help her uterus contract after its long labour and we took her back to her mate, who fussed over her for a long time.

In the scuffle the other little baby had fallen and was now ignored by the parents. I picked it up and when I saw it was still alive I wrapped it in a soft tissue and stuck it in my bra between my breasts for warmth. Then I went on a frantic search for a baby bottle with a nipple small enough to feed this tiny creature. Unfortunately I was not successful and the poor thing died after a few hours. Later I learned that the thing to look for was a toy set for a baby doll that included drinking bottles with tiny nipples.

A while later I needed the vet again. The male marmoset of the original young pair, Jip, had stopped eating and ran a fever. I took him to the veterinary hospital, which happened to be just around the corner from my house. The vet was British and he still followed the English custom in which people who take care of wild animals are not charged for veterinary care. I was very grateful to him, for I was already struggling with the food bills of my menagerie. Jip turned out to have hepatitis. There was not much we could do and I fully expected him to die, but he recovered. However, soon he developed a tendency to have fits. Once I was alerted by an outbreak of panic cries from the group. I found Jip lying unconscious on the floor of the night cage. Quickly I picked him up and put him on the kitchen sideboard. CC had once told me about an event in which he had resuscitated a small Capucin monkey with mouth-to-mouth respiration. Jip was not breathing, so I gave his chest a short squeeze and then started to blow quick short breaths into his nose and mouth. After a few seconds he stirred and before long he started to get up, so I put him back in the cage. A few weeks later it happened again, this time when he was excited over a helping of meal-worms. He improved again on my mini-CPR and lived another year or so, when he had a relapse of hepatitis from which he did not recover. I buried him in the garden under the banana tree and put a large fossil on his grave as a marker.

That summer I also lost the female of the pair, Janneke. Contrary to what the books (and CC) said, not all marmosets are monogamous. The old male had impregnated his eldest daughter as well as his old mate and both were due to deliver during the time when CC and I were going to be on vacation. Due to her poor start in life Janneke could be expected to have problems during delivery, but I had not thought of that before we left. Most of the marmoset births up till then had been so easy and quick.

We were vacationing in Spain. One day I felt very restless and out of sorts. I noticed it but could not figure out why I felt that way. That night we stayed in a small hotel but I was unable to sleep, my thoughts turning constantly to the animals in Dubai. I was sure there was something wrong there. As soon as it was morning I went downstairs to see if I could use a telephone somewhere. It took a while to get the connection, but finally Nambi answered.

'How are you and the animals, Nambi?' I asked.

'Cats are fine, madam,' he replied, 'but monkey is dead.'

'Which monkey?'

'Mama monkey, madam.'

'Old mama or new mama?'

'New mama.'

I was shattered. 'What happened, Nambi?'

'Baby not coming, two days trying, not coming. Then she die.'

I felt terrible at not having been there when Janneke needed help, at not having given clear enough instructions to get a vet if anything went wrong with the birth, at not having listened to my feelings so that I could have called earlier to give instructions. The rickets that she had had as a baby must have deformed her pelvis so badly that she was unable to give birth.

The rest of the clan kept doing well, and some time later we even established a second breeding pair, when I rescued a single male from a lonely existence in a cage on the grounds of a hotel. We built another night box, chicken wire run and outside aviary and gave the single male one of our younger females to create his own clan.

10

EXOTIC BIRDS

PEA-BRAIN PIGEONS

Now that I lived in Dubai and CC in Al Ain, we only saw each other on weekends. Even these were never complete weekends. While Friday was everyone else's day off, CC was off on Thursdays and came by taxi from Al Ain on Wednesday nights. I picked him up at the taxi stop on the outskirts of town and we would both be tired from a long week of hard work. Most of the time I still had to work a half-day on Thursday, so we rarely had a chance to go out into the desert any more. CC was completely happy spending the Thursday morning inside in air-conditioned comfort, reading his favourite magazine. He worked outside in the zoo all day, six days a week, and in the summer that was extremely exhausting.

Since I worked all week in a windowless room at the clinic, I was aching for some sunshine and exercise, but I could only get that on Fridays if I organised an outing with friends or went by myself. Camping overnight, one of the most wonderful things to do in the desert, could only be done during longer holidays.

One Thursday morning CC had gone out to buy his *Spiegel* magazine and had obviously spent some time at the *suq* also, because when I came home from work that day, I was introduced to four new housemates: tropical fruit pigeons (Jambu pigeons).

'Jambu pigeons come from the rain forests of the islands of Sumatra and western Java in Indonesia, from Malaysia, Thailand and Borneo', said Claus.

I reflected that I had probably heard them coo when I lived in West Java in the seventies, but I had never seen them there, because they are shy and behave inconspicuously in perfect camouflage.

'In the wild they will defend their territory by raising their wings and bobbing their bodies up and down, while cooing. If that does not work, they'll peck hard,' Claus continued his lecture. 'They lay one or rarely two eggs in the typical flimsy nest of a pigeon and the male and female share the incubation as well as the raising of the young. Both secrete "dove's milk", a nutritious fluid made in their crops. The young leaves the nest soon after opening its eyes on the tenth day but stays dependent on the parents for around ten weeks.'

'Are they endangered?' I asked.

'They are not on the endangered list but because their favoured habitat is rapidly being destroyed, they are considered threatened.' Looking lovingly at the quartet that sat huddled together in a small birdcage CC murmured: 'I have always wanted to have these. Just look at their beautiful colours.'

They were indeed lovely: the males had glossy dark green backs with a dark red head. On the white chest a red "drop" extended below their throats. The females' heads were a duller red. A pale blue circle outlined their golden eyes. Their bellies were white while the underside of the tail was chestnut. Their beaks were yellow and the feet dark red. And, as it turned out, they had no brains.

'Where are we going to put them?' I asked CC.

'Oh, there's plenty of space for a cage in the back garden in the shade of the mesquite tree.'

'And who is going to build that cage?' It was late Thursday afternoon by now. Guess who! The person who had the Friday off!

'What do they eat?'

'Fruit, of course. Apples, banana, some greens.'

The next day Nambi and I went to work. Fortunately we still had enough materials lying around from the time we built the marmoset cage. We attached the aviary to this cage. so they had one side in common. I bought a small tree in a pot from the flower market and attached some horizontal sticks at different levels to the wire netting. Then we let the pigeons into their new home. They emerged from their cage and sat on the ground.

I wondered if they were unable to fly. We tried to shoo them into action and they started to flutter around. One landed as if by accident on a perch, but the others just fell back to the ground. I decided to let them sort it out by themselves. They never did. They ate well, but never really learned to fly. In the morning, after they had eaten I'd pick them up and put them onto their perches where they'd sit preening themselves happily, until they fell off again.

I was not really a bird fan. I had not kept the chickens I had inherited from Gerard. I did not like to touch birds and had to learn to be decisive when picking up the pigeons. If you did not grab them firmly in one go, they would slide from between your fingers, shedding half their feathers in the process. CC was furious when he found two of his lovely pigeons half-nude next weekend. When he started to scold me, I yelled back at him:

'Next time ask me first before you unload creatures on me. I don't know how to take care of birds and I do not like birds, no matter how beautiful.'

The pigeons stayed with us for a few years until one after the other died of old age but I never learned to like them. They never showed their territorial display and had no interest in starting a family, even though nesting materials were available. They remained shy and stupid, and just sat and shat. They never used the large space we had created for them and I could not tell if they were content to be there or not.

In the end, the cage was used for the second group of marmosets – and with those at least you had no doubt that they loved the space!

A CCC IN THE WC

One day in June the phone rang and a man who had seen an article about me in the newspaper announced that he had found a bird. It had landed in the parking lot of his office and sat all day without moving. It seemed exhausted. He had been able to pick it up but now he did not know what to do with it. Could I please have a look?

'Sure,' I said, 'Come on over.'

Sometime later a large car drew up. The driver introduced himself as Mehmoud Rai. He walked around the front of the car towards the passenger seat. There sat the bird, absolutely still and seemingly tame. I picked it up and carried it to the spare bathroom where I put it gently on the floor.

It was a medium-sized bird, mainly beige in colour, with striking black wingtips. There was a white band above the eye, while a black band started from the corner of the eyes – both bands circled the head to meet at the back. The feathers at the back of the skull and nape of the neck were grayish. The beak was one-inch long, slightly curved downward. The bird had a very peculiar stance, stretched out high on long creamy legs, almost vertically, as if it wanted to look over a barrier into the distance. It moved in little spurts, like a plover, sometimes crouching low.

I had to find out what it was in order to know what to feed it. The few bird books I had did not help. In the evening I had to go to the committee meeting of the Natural History Group and this happened to be at the house of the bird recorder. As I waited for the meeting to start I leafed through one of his bird guide books. Soon I found a picture of my guest: it was a Cream-coloured courser (*Cursorius cursor*). I showed it to the bird recorder, who said: 'Until yesterday I'd never seen one. But this weekend I travelled four hours to the far West of the country to see a flock of these that had landed there on their migration and then I drove four hours back.'

I chuckled. 'You could have saved yourself a trip – I have one of these CCC's in my WC!'

Colin, the bird recorder, also thought the bird must be suffering from exhaustion, as it could not be someone's tame pet. He knew of no one who had ever tamed one. He told me:

'It belongs to the plover family.'

'I thought that,' I remarked, 'from the way it stands and walks! Is it a resident bird?'

'Its range is along the whole of North Africa and the Sinai peninsula, as well as further inland in Egypt along the Nile. Only when it migrates can you find it here, for then it goes all over Iraq and the Arabian peninsula, though probably not into the Empty Quarter. It prefers to be in stony and sandy desert areas, with a thin vegetation cover and nests on the ground in the open.'

Back at home my bird did not touch any of the food I put down. When CC came home that day he showed me that it was indeed worn out from its migration flight: it had no meat left on its breastbone and until it had grown muscle again it could not fly. He taught me how to make a food mixture from the yolk of a hardboiled egg, minced meat and soaked pellets of mynah food, all glued together with honey and butter. This I fed by hand. The bird sat quietly on my lap while I rolled small pellets of the mixture that I stuck into the back of its throat. When he swallowed it you could see the food go down the side of its neck into a gullet pouch on the right side of its chest. As soon as it had enough, it would shake its head vigorously and avoid my feeding hand.

With five or six feeds a day it slowly started to gain weight and strength. I always left a bowl with the pellet mixture and some mealworms with him and soon he started to peck at the mealworms. After a few weeks he started to put up stiff fights whenever I wanted to hand feed him, so I left him with a good supply of food all the time. His breastbone was now covered with a firm layer of muscle and he was ready to be free again.

Colin and I took him to one of the local parks. Both of us wanted to use the opportunity to get a few good pictures of the bird in the wild. I let it out of its travel box. It stood still for a few minutes, taking in the surroundings before flying off with a raucous call, the only sound I ever heard it make. I could not quite decide whether it meant: "thank you" or "good riddance"!

Half an hour later we saw it again in a different area of the park but by then it would not let us approach within 15 meters before flying off again. It obviously had not been tamed by living for almost four weeks in my bathroom.

PARROTS IN THE GARDEN

During the first month of my time in Dubai, I did a cat-sitting job at the house of some friends who were away on holiday. The house was in a compound with a swimming pool and in the evenings after work I spent some wonderful times there relaxing in the warm water. Every evening I could see flights of ten to fifteen noisy large birds fly over in a strong, straight flight, all heading in the same direction. *Going to their happy hour*, I thought.

Soon I found out that these were Ring-necked parakeets (*Psittacula krameri*) and that they all gathered at dusk in the garden of one of the palaces. This is where they roosted after a day of

61

flying all over the city to find food. Later, when I had my own garden they often came during the day to feed on the kernels of sunflowers or on the fruits of the mesquite tree. They were the most lovely and funny birds to watch as they waddled back and forth on top of the wall that served as a support for my sunflowers. Once I watched one as it did gymnastics on the telephone wire, holding on with its feet and beak, twirling around like a high-wire circus performer.

Ring-necked parakeets are very colourful. The adult male has a bright green body with long tapering turquoise tail feathers. A black band around its throat turns into a thin pink line that circles the neck (it is also called Rose-ringed parakeet at times). The beak is very sharply hooked, strong and bright red. Females and juveniles lack the ring and have a duller-coloured beak. The legs are slate green. Originating from the Indian subcontinent, they have thrived in many places after escaping from captivity. When this occurs in warm places with plenty of food like the Middle East that is not surprising. But there are even escapee colonies in cold places such as Bonn, Amsterdam and London! In the latter city there were 30.000 of these birds counted in the first decade of the 21st century. They nest in holes in trees or old buildings. In the Emirates they were present in all the cities, brightening up many gardens with their lively behaviour and colourful appearance.

My second house-sit in Dubai involved taking care of a captive parakeet. Judging by the fact that she did not have the characteristic rose-coloured ring at the back of her head, I assumed she was a young female. She amazed me with her repertoire of sounds: apart from the raucous screams and ear-splitting shrieks, she could do a perfect cat-call, she had melodious whistles, pleading whines, whispers and clicks, she tutted and creaked and sometimes even sang a six-note song. She went through the entire repertoire twice a day, at dawn and at dusk, when her free-flying fellow birds passed the house to wherever they were going. The early morning concert earned her the name of Wring-neck parakeet!

I liked to watch her eat. She could crack a watermelon seed and extract the thin sliver of kernel from the centre without dropping any of the pieces – and she could do this either hanging upside down or sitting up.

Even though these parakeets were so common, I enjoyed watching their antics in my garden, with the sun glowing on their bright green bodies and turquoise tails. In fact, I grew sunflowers just for them.

11

CATS FROM THE DESERT

During the time that Gerard was writing his report on desert wildlife for the sheikh, he managed to catch a cat far out in the desert. He knew that true wildcats occurred in the area, but also that they were rarely pure because they crossbred so easily with domestic cats. He examined his cat thoroughly and measured and photographed her. This had to be done while the cat was sedated, for wildcats live up to their name – they are extremely uncooperative!

The cat seemed to be the one described in *Mammals of Arabia*, the authoritative work on desert mammals by Dr David Harrison. Still, Gerard decided to send the photographs and measurements to Dr Harrison in order to verify the identification. Soon the answer came back.

"She has all the identifying marks of the Gordon's wildcat," Dr. Harrison wrote, "the mottled markings, no white fur anywhere, the tail with some black rings and tip, the cream-coloured spectacles around the eyes, the tiny tufts on the ears."

She also had a black stripe on the inner side of both elbows, and the undersides of her feet were black all the way up to the heels. On the back of the ears the fur was ginger-coloured. The fur was very fine and silky, covering black skin. During cold weather the fur was puffed up and became almost silvery. The black skin is probably an adaptation to protect the cat against the effect of the ultraviolet rays of the sun.

Wildcats have a lovely Latin name: *Felis sylvestris* – the cat of the forest, because it lived in the dense deciduous forests of Europe. In the nineteenth and early twentieth century these wildcats were almost wiped out through loss of their habitat. They were hardly missed because as secretive and nocturnal animals they were hardly known. Even those who had come across the wildcat had little cause to love it because wildcats are among the most ferocious of animals. Being smart and wary, they are extremely difficult to catch and if they are caught they put up such a fight that few captors remain unscathed after an encounter with a wildcat. It is amazing that our peaceful, strokeable domestic cats have evolved from this wild creature. For *Felis sylvestris* is the early forefather of *Felis catus*, the domestic cat.

The earliest evidence of wildcats comes from Europe, where fossils of wildcats have been found dating back to the Pliocene era (five to two million years ago). This means they were around before the last Ice Age. At that time they probably looked more like the wildcats that are now found around the Mediterranean. As the climate changed the cats of the northern regions developed their bulky shape (to conserve body heat), shorter legs and tail and smaller ears (less chance of frost bite). By this time Felis sylvestris had a very wide distribution. From the wooded hills of Scotland and the deep forests of Scandinavia, their range covered all of Europe and penetrated into the deserts of Africa, the Middle East and Asia. As they reached warmer climates, their outward appearance started to change to adapt to the different living conditions. The long winter coats gave way to smooth short hair and the bulky shape changed to a thin, long-legged form. The ears became larger, not - as in Little Red Riding Hood's tale - in order to hear better, but because they were needed to function as a cooling system. Blood circulating through the ears just underneath thin skin is cooled by the air. The larger the surface of the ears, the more efficiently the blood is cooled.

The next evidence of wildcats comes from Jericho, where archaeologists have found drawings from as early as 7000 BC.

Anatolian statuettes dating from 6000 BC show women playing with cats, indicating that at least occasionally cats were kept as pets.

General domestication of the cat did not take place until around 1600 BC. Around 900 BC in Egypt cats were revered as deities and treated as such. Being a great believer in the mystic power of cats, I favour the theory that the ancient Egyptians admired the wildcats for their beauty and cunning and that the cats, knowing they had stumbled onto a good thing, decided to bestow the favour of their close companionship on their admirers. But authorities on this matter insist that the domestication of the wildcat preceded the cat cult in which the goddess Basset was revered.

The awe in which cats were held in Egypt is illustrated in accounts of one battle in which the enemy held captured cats in front of themselves as they advanced on the Egyptians, who would not kill the cats and could therefore not hurt the men who held them!

Cats were buried with their Egyptian owners to accompany them into the next world. The British Museum in London has a room full of cat mummies from the pyramids. There is also a mural in that museum which shows a cat helping an Egyptian to hunt birds in a marsh. Although in general it was the caracal that was used for hunting at that time, this particular picture shows a tabby cat that does not resemble a caracal at all. I like to think it was an early descendant of *Felis sylvestris*.

Gerard had intended to release the cat again, but when he returned to the area where he had caught her, the site had been bulldozed for the construction of a new housing project. As he was trying to decide about an alternative place, he came across an old male wildcat in the zoo of Dubai. He managed to get this cat on breeding loan and put the two together. In spite of his advanced age, the male performed and on 4 May 1986, the female gave birth to the first litter of Gordon's wildcats ever born in captivity. The litter consisted of two males and one female and they grew up without problems. A second litter was born just before the old male died of old age.

When the second litter was about five weeks old, Gerard took them out of the enclosure for a few hours to take some photographs of the kittens in their proper habitat, out in the desert. When he put them back, the mother killed all three kittens. That was a hard lesson to learn. It is the way of the wild. Cats do not like disturbance when they are raising their young and if they feel too insecure, they will kill and eat their offspring rather than risk their possible loss to predators.

When Gerard returned to his home country I inherited the wildcats, together with the house, the marmosets, the chickens, the mealworms and Nambi. One pair of the cats had to be returned to the zoo where the founder male had come from. CC advised me to keep the mother-and-son pair for myself, since the mother was now a proven breeder and any offspring from the pair would have a slightly better genetic diversity than the brother-sister pair.

A few months after I had moved in, the first litter from this new pair was born. I made sure that the mother was left completely alone. We had put sacking on the wire cage and only opened the door once a day to push in food and a water bowl. Cleaning the litter box was not done for a while. The litter box was far enough away from the breeding box not to cause any problems. This way the mother would have all the peace and quiet she needed to raise her kittens. But the best laid plans…

One night about three weeks after the young were born, I heard a strange sound in my garden. It came from the back garden and through my bedroom window I could see the pale figure of a small barn owl sitting on the chicken coop next to the cat cage.

I remembered him. It was "Buma", a barn owl that Gerard had hand-reared and that had been given to another friend when he left. I found out later that Buma had escaped a week earlier. Apparently he had found his way back to Gerard's garden, even though he had been elsewhere for five months. He was obviously hungry as he sat there crying for food, expecting Gerard to come out and give him a juicy mouse. I tried to offer him pieces of chicken but Buma had always had an intense dislike for me, that he had shown by shrieking and making mock attacks at me whenever I passed his cage. So it was not surprising that he would not accept anything from my hand. In the end he flew away in frustration and was never seen again.

The next morning I left for work without checking on the cats. Fortunately Nambi noticed that something was amiss when he did his rounds. He saw the mother cat in the process of eating one of the babies. By the time he had fetched a broom to chase the mother away from the kittens she had wounded a second one. For several hours Nambi stood there, between the mother and her babies, waiting for me to come home. When I did, I quickly took the wounded kitten and its two unharmed siblings out. At the vet's we checked the tiny victim. Fortunately the wound was only a flesh wound on its thigh and it was stitched quickly.

CC was away on holiday when all the drama happened but fortunately he returned that night, in time to teach me how to raise three week-old kittens. First I went to the toy shops in the *suq* and bought a box with a toy baby doll including all the implements of mothering. Among these were a milk bottle and some nipples that were just the right size. The vet had some cat milk substitute. This product was so close to the real thing that kittens never had any problems with diarrhoea caused by incompatible proteins.

Getting it into them was another story altogether!

It is quite tricky to get the teat of a tiny milk bottle properly inserted into a kitten's mouth. CC showed me how to do it.

'You insert the nipple into the side of the mouth and then wriggle it into position so that it pushes softly against the palate, like this,' he said. 'You'll know it is in the right place when the kitten starts sucking. Never, NEVER, squeeze the bottle to force fluids down its throat. It'll aspirate and get pneumonia. You'll kill it.'

Every one of the feeds of that first week was a minor battle. I knew I had won whenever the kitten's ears would start to pump up and down with the effort of sucking.

After feeding would come the task of "making it go" – with a finger wrapped in a moist piece of tissue paper, I had to rub the kitten's behind very gently, until first some urine and then a little squirt of faeces was produced. On a good day, the whole process of feeding and cleaning would take about fifteen minutes per kitten. Multiply by three (kittens) and then by five (feeds per day) and add to that the time spent in making up the formula and sterilising bottle and teats, and it is easy to see I barely had time to go to work! It was a good thing that my workplace was five minutes away and my boss was extremely tolerant of my regular disappearances during the first ten days.

But the rewards were incredible. For the next four months my house was filled with happy cats. I take that back – my three domestic cats were not exactly overjoyed at the pranks the wildcats played on them. However, they were too well-mannered to hit back, so they withdrew to the bedroom whenever the wildcats were let out to play. I only let them out when I was home. The rest of the time they lived first in the guest room and later in the garage, which had a wire front, having housed Gerard's foxes at one time.

The kitten that had been injured by her mother turned out to be extremely accident-prone. One of her siblings scratched her eye in play and it became infected. When treatment with ointment did not help, the eyelid had to be sewn shut for sometime. And even this did not save the eye, which turned black and blind. Being one-eyed did not hamper her spirits in any way. She was always the most adventurous and naughty of the lot. One day she managed to get close to her father's cage. He reached out through the wire and grabbed her by a paw, which he stripped bare of skin and flesh in a split second. The vet held out little hope of saving the leg but tried nevertheless to sew whatever skin remained and put on an immobilising plaster.

She healed surprisingly well. With her one eye and plastered leg she looked like a pirate. By this time I had started to call her Calamity Jane.

Calamity Jane's sister had a habit that was as amazing as it was endearing. Whenever I came into the garage to feed the cats or play with them, she would launch herself from a sitting position on the floor straight into the air to land on my chest. She would never have her claws out, fully expecting me to catch and hold her. Her brother, on the contrary, liked to jump onto my back from the wall shelf where he spent most of his time.

Whenever I bent over to put the food bowls down he would land on my back with claws fully extended. I learned quickly to toss food bowls down without bending.

CC and I often discussed whether hand-reared cats could ever be returned to the wild. On one occasion I had the chance to observe that my hand-reared cats still had hunting and killing capabilities, even though they had never learned hunting tricks from their mother. Calamity Jane's sister, by now four months old, had escaped into the back garden. She scaled the wall of my garden to reach the neighbour's yard. There she proceeded to kill a chicken twice her size. She was dragging it across the yard, when the neighbours noticed her and tried to scare her away by throwing a pail of water over her, but she held tightly on to her prey and found refuge in the servant's quarters.

By this time I had heard a commotion and came running to see what had happened. The neighbours told me excitedly that an extremely ferocious cat had killed their chicken. They indicated that it was about the size of a Doberman and as fierce as a wolverine.

'Don't go into the room, madam,' they pleaded, 'the cat will attack you and you will be injured.'

I stuck my head around the door and called the kitten. She came running towards me, soaked and bedraggled but with her tail held high, waving proudly. When she jumped into my arms, I swear she was grinning.

The neighbours could not believe their eyes when they saw the kitten peacefully purring in my arms. I promised them a new chicken and quickly got out before they could change their minds about being good-natured about the incident. I realised that a chicken is easier to catch than a wild bird or rodent, but I was still reassured that the kittens had good instincts.

The kittens grew up and needed to be found a home, for the next litter was on its way. I could not keep all the cats for they were expensive to keep. I was always amazed at the amounts of meat they put away. If I did not give them at least three times as much as my domestic cats, they would become pencil thin. Of course they were de-wormed regularly. It was their high metabolic rate that burned away the calories. I only realised that this was the case during one of Calamity Jane's escapades.

She had escaped through the bathroom window and was gone for two days. I looked for her everywhere. Nambi scoured the neighbourhood and put the word out to other house boys and girls to warn us if she strayed into their gardens. I was sure I had lost her. Then one night at three in the morning someone knocked on my bedroom window. It was Julie, the British girl who lived in the house at the back of mine.

'Come quick,' she said, 'I think your cat is in my garden and my dogs are after her.' She had four huge dogs that were not used to cats.

I ran to the side of the house, where it was pitch dark. The dogs were standing in a semi circle, barking wildly and I could hear a cat growl ominously. Julie brought a flashlight and there was Calamity, puffed up to twice her size and looking unbeliev-ably fierce. No wonder the dogs kept a safe distance.

While Julie pulled the dogs away, I went to her, talking softly and she let herself be picked up. As I carried her into my house I noticed how hot she was. In fact I have never felt any living crea-ture as hot as that. Her body temperature must have been far over 40°C. The only animals I know who can tolerate such temperatures are camels that use this mechanism as an adapta-tion to the heat. Maybe a similar adaptation was at work in this desert cat. Afterwards I regretted that I had not measured her temperature, but at the time I was much too concerned about her condition to even think of that. It took several hours of panting and a great deal of drinking for Calamity to get back to normal. She never ran away again.

Calamity's brother and sister were sent to Wuppertal Zoo in Germany, which became the first zoo outside Arabia to have a pair of Gordon's wildcats. Wuppertal still holds the studbook for this species of cat. About a year after they had arrived in Germany, I visited them in the zoo. I was allowed to go into their cage. It took a few seconds of calling before the cats – now adults – came out of their den. When the female saw me she immediately did her flying leap into my arms, to the utter amazement of CC and the keeper who were watching outside the cage.

I could not bear to be parted from Calamity Jane, after the

troubles we had been through together. She still lived in the garage but spent much time with the domestic cats inside the house.

Over the next few years several litters of kittens were born to the breeding pair. One litter of three escaped through the wire mesh of their cage when they were about six weeks old. After I retrieved them from various bushes and trees, I did not dare to put them back with their mother, remembering what had happened some years earlier when Gerard had removed kittens from their mother. So I decided to see if I could tame these kittens a little bit so they would be easier to handle for vaccinations and examinations. Whenever we had to vaccinate the cats, CC brought a large net on a handle from the zoo. After removing most objects from the cage, he would launch into a rather lively ballet with the cats. They were fast but they were no match for CC's cleverness. He would predict where they were going to run to and with one deft movement swoop the net over them, immediately turning the handle so that the cat could not get out any more. Then he would hold the cat down with his shoe while I handed him a prepared syringe. On more than one occasion the cat bit completely through the thick leather of his working shoe! It was always a nerve-racking exercise.

So I tried taming this lot. I sat with them daily for hours at a time, trying to coax them out of their hiding places. One hiding place was behind a low bookcase. I'll never forget what they looked like as I peered over the top of the bookcase. The three little faces in a row looking up at me were heart-shaped, with their pointed chins and perfect triangular ears. They looked like little angels but to handle them I had to wear gloves, for they spat and clawed and bit whenever I approached them too closely. After four weeks I gave up. Wildcats are not easily tamed, after they have been with their mother for more than four weeks.

The kittens from the various litters were sent to zoos and breeding centres in Europe and Oman. Eventually the founder breeding pair was sent to San Diego Zoo in the USA, where they were doing well when I visited them years later.

Calamity Jane stayed for a long time. In the evenings she would be inside the house with us, where she loved to sit on the chicken wire tube that connected the night quarters of the marmosets to their outside aviary. The marmosets played with her tail as she watched my movements with her one eye. Eventually I sent her with one of her brothers to a private breeder in California, where they bred successfully. Her new "mom", Pat Quillen, obviously found out about the untameable nature of wildcats. She called the new kittens Rico and Shea, because they used to "ricochet" through the cage whenever they were approached. Eventually Calamity died at the ripe old age of thirteen years.

The last cats that I had went to the new Breeding Centre for Endangered Arabian Animals in Sharjah, where they were paired with newly caught ones and bred successfully.

12

IVAN THE TERRIFIED

The phone rang. 'Hi there. I was wondering if you could help me. The supervisor of my workers called me this afternoon and said that there was a strange bird in a tree near the fish ponds. It had four legs, he said.'

It was Kevin, one of Gerard's friends, who was employed by the same sheikh for whom Gerard had worked. Since he was an expert on fish as well as an avid sea-angler, we always called him Kevin the Fish.

'Four legs? What on earth did he see?'

Kevin giggled. 'Well, I went down there and when I approached, the animal jumped into the water and swam across the pond. We caught it with nets on the other side. It is very fierce and I have no idea what it is. Can you have a look?'

'I can tell you one thing without even looking at it - it is not a bird! But come on over and show me.'

A little while later Kevin walked down the garden path with a cat carrier. I peered into the box. A cat-sized brown animal sat in the far corner. Its face was remarkable. It had round ears like a bear, a pointed snout with a huge mouth that curled at the corners as if it was smiling.

It did not smile, but snarled.

'I've already called him Ivan the terrible,' said Kevin, 'Boy, can that small thing fight!'

'Ivan the terrified is more suited,' I countered. 'I have no idea what it is. It doesn't seem to have a tail. Did he lose it during the catching process?'

'Oh no,' said Kevin, 'We didn't hurt it at any time. Can I leave it with you?'

A call to CC at the zoo was in order.

'No tail?' he said. 'There are only two animals of that description that do not have a tail. One is an agouti and the other a hyrax.'

I knew agoutis from having seen them at zoos. This animal was much smaller. So it had to be a hyrax. CC told me that it would be best to feed it fresh alfalfa. I sent Nambi to the *suq* to get some and placed the frightened Ivan in an empty quail pen, while I went to my books to find out more about hyraxes.

It has been established from fossil beds that thirty-six million years ago hyraxes were the most important medium-sized grazing and browsing animal in Africa. Of the many different species that used to occur, nowadays only three main species remain: bush hyraxes and rock hyraxes, that often co-exist together, and tree hyraxes that have a much more limited habitat. Only the rock hyrax occurs naturally on the Arabian peninsula.

Rock hyraxes (*Procavia capensis*) are rodent-like, vegetarian animals that live in groups on rock piles in the African plains or in more mountainous areas such as in southwestern Arabia. They weigh between 1.5kg and 5kg, reach a length of about forty-five centimetres, have short legs, a rudimentary tail and round ears. Their feet have rubbery pads with numerous sweat glands that make them ideal for climbing, even scaling vertical rocks. Tactile hairs are distributed over their bodies, helping to orientate themselves inside the dark fissures and holes where they hide. They cannot maintain their body temperatures well so they huddle together for warmth and spend a lot of time basking in the sun. They have a complex digestive system that enables them to subsist on poor quality vegetation, while their efficient kidneys allow them to exist on minimal moisture intake. These kidneys concentrate urea and electrolytes and excrete large amounts of undissolved calcium carbonate. Since hyraxes always use the same places as latrines, the cliff faces in these spots are covered with calcium crystals. This substance, called hyraceum, was used as medicine in South Africa and Europe.

Hyraxes are related to both elephants and seacows. There are skeletal similarities in skulls and feet in these three groups of mammals. Their upper incisors are tusk-like. In addition, they all have nails instead of claws or hooves and they have two mammary glands between their front legs instead of in rows along their abdomen.

During the mating period the territorial dominant male becomes very aggressive. The weight of his testes, which are internal (a feature hyraxes share with elephants), increases twenty-fold in weight. The gestation period is very long for the relatively small animals: 7.5 months, after which one to four young are born. These are fully developed at birth and are weaned at around 3 months

I had known that they used to be found in the Hajar mountains that stretch along the eastern coast of the Emirates, because hyraceum has been found there. It was generally assumed, however, that in the UAE they were now extinct in the wild. This animal must have escaped from captivity somewhere. In due time I found out that some hyraxes were given as presents to the sheikh of Dubai in the past, and these had multiplied to form a sizable group that lived in one of the buildings on the sheikh's property. Some years later I found another hyrax in the area where I went for walks, not far from the sheikh's palace. It was another escapee, dead but still warm, obviously killed by a blow to its head from a needlessly frightened passer-by.

Finding fresh alfalfa for Ivan meant going to the vegetable *suq* every morning before going to work. The suq was in the centre of town and traffic was heavy at that time, so I was finding it quite a chore. Ivan solved the problem for us before the end of the first week. Nambi came running: 'Madam, madam, big mouse is out!'

'Where is it, did you see where it went?'

'Is in tree, madam.'

Sure enough, high up in the mesquite tree that shaded the back garden sat the hyrax, huddled in a fork of branches. The mesquite tree was huge. Its branches reached far over the roof of my house and that of my neighbour, Julie, as well as over our two garages.

It was mid-afternoon on the day that CC usually came to Dubai. So I told Nambi to keep an eye on the animal and decided to drive to Al Ain to pick up CC and some catching equipment. A few hours later we were back. Ivan had not moved. CC unfolded his plan of action to us:

'Nambi, you go on the roof of Julie's house. I'll go on the roof of the garage and start shaking the branches of the tree.' To me he said: 'The hyrax will jump, and it can jump incredibly far, so you go and stand in the back garden. Open all the windows and doors, also of the corridor along the wildcat cages, then you can shoo him in somewhere.'

It turned out to be a good plan. After agitating the tree for just a few minutes, the hyrax took flight (was he a four-footed bird after all?) He jumped from his perch four metres high in the tree to a spot in the back yard that was some six metres away from it. He shot into the corridor along the cat cages, where he was received with enthusiasm by our male wildcat. When I followed with a net, quickly closing the door behind me, I was able to rescue the poor creature from the grasping claws of the cat, who had stuck his paws through the wire of his cage to catch this interesting prey.

We restored Ivan to his own cage, having first repaired the hole through which he had escaped. That evening I told CC about my problems getting fresh alfalfa for the little animal. Since there was no place where we could release him into the wild, we decided that he would be better off in the zoo. So, the next day CC took him back to Al Ain and decided to put him into a cage that was already home to a few small nocturnal monkeys. At the end of the first morning he went to check on Ivan and could not find him anywhere in the cage. Had the escape artist performed a vanishing act again?

Then he noticed him, sitting on a high shelf, huddled in between the monkeys, who obviously did not mind the company.

CC was pleasantly surprised by this interspecies adoption, for the Ivan, being a herd animal, would have been unhappy on his own.

'These adoptions happen quite often in the animal world,' he told me when I asked him about it. 'In captivity sometimes orphaned or lonely animals are put together with another species, as in the famous cases of apes in laboratories having kittens as playmates. And remember when that little boy fell into the gorilla enclosure at Jersey zoo a few years ago? The huge silverback gorilla sat by the boy and protected him from the younger, more aggressive gorillas until he could be brought to safety. It is nice that my monkeys turned out to be peaceful too.'

Ivan was no longer terrified and spent the rest of his many years happily with this ersatz family!

13

ZOO VISITS

Summer vacations with CC were extremely interesting if not very restful. His vacations were always busman's holidays. He selected specific zoos where he wanted to see specific, usually very rare, captive animals that he had not yet seen or wanted to see once more.

I always marvelled at CC's brain. It stored an enormous amount of trivia that he could recall in great detail at any time. He knew a lot about European history and politics, but mostly his knowledge concerned wild animals. He knew exactly which animal was kept where and since when, and where they had come from, whether there was any offspring and where those had gone. It seemed he had every studbook of every zoo at his fingertips.

Even though at times I would have liked a few days' holiday to read a book or so, I was happy to trail along on the zoo visits. Having a personal guide made the visits much more interesting. CC would explain why an exhibit was good or not so good. I remember a beaver enclosure somewhere. It consisted of a model of a beaver hut at one side of a pond, with a small trickle of water running down a fake rock on the other side.

'I wonder if they ever turn that trickle off,' he said. 'You see, the sound of trickling water stimulates the beaver to do something. To him it means there is a leak in his dam, so he wants to repair it. In a sense it is great if you can design an enclosure in such a way that the animals are stimulated to be active. But I see no building materials in this pond, so in this case I fear that trickle will make the poor animals mad with frustration.'

In another zoo birds were flying freely in a well-lit forested space, while the area where the visitors were standing was pitch dark. I was amazed to see that there was no wire mesh or glass between the birds' area and the visitors' area. Again CC had an explanation: 'Birds do not fly into a dark space – unless they are nocturnally active, of course. And any bird that strays into the visitors' area accidentally will soon find its way back into the sunlight!'

If a cat in a zoo enclosure would be sitting comfortably in a very visible spot, rather than be hidden in the bushes or behind a rock, CC would explain to me that the trick is to give the cat a heating pad in that spot. Conversely, in hot climates an animal could be enticed to sit in a prime display spot by providing some cool air there.

CC was always looking for new ideas for successful exhibits and was enthusiastic whenever he discovered a good engineering trick or a special lay-out, just as he had caustic criticism for bad exhibits and signs of improper or insufficient animal care. As I spent time with him in his professional environment I realised that he must be a very difficult boss to work for. He tolerated no slack work, accepted no excuses for lack of knowledge and did not forgive oversights or mistakes.

Rare animals were a passion with CC. One summer we visited Port Lympne zoo in the UK just to see the newly arrived Sumatran rhinoceros (*Dicerorhinus sumatrensis*). This species was believed to be so rare that a captive breeding program might be the only way in which to safeguard the animals' continued existence. When CC saw the small rhino, his eyes filled with tears. Tears of joy to see an animal he had never seen before, and tears of sadness that the reason for being able to see the animal meant that it was in great trouble. A few years later we were travelling in Malaysia. There is a small zoo in Malacca on the southern coast. The town itself was a living museum of Dutch colonial architecture, with many things of interest to visit, such as the churchyard, where early Dutch colonials were buried.

Reading the carved and weathered headstones we realised that hardly anyone lived beyond his thirties in those days, while the number of graves of small children was astounding. Malaria, dysentery and cholera obviously took their toll.

The zoo was rather nice, in a park-like area with simple cages under shady trees. We knew there were at least two Sumatran rhinos in this zoo, but we had been told they were not on display and could not be visited. We spotted the rhino house with its empty outside enclosures. A couple of animal keepers were having a smoke at the entrance. I chatted with the keepers in my best Malay which is quite similar to the Behasa Indonesia that I had learned as a child and used when I worked in Indonesia some years earlier.

'Yes, we have a male and a female Sumatran rhino here,' they told me.

'How are they doing?' I asked. 'They were caught wild, right?'

'Yes, they have been here only since a year or so, but they are doing fine. We even have a baby!'

Quickly I told CC this amazing news that had not reached the outside world as yet. He did not believe I had heard right. I asked the guys again. They assured me there was a newborn baby in the house. I cast a longing look into the open door.

'Is it really not possible to have a look? We are professional people and would not do anything to disturb the animals and we are so very interested!'

There was a *sotto voce* palaver between the keepers. Then they opened the gate and let us through. We walked down a dark corridor past a pen where the male rhino minus his horns was sending us malevolent looks. Sumatran rhinos are much smaller than their African counterparts. This male was only about 1.5m high and not much larger than a Shetland pony. His hide was covered with patches of long coarse hair, with mud clinging between the hairs. This is an adaptation to a hot climate: the mud keeps the animals cool while at the same time it protects against annoying insects.

On the left a pen of four meters square held another rhino, and between her legs a tiny creature was hiding. It was no larger than a medium-sized dog but already a perfect rhinoceros. It looked like a toy. CC was excited but at the same time worried, because instantly he had seen a few features of the pen where a small animal could get hurt. He pointed them out to the keepers – a space between a wall and a fodder trough where the baby could get stuck, a few metal bits sticking out of a wall. I translated as best I could and we hoped that the message got through.

On our way out CC turned to me and said: 'They must have caught that female while she was pregnant. The baby cannot have been conceived here, there has not been enough time.'

We never found out what happened to the rhinos of the Malacca zoo, whether the baby survived to adulthood and whether they managed to breed any in captivity. The first officially recognised breeding was in 2001 in an American zoo.

We ended that vacation in Singapore, the true target of this trip: a visit to the Golden monkeys (*Pygathrix roxellana*) that were on display for the first time outside China. These amazing animals are covered in long gold-coloured hair, while their (incredibly fat) lips, the "bags" beneath their eyes and their private parts are a bright turquoise – and when I say bright, I mean unbelievably, startlingly bright! Other than their amazing colouration I did not find much of interest in them. To me they seemed a caricature of an animal. I asked CC why he was so fascinated by this animal. He explained: 'Well, you know that I always want to see what I don't know yet. This monkey is so unusual in its appearance. But the things I read about it were interesting too. They live in groups of up to six hundred in the bamboo jungles, coniferous forests and rhododendron thickets of the central and western mountains of China. Since the winter is cold in those areas, their fur has become very long, especially around the shoulders. When they jump they seem to have golden wings. Their fur was highly-priced in the past when Manchurian officials were allowed to wear cloaks made from their pelts. The large groups split up in smaller bands of around seventy animals in winter, when they have to live off tree bark and lichens. In summer they also eat leaves, bamboo shoots, insects, worms, small birds and eggs. Males and females have different calls and members of the groups of Golden monkeys are known to sing together.'

'Really, they sing? How fascinating! Are they endangered?'

'Yes, they are poached for their bones and heart that are believed to have medicinal properties but like almost everywhere else in the world it is loss of habitat that endangers them most.'

I looked at them with different eyes now that I had consulted my walking, talking encyclopedia.

In Europe we travelled many times to various zoos. In Barcelona we saw the famous white (albino) gorilla Snowflake, but far more interesting were a few forest elephants that did not receive any special mention. Forest elephants are quite a bit smaller than other African elephants and were considered to be a sub-species until DNA analysis in 2001 showed them to be a distinct separate species. In fact CC had once kept one in a zoo in Liberia long before it was described scientifically. At that time he thought he had a young elephant, or one that had been stunted in its growth. Had he realised what he was taking care of, he could have made a name for himself in the zoological world.

The discovery of this second species of African elephant was a chance one. When DNA identification was set up to trace where poached ivory was coming from, it was found that there were two genetically different species, that had evolved some two and a half million years ago. The forest elephant, now known as *Loxodonta cyclotis,* lived hidden from view and virtually unknown in the forests of central and western Africa. Much smaller than the savannah elephants, the largest forest elephant only grows to about 2.1m in height. They have rounded ears and their tusks are straight and thin with a pinkish tinge to the ivory. They are darker in colour with a long narrow face and live in smaller family groups. Poaching and habitat destruction are the main threat to forest elephants, of which probably less than 200.000 remain in the wild. Their ivory is more valuable than that of the other species of elephants because of its colour and higher density. The fact that they occur mainly in countries where hunger and war reign increases the danger that they will be hunted for both their ivory and their meat.

One of our favourite zoos was the Jersey zoo that was started many years ago by Gerald Durrell. I had always been a Durrell fan and I had been to the zoo once already, long ago. What I liked about it was that the animal enclosures were especially tailored to the needs of the animals. The cheetah had a space equal to a couple of football fields to run in, the marmosets had jungles in which to hide. At times you had to be very patient in order to see an animal at all, but your patience was rewarded when you saw some very natural animal behaviour. When CC and I were there the big attraction was a pair of aye-ayes (*Daubentonia madagascariensis*). These big-eyed nocturnal animals from Madagascar are not only cute, but they are fitted out with one very long digit with which they pry insects out of small holes and crevices in tree trunks. It looks very odd, but it must be quite handy to have a tool like a Swiss army knife "at hand", so to say.

People have often told me zoos are terrible places for animals. During our travels we have seen many mediocre zoos and some very bad ones. I remember one in Belgium and one in Spain that horrified me. Zoos everywhere get a bad name when bad or even mediocre zoos are allowed to operate. And yes, these places are not good for the animals, causing needless and often endless suffering. Fortunately the purpose of zoos has been changing over the past few decennia. They are no longer just collections of animals, but almost every zoo nowadays tries to be involved in both breeding and teaching programmes. Some zoos have become specialised. There are desert zoos, there are safari parks and there are zoos with very extensive teaching programmes in special areas, such as insects.

It would be wonderful if zoos were not needed, because every animal could live its life in safety in its own habitat. But the world is getting too crowded and the space that animals can live in is getting forever smaller. So the zoos are acting as Noah's arks, where some specimens are saved for the future.

CC often pointed out to me that breeding is a sure sign that animals are happy in a zoo. The enclosures do not necessarily have to be large or luxurious. Basel is a small zoo with noisy surroundings. But somehow the animals feel at ease there and the breeding successes of this zoo are well known. Other zoos do well because they only keep those animals that occur or used to occur in the region around the zoo. These animals are used to the climate and the available food and no special adaptations need to be made to their environment.

In general, zoos have shown me many wonderful things. I learned about animals that I would never be able to study in their natural habitat. I saw display behaviour that would have taken months of observation to see in the wild. I marvelled at the diversity of animals and at the ingenuity of their adaptations to the environment. In this world, zoos are necessary and fortunately really bad zoos are few and far between, and thanks to the proper example of good zoos even those are disappearing.

CC was never sentimental about the animals in his charge. I remember that once as he was observing his eagles in the huge aviary in Al Ain, two elderly British ladies stood there watching too. One said to the other: 'I think it is so sad that these birds can never soar!'

CC turned towards them and remarked: 'Madam, eagles only soar when they are hungry and looking for food. These are not hungry and have little reason to want to soar.'

When he told me about that incident, I did not quite agree. I am sure that birds that can soar do so for fun at times. They like taking advantage of natural updrafts and can float around for hours doing absolutely nothing. In fact, it was CC himself who had alerted me to this. Once we were driving through Switzerland when CC said: 'Somewhere around here I have once seen a huge number of buzzards playing in an updraft caused by the landscape.' Minutes later we rounded a corner, following the contours of a valley, and there were the buzzards – at least twenty-five of them circling in a column that reached so high that you could barely see the birds at the very top. CC's earlier observation had been many years prior to this second sighting - and one can assume that the birds were always doing this particular game in this particular spot.

So why did CC make that remark to the ladies? I think he just found it difficult when anyone criticised the way his animals were kept. He did all he could to give them optimal conditions and felt it as his personal failure if things were lacking, although often he could not execute his plans due to the municipal bureaucracy. Below the surface of competence and male chauvinism there was a rather insecure person who could not cope with criticism.

14

A GAZELLE IN MY HATCHBACK

When I was still living in Al Ain, CC already used to bring home orphaned baby gazelles. The zoo regularly had deaths in its ungulate groups, often due to nocturnal attacks by feral dogs. There was a night watchman whose task it was to guard against these attacks but he never seemed to be able to prevent them. Maybe night watchman was not an appropriate title for him.

Another problem was the way in which the enclosures had been constructed in the years before CC arrived. CC had told me about the stays of the fences having been put on the inside, causing deaths by decapitation every time the skittish ungulates had a panic attack. Needless to say he immediately changed this situation, not without a major fight with the financial department of the municipality that ran the zoo.

One of the orphaned baby gazelles joined us in the Al Ain apartment because CC had to bottle feed her twice every evening. When her stomach was full she would become quite playful, skipping about the slippery dining room floor and butting her little head towards the cats. The three cats never minded the intrusion of strange animals in our household. Cato was always very shy and retiring but curious Catryn more often than not tried to get the visitor to play. The gazelle was happy to oblige, prancing through the apartment and chasing the cat around the furniture. Sometimes Catastrophe would join in and the game usually ended with the two cats chasing each other under the bed. The gazelle had a herd of sorts and grew up happily until she was big and strong enough to join her herd at the zoo.

She was an Arabian gazelle (*Gazella gazella cora*), the most common ungulate of the region. This is a small slender antelope, with a shoulder height of about sixty centimetres. Its body is a reddish sandy brown with a distinct black flank stripe, a pure white belly and it has a short black tail. Both males and females have ribbed horns with the tips hooked forwards and upwards. In the male the horns are S-shaped, while the female's horns are straight, shorter and thinner. When trying to escape danger they can reach speeds of up to 65km per hour. They live in small groups of up to seven individuals, led by a dominant male. Their range in Arabia largely coincides with the presence of Acacia trees, of which they eat the leaves and seedpods while making use of its shade. They will drink when water is available but mostly they obtain their moisture needs from their food, grazing and browsing at dawn when there is dew on the plants.

Its local name is *dhabi* and the name of the city Abu Dhabi literally means "father of the gazelles". In the wild these graceful little gazelles almost disappeared in the Emirates until a hunting law was drawn up and a few reserve areas were set up. Quite a few captive bred gazelles were released into the desert by the wildlife department of the Abu Dhabi government. In recent years its survival in the wild is threatened again – this time not by hunting but by the ever-increasing population and development pressure in the country. Soon it will only survive in the remotest areas of the mountains and in the zoos, wildlife parks and private collections scattered about the country.

When I moved to Dubai and CC came over on weekends only, taking animals home overnight was more difficult. Small animals were carried in CC's weekend bag, but a gazelle, even if still a baby, is too large for that. One day CC called the day before the weekend. 'I am not sure that I can come to Dubai for the next few weeks. I have a Morrh gazelle to take care of and she is too big to take in a taxi.'

I was not happy about foregoing the weekends. We had so little time together as it was. So I said:

'What if I put down the back seat of the Saab – a gazelle can easily stand there. I'll put some cardboard on the floor and I'll come and pick you up tomorrow and take you back to Al Ain after the weekend.'

'OK, let's try that,' he said.

When I arrived at the zoo the next day CC approved of the car arrangement and put some straw on the cartons to prevent the gazelle from sliding around. Then he brought out the animal.

'Oh, she is lovely,' I exclaimed. For a baby she was already big, with very long legs and a long slender neck. She was mostly white with a light brown saddle and neck and on her throat there was a white spot, like a pendant.

We started driving back. Soon we found out that another adaptation was needed for the gazelle transport. The gazelle who considered CC to be her mother wanted to be near him all the time. She pressed herself between the front seats trying to get to CC's hands that always held such nice milk bottles. Since CC was driving I had to keep pushing the animal back. She might have been a baby still, but she was quite strong and very persistent. So the next day we made a cardboard wall to separate the front from the back. It still needed a hole in the middle – both to enable the use of the rear view mirror and for us to keep an eye on the animal. She immediately stuck her head through this hole so she could keep an eye on us. The rearview mirror could only be used to admire her beauty. In this way we carted her back and forth between Al Ain and Dubai for many weeks until she was weaned off the bottle.

The Morrh gazelle (*Gazella dama morrh*) is one of the larger gazelles of Africa, also called the Western Dama gazelle. It gets its height from its long neck and legs. The neck and back are reddish brown and the rump is white. There is a white spot on the throat and a white patch from beneath the tail upward onto the back. The horns are relatively short and sharply curved back. The animal can reach a shoulder height of over one metre, with large males having a weight of up to seventy kilograms. Their home is in the steppes and deserts of the Eastern Sahara where they used

88

to live in groups of ten to thirty females and young controlled by an adult male. However at present they are extinct in the wild.

Several years later we were on vacation in southern Spain, where we visited a large safari park near Almeria. Here lives the largest herd of Mhorr gazelles in captivity. The habitat of Almeria is very similar to the gazelle's home range and they obviously thrive there. There are groups of these gazelles in many different zoos in Europe and America, but it is unlikely that they can be re-introduced into their native areas, where famine and war are rampant.

15

DWARF HAMSTERS AND
A FAREWELL TO OLD CATS

CC came back from a holiday on his own to Germany. He brought me a small box that made scratching noises. I peered inside carefully and made out four small balls of dark grey fur.

'What are they?' I asked.

'They are Russian dwarf hamsters. I had never seen them before when I found them in the pet shop. They are still quite rare as pets and I just could not resist them. I got one male and three females, so we can breed some.'

I still had a perfect hamster cage – one of Gerard's former snake terrariums. We put the huge glass box on the low chest of drawers in the second bathroom and filled it with a mixture of hay and newspaper shreds. An earthenware jug with a long narrow neck could serve as a burrow. A hamster water bottle was fitted to the side of the cage. CC showed me what to feed them (grains and fruit) and we stood back to watch them as they settled in.

They were incredibly cute – less than ten centimetres from nose to butt. They sat and scuttled around with rounded back, not showing the tiny tail. Their round ears were quite small but their eyes were large and limpid. They were dark grey on top and pearly white below. Across the middle of the back there was a black stripe that faded gradually into the lighter grey and a similar stripe that was wavy ran along both sides separating the grey from the white. Their fur was soft and glossy, very thick. They tamed quite easily and came to sniff my fingers whenever I put my hands inside their cage, even if I was not carrying food.

I asked CC for more details about the little creatures.

'Their scientific name is *Phodopus sungoris sungoris,*' he said. 'They get their common name Dwarf Winter White Russian Hamster from their tendency to turn white in the winter. It's a sociable hamster and you'll find that you'll have a large group in no time at all, for they can have three litters of up to ten babies per year. But their lifespan is short, no more than two years, even in captivity.'

Within a few weeks after their arrival, one of the hamsters died. I could not see anything wrong with it so I wrapped it in a plastic bag and kept it in the fridge till CC could have a look at it. But his veterinary eye could not detect anything wrong, except that it was rather thin.

'Too bad,' said CC, 'it's the male, so now we won't be able to have babies!'

Not long after I noticed something odd in the terrarium. I turned on the lights to investigate and saw the tiniest replica of a dwarf hamster pushing through the hay. It was a baby, already independently foraging, perfect in every detail of its two centimetre long body. I saw more movement and there was another. And another. I called to CC, who was reading in the living room.

'Hey, you know what? Either we have a case of parthenogenesis here, or that male had some fun before he died.'

That day we counted seven baby hamsters. A few days later I saw an even smaller baby sitting in the food dish. I poked around a bit among the objects and toys that were spread around the cage. It seemed that there were five of this size around. Behind the treadmill wheel I found a nest with squirming nude blind babies, at least half a dozen. I added a new cause to the list of possible causes of death for the old male!

So now I had twenty-one dwarf hamsters. They all did fine

and grew up quickly. They would start to reproduce in another month or two, so I needed to separate the sexes before that could happen and I needed to find homes for the surplus hamsters. Mine had been admired by many friends, especially a couple of families with young teenagers. It did not take much to persuade the parents to let the youngsters have Russian dwarf hamsters as pets. CC gave them a lesson in hamster care, so they went and bought cages, food and toys and carried off their pairs with pride.

With some new virile male hamsters in my terrarium, the hamster breeding went on and on and I was running out of options for placing the young ones. Finally we decided to take the males out completely. One of the hamsters became very thin and when I picked him up to examine him, I saw that for some strange reason the teeth of his lower jaw had grown out to a horrendous size, cutting through his upper lip and preventing him from eating. I felt terrible for not having noticed it before. When I called CC that day, he said: 'You have to take care of him. Remember what I taught you to do?'

I had always had an abhorrence of killing animals, even when I knew it was necessary, mainly because I was afraid that out of inexperience I might hurt rather than kill. One day I had found a badly damaged seagull on the beach. It had been the target of some cruel games of local boys, who tortured it so it could no longer see or fly and then just left it in the burning sun. I was alone and there was no one to help me, so I had to put the poor thing out of its misery by myself. I found a large stick and hit the bird as hard as I could, but the soft sand underneath lessened the impact of the blow and the bird did not die. So I had to do it again, this time making sure I had placed the bird on a firm plank. Then I walked to the sea and was violently sick. After that incident I asked CC what I should do if I ever had to end an animal's life in the future. So he taught me a few of the less pleasant tricks of his trade.

Now I took the little hamster outside to the cemented part of the back yard. I nuzzled his silky soft fur and whispered to him as he sat quietly in my hand. Then I lifted him high above my head and threw him onto the hard floor as hard as I could. It killed him instantly. I buried him under a flowering hibiscus bush.

A few days later I faced another terrible decision. Cato and Catryn, the two older cats that I had brought from Holland were sixteen years old now. Catryn had had multiple health problems the last few years that seemed to be caused by infections of her brain. She would start to lose her equilibrium and no longer recognise me. A shot of cortisone would put her right again for a couple of months. I had a feeling she was in terrible pain when it happened but I could not be sure – between bouts she was her own always playful self. But then the incontinence started. And this time it was both cats that were affected. We tried medication for several months but it did not help. I removed the fitted carpet from all the rooms and laid PVC tiles. Still the house started to reek of cat pee.

When I consulted the vet about it once again, he said: 'You've got to put them down, otherwise you'll start to hate them.' As I walked home I contemplated that the animal-loving English do not have a very nice word for animal euthanasia: "putting them down" sounds like a final insult. In Holland we say: "helping them to fall asleep".

I found the two cat cages and rounded up Cato and Cathryn, both fast asleep in the sunshine in the garden. My heart was full of doubt. They were so peaceful and obviously happy and comfortable. But that morning I had wiped up and disinfected seven puddles. It was an untenable situation. When I came back from my sad mission Nambi and I buried the two cats underneath the banana tree. I could not stop crying as I stroked their glossy fur for the last time. Had I really done the right thing? At least they lived and died together – and they had had a good run. To my surprise both Catastrophe and CC were extremely upset. Catastrophe had never shown the slightest interest in the two sisters and I thought she'd be happy to see the last of them. CC usually took the death of animals in his stride. I wondered if he was upset because he realised how I was feeling.

16

PUSH

Although I was now down to one cat, I was not actively looking for another. Catastrophe had just regained her tranquil balance after the loss of her housemates and would not welcome a new intruder.

But sometimes an animal crosses your way – sometimes it even happens quite literally.

Dubai in the eighties was still a city of manageable size. There was an old centre on both sides of the creek where it opened up into the Arabian Gulf. Little boats plied back and forth, carrying passengers across the water for work or shopping. On the southern shore the old windtower houses of Bastakiya could still be seen here and there, some having been renovated by expatriates. Much later the government realised that the antique buildings needed protection and started renovations also.

The windtower or *badgeer* is a very effective ventilation and cooling mechanism, probably having originated in Persia. It is a square tower that is made of two intersecting walls forming a cross that runs from the ceiling of the first floor to a height of ten or fifteen metres above roof level. The four open triangular areas that are thus created catch the wind from whatever direction it is blowing. The base of the tower is also open allowing the down draught to enter the building and provide cool relief to those sitting below. Apart from the positive pressure on the windward side of the tower forcing wind down the tower, there is reduced pressure on the leeward side which sucks air from the room below and thus contributes to the air circulation. The old coral stone houses have stone towers, but you can also see windtowers implemented on the shacks of local fishermen, this time made out of burlap or of woven palm leaves (*barasti*). The cooling is quite effective. One time when I tried staying underneath a tower in the winter I found it freezing cold.

The northern part of the city, called Deira, was the commercial heart of the city. When I arrived in the eighties there were a half dozen hotels along the creek and the quays were full of stacked wares being loaded on and off the rows of quaint *dhows* moored alongside. A late afternoon walk along this bustling trading quay was always very interesting. I liked taking pictures of the *dhows* with their external poop boxes and gaily painted railings. Stacks of "Paki mats" – thin foam mattresses with flowery covers – contrasted strangely with the gleaming white high-rise buildings along the boulevard. There were the smells of spices and cigarettes, the sounds of Indian dialects and the sparkle of the sun on the choppy waves of the creek. Once I found a large crate with the intriguing words: "Remains of Mr. Chandrapawatty." It did not look like a coffin, so I assumed it contained ashes.

While towards the north the city of Dubai joined up with Sharjah, towards the south the former villages of Jumeirah, Umm Seqeim and Bada'a became suburbs. Three parallel four-lane highways ran for miles along the coast, separating posh residential districts from each other. In those days small fishing harbours were still strung out like beads along the coast. In the early morning you could see the boats come in with their catch and you could buy wonderful *hamour* and crabs for a pittance. In the evening you could watch the sun setting while having a picnic seated on large boulders with the shady date palms of an oasis at your back. Life was peaceful and gentle there. There was poverty too, but in the mild climate of winter it did not weigh too heavily. And in the hot summer life just came to a standstill at noon.

I was driving along the middle one of the three parallel highways, heading for home in al Bada'a, when suddenly a cat shot out from the planted road divider and ran against my front wheel. I heard the dreaded thud and looked in the rear view mirror to see a still shape on the road. Distraught at having caused death, I did a quick U-turn at the first possibility and headed back to where I had hit the cat. I wanted to take it off the road so it would not be squashed any further. It was a beautiful Siamese cat, velvety beige with black feet and ears. As I picked it up to transfer it to the road verge, I saw its whiskers tremble. It was still alive!

I put it on the floor of the car and drove to the veterinary clinic. There some X-rays revealed that the cat had a broken jaw, but no other injuries besides the concussion that had rendered it unconscious for a while. I left the cat with the vet to have its jaw wired and picked it up later that afternoon, having been instructed to give it liquid food for the next four weeks.

The cat, a gorgeous male, recovered amazingly fast. Within days he was walking around and crying through clenched jaws for his "drink" of mashed sardines, which I had to pour in with a small spoon. It was a messy and time consuming procedure but well worth the effort, for he turned out to be a wonderful creature. He was a real cuddler, loved to be carried around, slung over my shoulder like a rag, purring like a little generator. At any time you could push him over on his back so you could tickle his belly. That earned him the name Push.

At the same time that Push was with us, we were also taking care of a baby leopard. This animal had a disease of some kind that would cause it to topple over and be completely disoriented for a few days at a time. During this time it had to be force fed, as it had no appetite and was generally listless. Then it would recover, regaining its strength and becoming a happy, inquisitive leopard cub again. Push was very interested in the cub that was only slightly larger than he was. They would play together and Push seemed to be genuinely concerned whenever the cub had a relapse of his disease. Eventually the leopard succumbed to his ailment and on section it turned out that it had a string of abscesses in his brain. Every time a new abscess formed this would cause his symptoms, then the abscess was contained by its body defences and it would recover, until at last most of its brain was affected and it died.

Push's dental wires were removed and now he really came into his own. I had to go home to Holland for a few days and when I came back, CC told me that we had a problem. Catastrophe, who had always given the newcomer a wide berth, was suffering. Whenever she wanted to walk around the house, Push would chase her out. Outside a huge ginger tomcat belonging to one of the neighbours would chase her around the garden until her only refuge was found in Nambi's room. Since Catastrophe had the oldest rights, I needed to find a home for Push. Luckily Dubai had an active Feline Friends organisation and through them I found a family with young children that was willing to take him. I knew they were the right family for him when I watched Push being carried to their car, slung perfectly relaxed across the shoulder of the seven-year old boy.

17

SANDY

Friends had invited me to join them on a trip to the sandy desert. I had not been on many sand trips before because I did not have a 4WD vehicle. My car was able to travel the gravel roads in the mountains and along the coasts, but the sandy dunes were unexplored as far as I was concerned. As we drove down there along the four-lane highway that led through the outskirts of the city, I saw something small and alive on the fast lane of the road.

'Please stop,' I called, 'I want to see what that is.'

I thought it might be a rodent of some kind, but it did not move away as I approached. In fact, it was not moving at all. When I picked it up, the tiniest puppy face looked at me with large brown eyes. It was so small that it fitted on the palm of my hand. I looked down on the little ball of fur and thought: 'Oh, oh, fifteen years!'

Sandy had arrived.

As we were out on a trip, the little puppy had to come along. It was very tired and fell asleep immediately on my friend's new blue pullover, which it later peed on as a "thank you". When we stopped for a picnic, I had a chance to look at it more closely. It was a she, of very slender build. Her face was brown with a broad black stripe over the bridge of the nose. Her overall colour was greyish – the colour of wild animals – with a white patch on one shoulder. Her worm-like tail had a dinky white tuft. The paws were thin and long, so I surmised that she would be a small to medium-sized dog when she grew up. That suited me fine. A few days later a friend who had been in the Emirates longer told me that small paws mean nothing in a desert dog. I did not believe her then. However, little Sandy grew at tremendous speed, causing CC to quote an old German saying: 'Millet and puppies double in size overnight!'

We estimated that she was about three and a half weeks old when we found her. Since that was on 25 January, I put her birthday on 1 January – easy to remember. At the time I was between jobs so I had lots of time to devote to the puppy. She was my first dog. Our family had always had dogs, but they were either my mother's or my brother's. I had always longed to have a dog of my own, but my lonely lifestyle and long working hours left no time for a pet other than cats who are more independent. I did not think it was fair to have a dog when I was never home.

I fussed over Sandy as over a child and she became the world's most spoiled animal. Several of my friends remarked even years later that in a next life they would like to come back as a dog in my house! CC laughed at me when I wanted to go on a beach walk with the dog when she was barely six weeks old.

'Puppies don't leave the neighbourhood of their den for up to four months,' he said. 'She is not ready yet for walks.' He was right, of course, but I felt that dogs needed walks.

One housemate who did not like the intrusion of a puppy at all was Catastrophe. I had put the large glass terrarium with the dwarf hamsters on the floor in the sitting room, so that they would get some sunshine. Catastrophe decided that she was safe from the puppy's enthusiasm inside this glass cage, where she could enjoy the sun as well as peace and quiet. When CC saw her jump into the glass box one day, he said:

'Well, I guess the dwarf hamsters will be cat food now.'

'No,' I said, 'Just watch!'

Before long one of the tiny hamsters came out of the earthenware jug that was their burrow. He scurried over to where the cat was sitting, with all her loose ends tucked in. Then he stood up against her face and sniffed her whiskers. A little while later, he was fast asleep curled up on Catastrophe's neck. CC could not believe it.

I told him: 'Somehow my pets know that the other animals in the house are pets and not prey. No one ever harms anyone!'

That night Catastrophe went out and caught a mouse in the garden that was about the same size as the hamsters. It was lying in front of the bedroom door the next morning - did she just want to prove to me that it was not her lack of hunting skills that left the hamsters alive?

I found a new part-time job. To transfer the work permit and visa to the new employer I had to leave the country and re-enter. I took the well-known visa-flight to Doha. In the airport someone had mopped a ceramic tile floor and left no warning signs. I slipped and fell on my back, spraining my ankle. The airport emergency unit taped the ankle and sent me on my way to Doha. It was not a pleasant trip with the throbbing ankle and the beginnings of a back pain. The next few days my back stayed a bit sore. A few days later I lifted Sandy up to put her outside for a pee. As I turned towards the door I heard a popping sound in my back. I thought nothing of it and went to work. Within half an hour a fierce pain started in my back. I had to lie down between examining patients. I was sure I had slipped a disc in my back. I remember thinking:

'Now I will HAVE to lose weight. This is the turning point for me as a fat person.' After a couple of hours I could not take it any longer and took the rest of the day off. The pain got worse and worse. Painkillers did not help a bit. Great waves of pain engulfed me. I remembered that one of my colleagues at the hospital in Al Ain, a Swedish orthopedic surgeon, had moved to the Rashid Hospital in Dubai. I crawled to the phone on all fours and called him for advice.

'Lie down flat with your legs elevated at right angles resting on cushions,' he said. 'Not every hernia needs to be operated.'

I tried to do what he said but after a while I was reduced to tears by the pain. It was a long and horrible evening but finally I fell into an exhausted sleep. In the morning the pain was gone.

But so was the strength in my right leg. This was not good. I called the surgeon again. When he heard my news, he almost yelled at me: 'Come to the hospital instantly. I'll meet you at the door.'

I called to Nambi to get me a taxi, while I hopped around on one leg getting some overnight things together. Before I left I managed to instruct Nambi to give food and water to little Sandy, but my brains were not functioning very well and I did not say anything about keeping her company or playing with her.

In the hospital an MRI quickly showed that one disc had completely herniated, at the site where apparently some ligament had broken during the fall at the airport. I was to be operated on immediately. I was very grateful to be able to put my fate into the hands of a well-trained European surgeon. I just had time to call my father, whose birthday it was that day, and CC. I told the latter that I would be very groggy the next day, so he should not bother to come right away.

When I came to in the recovery room, I noticed that it was four and a half hours later, instead of the expected three-quarters of an hour. The surgeon's face looked grey with tiredness.

'I'll tell you about it later,' he said. 'It was difficult but it went OK.' Apparently the disc had slipped forward to the front of the spine – an unusual situation. The surgeon had had to work very carefully around the spine, chipping bits off the disc little by little. This was even more difficult because of my obesity – he had to make a larger incision than normal and even then it took much longer than expected. The next day the surgeon asked me to wriggle my toe. To his amazement and alarm, I lifted my whole leg.

'Don't do that,' he warned, 'give it time to heal. I did not think that you would ever be able to use that leg again. The nerve had the colour of an aubergine. It had really been badly compressed.'

I had to stay in the hospital for twelve days. I remember the first few days best, lying on my back with incredible pain, thinking: *This really is hell*. Although I knew I had told CC not to come, I was very disappointed that he had not shown up anyway. It was unreasonable, but even so it hurt. The one time I needed him, he was not there.

When I came home, Sandy had grown tremendously. She had been so bored that she had chewed everything that she could possibly find: shoes and slippers from the closet, towels from the bathroom, all the bindings of the books on the lower shelves of the bookcases. Poor thing. My mind had been so occupied with my own misery that I had not provided for her adequately.

A month later she reached the age to be sterilised. I brought her home after the operation and as we walked from the car to the house, she decided that she was tired and lay down on the path. It was the end of June and far too hot to be outside. I could not pick her up, because I was not allowed to bend over yet. I nudged her with my foot but she wouldn't budge. When I insisted, she bit me. That was the one and only time that she ever bit anyone. I am sure it was because the remnants of the anaesthesia had weakened her normal inhibitions.

Sandy was my companion and best friend for many years. We spent every minute that I was not working together. She came along on desert trips and *wadi* walks, camping and swimming. When she was still quite small the walks on sharp hot stones would hurt her feet and then she would sit in my backpack and enjoy being carried. Water was her favourite element. She was a strong swimmer. Once she even followed me on a half-hour swim around a small offshore island.

I soon found out that walking your dog on the beach was the dog-owners' equivalent of baby-sitters socialising in the park. I encountered a Finnish lady who walked her young boxer there. The two dogs and their owners became best friends – a friendship sustained over many years. The dogs raced each other on the wet sand of the beach at low tide. Sandy was an extremely fast runner. I always felt that she had a fifth gear. When other dogs were going as fast as they could, Sandy would suddenly spurt ahead, leaving the others to eat her dust.

Much later, a zoologist friend remarked that the bone structure of Sandy's head was very similar to that of wild wolves. We concluded that she was probably a cross between a wild Arabian wolf and a saluki, the desert dog beloved by the Bedouins. The latter's genes would explain her great speed and more slender build, as well as her pleasant smell. Many years later when I could observe some Arabian wolves at close quarters, I noticed that the way these animals moved and other small mannerisms were exactly those of Sandy.

Her half-wild origins gave her some special qualities that everyone who ever met her soon recognised. She was extremely intelligent. She learned to open doors by manipulating the door handle. To open a door inwards, she would stand on her hind legs, press down the handle with her front paws and back up. She also worked out how sliding doors and windows worked. The fridge door gave no problems until I fitted it with a padlock. This was very necessary, for she was the world's greatest thief of food. Even when she was very old and could barely walk due to the arthritis in her hind legs, she still managed to steal anything edible that I had left within reach on the kitchen counter.

She had an uncanny ability to know when I was coming home. My working hours were irregular but CC said: 'I always know when to expect you, because Sandy will suddenly get up from what seems to be deep sleep and head towards the gate. There she'll lie down with her nose stuck underneath the door to look for you and ten minutes later you'll be there.' My clinic was less than ten minutes driving away. If she got up ten minutes before I got home, that would be just about the time I would pick up my things to go to the car.

The same would happen at the end of vacations. Nambi told me that she would be fine for the whole month, until the last day. That last day she would spend the entire day lying with her nose in the small space beneath the gate, waiting.

One thing that spoke against her wolf-saluki origins was something that happened when she was about a year old. We had gone on a little drive and I stopped the car along a road that led through a nice part of sandy plain with a rocky outcrop a few hundred meters away. As we got out of the car to go for a walk, Sandy became very alert, looking at the rocky hill. Just as I noticed a small herd of goats there, she took off like a rocket. There was nothing I could do except watch and hope for the best. What happened was totally unexpected. Sandy circled the animals, driving them together and then herded them down the hill towards me on the road. There she kept them together, avoiding the butting heads of the goats. I was totally amazed. This dog had never seen a goat before in her life and had certainly not been taught to herd them. Both wolves and salukis would hunt small hoofed animals, not herd them together. Throughout the rest of her life Sandy never chased or killed an animal on her own, although she would join in a chase with other dogs, if there was a chance.

She was extremely friendly to both people and other animals. Complete strangers could pet her, children sat on her and pulled her ears, young cats played with her tail or used her as a cushion to sleep on – she could be depended upon never to bite or even growl. She was enthusiastic to meet new people, jumping up to greet them. Of course people were scared of her, as she was so large, but I used to say: 'She only kills with kisses!'

In fact, she was so friendly that I doubted that she would be any good defending me in case of need, but I need not have worried. One evening we were walking around the block in my Arab neighbourhood, when a dog suddenly rushed at me out of the dark and nipped at my ankle. I yelled with alarm and immediately heard a terrifying growl from Sandy who hurled herself at the dog and chased it away without much ado. Having seen her in action I was happy to be her friend and not her enemy and never again feared anything on our trips in the desert.

In general her behaviour was quite different from that of normal domesticated dogs. Often I thought she behaved more like a cat, and a Siamese cat at that. She was relatively aloof, giving her affection only at moments of her own choosing. Although she would never growl at me, she made it very clear (by turning her head away) when she did not want to be fussed over. When she did decide to come for a cuddle, it was often at unexpected moments. When I was weeding the flowerbeds on my knees, I would suddenly feel her front paws on my shoulders and her head pressed next to mine, with her whole body resting on my back. Sunbathing was a favourite pastime and if I lay down on the sun chair she would immediately jump up and stretch out on my legs and tummy.

She had extraordinary eyesight for a dog. One incident was interesting as well as funny. We were walking on the beach where some kids were flying a large kite. It was a purple dragon with a long undulating tail. Sandy caught sight of it and stared at it. I saw her head swivel to follow some gulls in flight and then return to look at the kite. I could imagine her thinking: *I know what they are, but what the hell is this!?*

She started to bark at the unfamiliar thing. At that point the kite caught a down draught and plummeted towards the beach, in that erratic way of kites and deflating balloons. Sandy turned around and ran, looking for a safe place to hide. She found it in an ambulance that happened to be standing on the beach with open doors. Sandy took a flying leap through the door, across the lap of the attendant and hid behind some oxygen tanks. I was concerned that the attendants would be very angry to have a dirty dog in their ambulance, but fortunately they had seen what had happened. They were falling about with laughter as I tried to extract the quaking Sandy from behind the oxygen tanks. The dog refused to go to the beach for several weeks after that!

One other incident that had me marvelling at her intelligence took place about eight years after CC had left us. We were stopped at a red light when Sandy suddenly pricked up her ears and stared intently at a man approaching on the sidewalk of the cross street. It was a tall, well-built Asian man, unknown to us. But as I watched him approach my brain also itched with a faint memory. Suddenly I realised what it was: the man's gait and posture were almost identical to what CC's had been as he crossed the street from his taxi to our car, during the many Wednesday evenings when we used to meet him as he came from Al   Ain.   That Sandy would recollect this after so many years had passed was extraordinary.

She showed intelligence also when the municipality put some "sleeping policemen" in the long straight road that led up to our house, to prevent young idiots from driving too fast. Since these bumps were dangerously high I braked to almost standstill before easing my car over them. Sandy, always in the front seat, usually braced herself with one or two paws on the dashboard bar as soon as she felt the car slowing down. One day I was not paying attention and approached the bump without decelerating. Sandy stretched out her paw when she saw the bump getting closer, before she could feel the car losing speed. Clever girl!

People often say that dogs are unclean and that you must avoid being licked by a dog. This may be true of feral dogs that eat carrion. Sandy had bones every day of her life and her teeth were the strongest whitest teeth ever seen in men or dog. The vets always commented on her cleanliness. Once, when I had been stung by an insect in the garden, I developed a frightful rash. It was an allergic reaction, hives of some sort. The bright red bumps that formed in and under my skin itched so bad, I wanted to cut off my leg at the knee to be free of it. For many months I tried every remedy under the sun, from expensive cortisone creams to the potassium permanganate that was so popular in the region, without effect. Finally I gave up and let it be. Then one evening as we sat watching TV Sandy started to lick my leg. Her soft warm tongue was so soothing that I felt the tension drain out of my body. The itch had gone! Sandy kept on licking. This was unusual, for she was not the licking type of dog. She systematically worked up and down my leg, even including those parts of the skin where the rash did not show yet, but was already burning below the skin. She continued for twenty minutes. The next morning the rash was practically gone. In the evening Sandy gave me another treatment and that was the end of my problem. My skin was smooth and soft again, the ugly bumps had disappeared and the scratch marks healed without infection.

Later in life Sandy became more affectionate, especially after she lost her hearing. Then she would sometimes give me the lightest of licks on the tip of my nose – like the brush of a butterfly wing. Once she was sleeping at my feet as I was watching TV, stretched out on the bed. Suddenly she woke up, stood up, walked to the top of the bed and gave me one of her butterfly kisses. Then she turned back to the foot of the bed, curled up and went to sleep again. It brought tears to my eyes. I'll never forget that moment.

There was something about Sandy that set her apart from other dogs, something mysterious and powerful. One day I read this remark in Biruté Galdikas' book about orang-utans:

Communicating with a (wild) animal of another species means glimpsing another reality. Perhaps the closest analogy would be visiting a parallel universe. ....the impact of interspecies communication compares to a near-death experience in intensity. One is never the same again.

Immediately I recognised this emotion: *Yes, YES, that's why I have always been so in awe of her!*

I realised that it must be the wild part in Sandy that made her so fascinating.

Sandy died when she was sixteen years and two months old. She was happy and alert till the last day but had been suffering from epilepsy. After a really bad night I called the vet. She greeted him politely and followed us to her bed. It took just a second for the injection to take effect. She had felt no fear or pain. Now she lies buried under a huge rosebush in a spot covered with forget-me-nots.

18

WEIGHTY PROBLEMS

Even though CC and I did not see each other all week, we managed to have a good time together on the weekends and during the holidays. However, it became clear to me by this time that the relationship lacked depth. We could talk about many subjects, but rarely broached anything very personal any more. If we had a quarrel, CC would mope and refuse to talk things over. He hated confrontations of any kind. From time to time we discussed our future. CC was still married although he never seemed to have any contact with his wife.

Once my parents came for a holiday. I was still living in Al Ain at the time. During one memorable dinner, my father asked CC what his intentions were towards me. CC avoided answering and mentioned that he had difficulty persuading his wife to divorce. My father countered: 'If you find it so difficult, I can go to Vancouver and talk with her!' I knew that my father was serious. He would do that without batting an eyelid. CC almost choked on his food and promised there and then that he would talk to his wife during his next vacation.

So on his next vacation he went to Canada with the intention of asking his wife for a divorce. I waited for his return with some anxiety. When we were together the first evening after he came back, I asked him: 'Did you talk to your wife?'

'Yes,' he said, 'I tried, but when I mentioned divorce she started crying and I did not mention it again. We did not make any decision.'

'And what happens if I start crying now?' I asked him.

The trouble was that I never was a cry-baby. So we continued spending our free time together without a commitment.

When I had my back operation and CC did not come to see me at the hospital until the third or fourth day, I had plenty of time to think about our relationship. I realised it was not going anywhere permanent. Even though by now we had been together for six years, there was no growth, no development. He usually wanted sex when he was with me on the weekends, and I was rarely up to it because it was the end of the week and I was really tired. He often wanted me to dress up in lacey nylon underwear, which was unbearably hot, even inside the air-conditioned house. It also did not help that I was getting forever fatter and became very unsure of myself and my appearance. I should rephrase that. I wasn't unsure. I was sure that I looked horrible. Not to mention ridiculous in that lacey stuff.

I dieted during the weekdays and undid any good results during the weekends, when CC liked to have big home-cooked meals. I tried every diet under the sun, had weekly appointments with dieticians. I tried pills and powders, ayurvedic herbs and acupuncture. I even joined WeightWatchers, where quite a few of my patients had had success. It was embarrassing to follow the programme together with people that knew me as their doctor.

The pattern was always the same – I'd lose three or four kilos straight away and then remain on a level for weeks on end, no matter how little I ate. After two months I was usually back to my previous eating habits. They were not particularly unhealthy. I ate no potatoes, rice or bread, but lots of vegetables. I never fried food, but used the microwave and grill.

The problem was with sweet things. I craved them – if I left them out of the diet, I could only go for a few days before going on a sweet binge. Trying to stick to one small sweet a day worked when I was really motivated, but often it deteriorated into "finishing the pack"!

It had been like this my whole life. I remember that even as an eight-year old I was sneaking slurps from the syrup jar in the kitchen. At that time I was as fat around the middle as I was tall!

Over the years I had a few thin periods, when for no apparent reason I would suddenly start losing weight and be reasonably slim for a year or so. Then there would be a break in the routine (yet another change of house or country) and I would be craving those sweets again.

My last relatively thin period had been when I first met CC. But in the hot desert climate, with a constant lack of exercise and an overload of stress, I just grew fatter and fatter, until my body weight levelled off at "gross obesity" (as it said in the report of the back operation), where it has stayed ever since!

It was not that I did not take any exercise. I walked with the dogs first thing in the morning, a brisk half-hour walk at dawn. In the summer I swam for at least one hour a day, while in the winter I did day-long walks on the weekends, often climbing hills on rough ground. I tried gym classes, but the sweaty stink of the buildings put me off and I hated to be the fattest in the group. I often could not do the exercises, because fat got in the way of a particular movement. Water gym seemed fun, but in order to take the class you had to be a member of the hotel club and I could not afford it.

I felt discouraged, guilty, and unlovable. I loathed my lack of self-discipline in this regard – so unlike me, the person who was really quite well-disciplined in every other way.

CC never referred to my weight. He did not seem to mind, though later that turned out to be false. I felt, however, that he did not love me. Maybe he never had. Maybe for him sex had been the most important facet of our relationship and now that the excitement of the early days had waned, nothing had come in its place. He did not need me, he did not share much of himself with me. He was a friend, sure, and we did have good times together, but in a way, he just used me to have comfortable week-ends and shared costs on holidays.

I questioned my feelings for him, too. Once, after a particu-larly ugly quarrel, I considered ending the relationship. But when I thought of being alone again, of having no one to share things with or go on holidays with, I said to myself: *Better a relationship with shortcomings than none at all.*

I had never succeeded in finding a partner who was really good for me. In the past I had often been on the receiving end of abuse and neglect. This time it was to be no different.

19

SAND FOXES

I was still at work when there was a phone call from CC. This was unusual, he rarely called. Since it was Wednesday I was supposed to meet him at the taxi stop that evening.

'I wonder if you can come to pick me up in Al Ain after work,' he said, 'I have a surprise for you.' I readily agreed to drive to Al Ain, relieved that his call did not cancel our short weekend together.

When I arrived at the zoo a few hours later, CC approached carrying a large carton box.

'What have you got,' I asked, 'another bottle baby?'

'No, these are for you!'

I peered into the box. Two tiny, creamy white faces stared up at me, four eyes and two noses like buttons of black licorice, stubby muzzles showing tiny pink tongues, fuzzy hair on the round little heads. I was instantly lost in love and admiration.

'They are sand foxes, aren't they? How did you get them?'

'A guy from Saudi Arabia came to the zoo and wanted to sell them, but we have too many already in the zoo, so the director refused to take them. As we walked away from the man, I saw him pick up a large piece of wood – he wanted to bash their heads in. I rushed back and said that I knew someone who'd want them.'

'How much did you have to pay him?'

'Only a hundred dirhams each – less than sixty dollars,' CC said, adding: 'a belated Christmas gift from me to you!'

'Boy, were they lucky that you were around,' I said. 'I am going to call them Mazzel and Tov.'

'Do you think that is wise? Someone might notice that that is Hebrew!'

'I bet no one ever notices. They had "*mazzel tov* – good luck" to be rescued, and that is how they are going to be called!'

I was over the moon with these new additions to my private zoo. The next day we resurrected the garage as a fox home. It had been that when Gerard still lived in the house and later the young wildcats had lived there for a while. Gerard had replaced the double doors with strong small-meshed wire covering the whole front, with a wire mesh door on one side. In the back was a small den made of rocks cemented together. I removed all the suitcases and other junk that had accumulated over the past year, leaving two large metal trunks in place. Then we went to the desert and got a carload full of sacks filled with clean sand, which we spread around a few mesquite tree trunks that we salvaged from a deserted lot. It looked really nice and the foxes immediately liked their new abode.

They had arrived a few weeks later than Sandy, and I calculated that they must be almost exactly the same age. Of course Sandy was already a lot bigger, but that did not prevent the foxes from getting excited whenever I walked by with her. When I went inside with the food bowls, Sandy came along. The foxes yapped and jumped, their voices shrill with excitement, furiously wagging their tails. Sandy stood there, wagging her tail more slowly and sniffing the cubs, then licking them gently. It was obvious that she was some sort of foster mother for the little ones.

Fortunately they were already weaned, so we did not have a feeding problem. We were feeding the wildcats with quails and the foxes loved those too. Consequently they thrived and soon reached adult size – a little smaller than a domestic cat. For a long time they remained gangly and thin, like teenagers. When the summer came and the garage became very hot I found a way to provide them with a cooler sleeping place. The garage building included a small two-by-four-metre room for Nambi with, adjacent to it, a toilet, still the Eastern squatting type. With Nambi's permission I built a square box of bricks covered with a thick wooden lid underneath his bed, and then broke a hole through to the garage wall. While we were at it, I also installed a shower in the toilet for Nambi. Since the foxes slept during the day and Nambi mostly at night, they did not bother each other.

In the beginning I went into the cage very often, and the foxes became quite used to me. The male, Mazzel, was more courageous than shy little Tov. He'd come and stand up against my leg as I sat on one of the tin trunks. I usually had some dog biscuits or broken cookies with me and he soon found out where I kept them. His inquisitive little nose pushed at my pockets until I produced the desired titbits. For fun I'd hold a piece between my lips, daring him to come closer. He'd jump onto the trunk and reach up high to take the cookie from me, his cute little nose right next to mine.

He liked being tickled under his chin, but seemed afraid of being touched on the back. I had noticed the same behaviour with the marmosets and I wondered whether it was an inborn fear of predators. In the wild, whatever preyed on these small creatures, whether it was a raptor or a mammal, would usually grab them by the neck. Even though neither the marmosets nor the foxes had ever encountered a predator, the instincts were still there.

Sand foxes, also known as Rueppell's fox (*Vulpes rüppelli*), are creatures of the sandy desert. They occur naturally in the eastern Arabian deserts, contrary to the similar but even smaller fennec fox that ranges from the North African deserts into western Saudi Arabia. They are similar in size to a domestic cat but much more slender. An adult male weighs less than two kilos. The creamy white coat is bleached to pure white at the tip of their bushy tail. Their footpads are covered with dense hair, enabling them to walk easier on soft hot sand. Their ears are enormous, functioning both as sound-gathering and heat-losing organs. They have dark "tearlines" on both sides of their nose. It has been said that these reduce the glare of the sun to the eyes.

They communicate by using a range of sounds, from soft barks to shrill bird-like whistles. In the wild they are mostly solitary, but sometimes they form pairs or even small family groups. They live in burrows, often made by other creatures, and change dens frequently. They hunt at night, but can often be found in the early morning or late afternoon taking a sunbath near their dens. Their hunting range can be as large as forty square kilometres. They feed on small mammals, insects, lizards, grasses and seeds, even fruit when it is available. They can live without water for long periods of time, getting the moisture they need from their prey animals or from the morning dew. During the winter months the female can have two to four blind cubs after a gestation period of fifty days. The cubs become independent after about four months.

CC was surprised to hear their calls, which were so bird-like. He remarked that he often heard those calls from his bedroom at night. His house was near the edge of Al Ain, close to where the huge Rub' al-Khali (Empty Quarter) desert begins. Either their calls carried very far in the silent nights, or the foxes ventured closer to human habitation than we expected.

One day a friend, Patrick, who worked for a wildlife research station in Abu Dhabi emirate, came to my house. As he admired my new arrivals he remarked:

'When we went camping during a survey in the southern Abu Dhabi desert a few weeks ago, I saw some of these in the wild. They were amazingly tame and came right up to the camp.'

My interest was fired immediately.

'Could we go there one weekend and see them, do you think?'

'Why not,' said Patrick, 'I am sure there are some others who would like to go camping in the Empty Quarter.'

So a few weekends later we set off with two 4WD vehicles, full of camping and survival gear. We drove south from Al Ain to the last town at the edge of the Rub' al-Khali. There we took a track that led us across huge dunes. These sickle-shaped barchan dunes lie perpendicular to the prevailing wind direction. The windward side on the south-west is very steep and it is practically impossible to ascend by vehicle on that side. Camels can do it but even they prefer to find easier routes. So we were approaching this forbidding terrain from the north-east.

Once we climbed the first dune on its more gently sloping

leeward side, we were committed. Now we had to continue traversing the waves of this sand sea or be doomed to walking! At the top, our trained desert-driver stopped to survey the route. The ridge looked sharp like a knife and the sand was deep and loose. The landscape in front of us was awesome. As far as the eye could see the dunes rolled on. Nearby the patterns in the sand were clearly visible, the wind having sculpted graceful wavelets and sinuous mini-ridges. Only the valleys between the dunes showed some vegetation. Coming down the steep side of the dune was excitingly frightening. The nose of the Landrover was pointing straight down as we plunged into the abyss. I was sure the car would go "hood over wheels" the next second. Then the land levelled out and we were driving on the hard surface of packed sand of the interdune salt flat.

Our trip continued for hours up and down the dunes, with some stretches on level ground. The lead car had a GPS system, so we knew at all times exactly where we were heading. It was late afternoon when Patrick announced that we had reached the spot where he had seen the foxes. It was in the middle of a rather wide salt flat with sparse saltbush vegetation. We lowered our weary bones from the vehicles and walked around looking for tracks or other signs, but the afternoon wind had swept the desert floor clean.

We decided to pitch camp and start preparing the evening meal. It was February and the days were short. As soon as the sun had set it turned very cold. While it was still light we had gathered wood and dried camel dung for a fire. The wood came from a few huge arta bushes and a lone ghaf tree that had managed to grow quite large, even in the harsh conditions that prevailed here.

Patrick and I left the roaring fire for a short foray with the car away from the disturbance of the camp. A powerful searchlight on top of the car picked out a hare. I had never seen a relaxed hare before. Usually you only see their backsides as they sprint off. This one sat, seemingly oblivious of the light that hid our presence, and munched the bead-like leaves of a saltbush. Then it leisurely walked over to the next bush. To my surprise it did not hop.

Small sand geckoes moved like lightning across the flat sand and disappeared in clumps of sedges. Patrick saw an owl winging its way across the dunes, but my night blindness prevented me from seeing anything outside the circle of our search light.

There was no sign of the sand foxes.

Patrick and one of his colleagues set some bucket traps to catch whatever creature might fall into them during the night. We went to bed early, enveloped in down sleeping bags. I had a small pup tent and slept with my head almost outside, so I could see the glittering expanse of the starry skies above. The Milky Way looked like a bridal veil, near enough to be touched. I located the Big Dipper and by extending the short side of the wagon five times I found the brilliant North Star exactly where it ought to be. On that comforting observation I fell asleep.

When I woke up the sky was becoming lighter in the East. As the darkness receded, pearly pink and soft gold colours painted the sky and the heavy mist that lay over the soft dunes. The light grew stronger and the mist became transparent, like the gossamer flowing robes of a dancer. This world had no limits and no sounds, light and colour filled it to overflowing.

As the golden disk of the sun rose over the horizon, the mist rose too and revealed the treasure it had carried: diamond dew drops quivered on every bush and blade, drops of life-giving liquid, precious in this arid land.

A Desert skunk beetle stood on the sand, with its head low to the ground and its back sticking up. Dew had gathered on its shiny black carapace and was rolling down its body to its mouth, providing the moisture it needed to survive another day.

A spider's web hung like a diamond necklace between two tussocks of desert grass, luring insects into its embrace with the promise of water.

All around my tent, tiny foxy paw prints could be seen, right up to the place where my face had been. The sand foxes had visited, but I had not even noticed! I recalled that another friend had told me how he woke up during a camping night to find a fox standing on his chest, checking out his face with his sensitive little nose! Obviously the foxes here were also not very shy and who knows, one could have been nose-to-nose with me!

I was disappointed that I had slept so well.

The traps yielded a range of small creatures: beetles, spiders and two species of geckoes. One of the geckoes was adorable (I thought) with a large head and enormous golden eyes. Its body was cream-yellow mottled with brown. It posed willingly for my photographs. Another species was only half a finger long and so thin that it was transparent – you could see its stomach and guts through the skin. They were both already known from this area, so we did not add anything to the scientific databank. Still, Patrick recorded everything in his notebooks. Even the absence of animals in an area is knowledge.

After we had taken all the pictures we needed, we had to carry on with our trip if we wanted to get to the inhabited world again that evening. The sun started to burn, even this early in the season.

The light shimmered on the silvery salt of the sabkha between the dunes, where a few camels were browsing the salt bushes, their hind legs stained with their liquid stool. The prevalent salt bushes were those that the bedu call harm. The word "haram" can mean either unclean, forbidden, or "poor thing". The salt water contained in the beady leaves causes diarrhoea, so the word "haram" applies when a camel eats harm. From a distance the camels' legs seemed ten feet tall, quivering stilts, standing in blue patches of water. But this was a mirage. There was no surface water in this desert.

We were now driving for long periods of time along the flat sand between rows of dunes, heading north-west towards the coast. Suddenly the lead car stopped. Patrick pointed towards a small hill that had a crescent-shaped burrow.

'I saw a Little Owl ducking into that burrow. Let's see if there are any owl pellets. They might contain the bones of whatever small reptiles occur here.'

Just as we started to walk towards the hill, I saw a movement over to our left. A tiny furry animal sprinted from one burrow to another.

'What the hell was that?' I asked surprised, as another appeared, running as fast as its little legs could carry it.

'They're sand fox cubs,' exclaimed Patrick, as delighted as I was. 'Let's go over and see if we can get closer.'

We crept as quietly as we could towards the burrow, taking advantage of small bushes and stands of sedge as cover. At about four meters from the burrow we dug in and waited. Before long the anxious face of the vixen appeared in the opening of the burrow. She did not see or smell us and was obviously reassured when she retreated. First one and then the other of the cubs crept outside. They stayed in the entrance and began to doze in the sunshine. Patrick and I started to take pictures, very carefully. Every time a shutter clicked, the cubs would jump a little, with unfocussed eyes, and then they'd doze off again. They were a little bit younger than Mazzel and Tov had been when they came to me. The baby fur on their little round heads and bellies was so sparse that you could see their pink skin underneath.

Lying there in the hot sun on soft sand, watching the baby foxes, I was as happy as I had ever been in my life.

Meanwhile, back in Dubai, Mazzel and Tov had settled into domestic bliss. By now Nambi was feeding them daily and I did not go into their cage as often. Remembering what had happened to Gerard's menagerie when he left his dogs unsupervised, I did not allow Sandy to go inside at all. I did not think she would ever harm her friends, but I was not taking any chances. Even though their food was not coming from me any more, every time I walked towards or past their cage, the two foxes would erupt into a frenzied dance of joy, yapping and whistling. They sank their tummies down to the floor, making sinuous movements with their whole bodies and wagging their tails so fast that all you could see was a blur.

Sometimes I went inside to take photographs. Once, I sat on the big trunk and focused on Tov as she stood nearby. I had put a second lens, my 100mm portrait lens, next to me. When Tov remained where she was, I wanted to take her portrait and groped for the other lens. Failing to find it, I looked around. The lens was nowhere to be seen. I stood up and looked on all sides of the trunk, thinking that maybe it had fallen off. Nothing. Then I noticed that Mazzel was in the sandy area at the back of the garage. I walked towards him and disturbed the sand where he had been standing – and there was the lens. Mazzel had buried his catch! I was amazed that his slender jaws could carry such a heavy weight. But then, I had also been amazed when I found out that this small predator could kill and eat desert jirds and jerboas that look far too large to fit in his mouth!

One Sunday, when Nambi was off duty, I entered the cage with the evening meal. I had not noticed that Tov was sitting on the shelf along the wall near the door. As I opened the door, she took a flying jump over my head and ran into the garden. Within seconds she was over the garden wall, and had disappeared into the neighbour's property. I ran after her, but could not find her any more. I was frantic.

'You stupid twit,' I blamed myself, 'you're never going to get her back, and someone will hurt her or she'll get hit by a car. She does not know how to get food. Damn, what am I going to do?'

Immediately I made flyers in English, Urdu and Arabic with a picture of Tov, asking anyone who saw her to contact me before trying to catch her. I left them at every door in an area of four blocks around the house. I handed them out at shops and at the mosque, where all the men from the neighbourhood came to pray. One of them carefully studied the flyer and then looked up at me, and asked:

'Would it not be easier to keep a dog?'

Nothing happened for a few days. I had managed to get an article into the newspaper about Tov's disappearance. It brought some scathing reactions from people who said it served me right for keeping wild animals caged!

Then the phone rang.

An Indian man asked: 'Are you the madam who lost the fox? I think it is in my garage.' He lived just a few houses away in the street behind mine. I asked him to please keep the garage doors closed and wait until I had arrived. Then I called the vet and

120

asked if he could come and help me catch the fox. He brought a catching net but we could not use it because the garage was chockablock with boxes and old furniture. However, Tov was so weak and exhausted that she did not resist capture and we managed to coax her into a cat-carrier without any trouble. She never tried to escape again.

And I, having learned my lesson, added escape prevention corridors to all the cages by wiring off an extra meter in front of each cage. The outer door of these corridors had weighted pulleys on the door so that they would close automatically once you had entered and before you opened the inner door. The article in the newspaper had drawn the attention of the Sheikh of Sharjah, with whom I was in regular contact about a Desert Park that he wanted to create. He told me that he had always wanted to have some sand foxes. That put me in a quandary, for in Arabia you are expected to give a person any object of yours that this person expresses a desire or admiration for. I did not want to give my foxes away, mainly because I was not sure that they would be properly taken care of by anyone else.

I plucked up my courage and told the Sheikh: 'I know I should give these sand foxes to you, Your Highness. But I have a problem, which you as a family man will understand, I think. I have no children and my animals are my children, they are my family. I cannot give them away.'

The Sheikh said nothing but did not ask for them again.

Mazzel and Tov were among the first inhabitants of the Breeding Centre for Endangered Arabian Animals that was established several years later. They lived to the ripe old age of sixteen years and no one ever commented on their names!

20

ABOUT RAISING A KANGAROO

On the phone CC sounded so sad and discouraged. My heart went out to him.

'It was terrible', he said, 'The whole enclosure was full of bodies, torn apart and bloody. It was amazing that there were any animals left alive.'

During the night a posse of feral dogs had entered the zoo and penetrated the large enclosure where the Grey Kangaroos lived. The night watchman had obviously slept on the job once again. The dogs had had a frenzied hour of chasing and killing the large marsupials, before finally someone heard the rumpus and fetched the vet who lived on site. A few well-placed gunshots had solved the problem – too late. One of the survivors was a "joey" – a young kangaroo that had fallen out of its mother's pouch during the chase. The mother had been among those killed and now CC was bottle-feeding the baby.

When CC arrived on Wednesday evening, I was eager to see the little guy. I knew practically nothing about kangaroos, other than that they lived in Australia and could jump very far. Now I learned that the babies remain in the pouch very long. CC's foster child was not small, already the size of a small cat. However, he was still totally dependent on his milk feeds. He drank very little at a time. His metabolism was obviously quite slow and he was also very inactive, one probably linked to the other.

The Grey Kangaroo (*Macropus giganteus*) occurs in the wild in eastern Australia and Tasmania, where it prefers an open woodland habitat. It is a sociable animal that lives in bands or mobs, foraging on grass and leaves. An adult can reach a metre and a half in height and weigh up to ninety kilos. An average mob is made up of a mature male, two or three females with young and two or three young males. Many mobs often graze together. Kangaroos can survive on poor quality grass and go without water for long periods. With their excellent eyesight and good sense of smell and hearing, they can quickly detect approaching danger. An alarmed kangaroo thumps the ground with its hind legs, rather like a rabbit does, to warn the rest of the mob. If necessary, the grey kangaroo can travel fast, bounding along using only the two hind feet and balancing himself with his tail held horizontally. It can easily jump up to ten metres.

When ready to give birth, the female leaves her mob, finds somewhere quiet and licks her pouch and birth canal clean. After a pregnancy of thirty-six days the tiny baby, called a joey, only 2.5cm long and weighing less than one gram, is born headfirst, pink, blind and naked. It grasps its mother's fur with the claws on its forefeet. The mother offers no help at all. In about three minutes, it has dragged itself up to the pouch, entered it and clamped tightly onto one of the four teats, which swells in its mouth. The joey spends three hundred days or more inside the pouch, growing very slowly for the first three months. After fifteen weeks, faster growth begins when the mother's milk increases its fat and protein content. The joey continues to suckle for another nine months after leaving the pouch. At this age it can run about and jump easily in and out of the pouch.

CC asked me to make a pouch from an old towel, which we suspended from the hat-and-coat stand. Here Joey sat contentedly between feeds, sleeping most of the time, but sometimes peering over the edge of his pouch.

My friend Carien was visiting at the time. The two of us

watched CC as he fed the lanky animal. Joey was light grey all over except at all his tips, which were almost black: his velvety diamond-shaped ears, his snout, the lower halves of his short front legs and his feet, the distal half of his tail. He had a rather expressionless face with large dark eyes. After his meal, he'd try a few timid hops on the bed. When Carien reached her hand out to steady him, he clung on to it with his tiny paw. That was when we noticed he had six digits on his front feet.

'Do all kangaroos have six toes on their feet?' I asked CC.

CC examined the little paw but said nothing. The next evening when I called him at the zoo, he said: 'Kangaroos normally have only five toes. I had to check our leftover animals to be sure!'

This was typical of CC. He would never take the risk of being wrong. I could learn something from him in this respect: only say something when you are sure it is the truth. I was more spontaneous though rarely irresponsible. Sometimes however, I would make statements that I later had to retract. From CC I learned to say: 'I don't know but I'll look it up!'

Little Joe stayed with us for a long time. He took forever to grow up. Maybe it had something to do with the fact that we did not change the formula of the milk. Had he remained in his mother's pouch, Joe would have had milk that would change in composition as he grew older. In the wild it can happen that the mother becomes pregnant again while she is still carrying a young in her pouch. The tiny new baby scrambles its way to the pouch, searches for a nipple and latches onto it with a vengeance. And then something quite incredible happens: the small baby sucks "small-baby-milk" from its nipple, while its larger sibling receives "almost-weaned-baby milk" of a completely different composition from another nipple.

In time the kangaroo group at Al Ain zoo recovered and Joey lived happily ever after (as far as I know).

It was around this time that on a memorable weekend CC saved my life on Thursday and almost killed me on Friday. I had come home from work early that day and was getting things ready for lunch. As I walked from the kitchen to the bedroom to put away some clean laundry I munched a grape from the bunch that CC had just bought. As I bent over to open a drawer, I suddenly choked. From one second to the next I could not breathe any more. I staggered backwards and tried to thump myself against my midriff, to no effect. Calling for help was impossible and the living room where CC was reading his magazine seemed miles away to my already dimming mind. For some reason Nambi passed by my bedroom window at that very moment. This was unusual for normally at lunchtime he was fast asleep in his room. He must have seen some of my frantic movements, for the next thing I knew CC came rushing in, grabbed me from behind and executed a whopping Heimlich manoeuvre. The skin of a grape flew out of my mouth and I deeply inhaled sweet, sweet air.

'Thank God,' said CC.

'Thank YOU,' I said, as I sank exhausted on to the bed.

'Thank Nambi!' CC retorted and then he told me how Nambi had come running in shouting:

'Madam trouble, come quick!'

'Imagine,' I said, 'if you had not been here, I would have died and the police would have arrested Nambi. They would have seen I had suffocated but they would never in a million years have brought to light that piece of grape peel.' Convicted of murder Nambi would have lingered in prison for years before being deported, if he survived.

I remembered the police investigation of a fire that had broken out in the house of my neighbour Julie some time earlier. She had dismissed a house girl for some reason and we assumed that out of revenge this lady had torched her kitchen. Julie had four dogs that thankfully were outside in the garden when it happened. Later she showed me the police report. Under "cause" the report mentioned: "The fire was started by an outside person or one of the four dogs on the premises."

Late that same afternoon CC packed some baby spur-thighed tortoises in travelling boxes. They were surplus animals from the zoo that were being sent to a place in Germany. The export papers were all ready and done, and I had promised to take the boxes to the airport the next day. CC tied plastic rope around the boxes and in order to prevent the ends from unravelling, he melted them in the flame of the gas ring of the stove. The stink of the melting plastic pervaded the house as we left shortly afterwards for the trip back to Al Ain. Although CC usually took a taxi to go home, sometimes I drove him back in my faster and air-conditioned car. The road to the desert city was usually deserted at this time and I had driven it so often that it felt as if the car knew the way by itself. When I got home two hours later, a bad chemical smell hit me as I opened the door.

'Oh yes, that stupid plastic,' I reminded myself, 'I'd better keep my bedroom window open.' In spite of that I woke up with a thumping headache the next morning. I staggered to the kitchen to make a cup of tea. Nambi was there preparing the food for the marmosets. A piece of fruit had dropped to the floor and I bent over to pick it up. As I did so, I glanced at the stove – and saw that the knob for the large gas ring was on the "on" position, even though there was no flame. CC must have left it on and the flame could have blown out when we pulled the door closed behind us. I reached over immediately to turn the gas off and in the same movement threw open the kitchen window.

'Get out of here, Nambi, there is gas everywhere.' I shouted. As we stood in the garden, I said to Nambi:

'Why did you not boil an egg this morning?' The marmosets always had a hard-boiled egg sprinkled over their salad and one of the first things Nambi did when he started work, was put some water on the stove for boiling that egg. If he had done so that morning, we would all have been blown to high heaven.

'No eggs in fridge today,' said my friend.

'And I also want to know what you were doing in the back yard yesterday at lunchtime.' I asked, remembering that other lucky event. Nambi looked down the yard and said:

'I no cleaning cat box in morning, madam.'

'I am very happy that you forgot, Nambi, and that you remembered in time.' I said sincerely.

We looked at each other in wonder at having had such narrow escapes.

21

HOUDINI

Friends of mine in Dubai had an African Grey Parrot that could talk. It had an amazing repertoire of learned answers to questions and spontaneous funny noises. I was quite envious. My lack of enthusiasm for birds did not extend to parrots. These I found not only beautiful but also interesting. The daily antics of the Ring-necked parakeets in my garden were much appreciated, but those were wild birds and did not react to me.

So I was overjoyed when Nambi showed me what he had caught in the garden one day. In the birdcage that had once housed the marmosets sat a Sulphur-crested Cockatoo. He was 30 cms tall, all white with a bright yellow crest and a round patch near his ears that had the same colour. His beak and feet were jet black. His eyes were dark grey (females have brown eyes, I knew) and I assumed he was an adult bird.

'Where did you find him?' I asked in surprise.

'Was sitting in garden, madam', said Nambi, 'very easy catching. I think maybe hungry!'

Of course I had to go out to get some proper food for my new housemate. When I had filled the two food bowls, the bird gave an ear-splitting raucous cry and fell to. As he balanced on one foot, he took a sunflower seed in the other claw, bent down his head with its yellow crest raised and cracked the seed open with his strong beak. Then he worried at the husk with his pink tongue to extract the tasty kernel. The small sounds of splitting husks were accompanied by soft chuckles and grunts.

I already had a bird in the study where we put the cockatoo – a canary that was recovering from an injury. His very small cage hung from the lamp in the middle of the room, while the larger cage stood on the table in front of the window. When I wanted to replenish the cockatoo's food bowls the next day, I slipped them out of the seven-by-three-centimetre slot that held them in place. I turned towards the low bookcase where I kept the boxes of seeds and filled both bowls to the brim. When I turned back again to put them back into the slots, the cockatoo was gone.

I could not understand it.

The door was firmly closed and I had not been aware of any noise or commotion. I looked around but there was no bird flying anywhere. Then I heard a squeak from the canary. The cockatoo was sitting inside his cage, having pushed up the sliding door and wriggled in. And now he was attacking the much smaller bird.

'Nambi, come quick,' I called, 'I need help!'

Nambi came running, tea towel still in hand. As he entered the room I told him to close the door. Then I opened the cage and shooed both birds outside. The canary flew to the top of a tall bookcase, while the cockatoo made for the curtains. Nambi then enveloped the bird in the curtains as I grabbed the tea-towel to wind around the cocaktoo to try and extricate him from the curtain folds. The cockatoo screeched and bit my finger - if I had not had several layers of towel and curtain covering my hands I would have lost the finger. Even so it hurt like hell.

Somehow we managed to shove the feisty bird back inside the larger bird cage. I left Nambi to catch the canary while I went to put some ice on my throbbing finger.

When peace was restored, I contemplated the birdcage. I would never have believed that such a large bird could have squeezed through the feeding slots of the cage in a matter of seconds and without making a sound.

'Well, I guess we must call you Houdini,' I said to the escape artist. He cocked his crest at me, flaring the yellow crest that set off the pure white of the rest of his body. He was a handsome bird and he knew it!

Houdini was great fun to have around the house. He was noisy, especially in the morning and evening when the flocks of Ring-necked parakeets flew over. But it was a cheerful noise and it harmonised well with the twittering of the marmosets and the bird-like calls of the desert foxes. He never learned to talk, but he mimicked any sound that occurred in and around the house. One day a visiting friend said: 'What is that strange noise from the other room?'

It was a strange murmuring noise that sounded like a large room full of talking people.

'It is my cockatoo, and I don't really understand what he is trying to say.'

'Do you know what that sounds like? It sounds like a *majlis* full of Arabs.' He should know for as one of the sheikh's employees he had to attend the morning "business" meetings of the sheikh every day.

'Maybe he belonged to a sheikh once,' I ventured.

Another day I was in the garden when I heard the wildcats mating. I was surprised. Although I knew that the female was in heat, the cats were usually only active at night. They had been at it for the past few nights. When I went to investigate, the cats were dozing peacefully. Then I heard the sound again – coming from the open window of the study – a new Houdini special!

As soon as I had moved the canary to the large aviary outside again, I let Houdini have the run of the room at least once a day. He loved flying around and interacting with the cats. He'd waddle sideways along the edge of the bed, wings spread showing the yellow tinge of the feathers underneath, talking like a maniac to Catastrophe, who was curious but cautious, ready to disappear under the bed in a second.

He would fly onto my shoulder and suck my earlobe. I admit I was a bit scared the first time, with my finger still black and blue. But Houdini in loving mode was harmless. His tongue was soft as velvet and tickled me till I giggled.

Even in the first week it was obvious that Houdini had a soft spot for Nambi. He would sit on Nambi's arm and lovingly take one short hair after another between his huge beak and tongue to groom them. This activity would be accompanied by gentle clicks and coos, reminding me of a mother comforting a child.

When CC came on the weekend, he identified Houdini as a Lesser Sulphur-crested Cockatoo. Houdini on the other hand identified CC as THE ENEMY. As soon as he laid eyes on this unknown male, he became very excited, hopping up and down and producing a stream of aggressive sounds. The one time that I let him out that weekend, he made a beeline for CC's head and it was immediately obvious that he meant no good. CC ducked behind the door and shut the bird in the study. Houdini must either have considered CC as a rival, or he had had bad experiences with white males.

At times Houdini did not want to go back into his cage. Nambi discovered the perfect way to tempt him back inside. He had noticed that other free-flying parrots were very fond of the fruits of the Indian almond tree that shaded the front yard. Two or three of the large fruits with their hard nuts inside would get Houdini back into his home immediately and then keep him busy for hours as he peeled and ate the fruits and then manipulated the nuts until he could crack them. It was a good thing to know as, true to his name, the bird escaped all the time. Padlocks lasted all of five minutes, wires were untwisted in seconds, nothing stood up against his powerful beak. Houdini was only ever inside his cage when he wanted to be. Since he had not yet figured out how to open the study door, he was at least safe inside the study.

My neighbour Julie told me that a friend of hers had a female Sulphur-crested cockatoo and was looking for a mate for her. Since I was sure Houdini would enjoy some company, I agreed to put them together.

The Lesser Sulphur-crested Cockatoo (*Cacatua sulphurea*) is an endangered species, originating in the Indonesian islands. There are probably less than 10,000 of this species left in the wild, having been collected intensively due to their popularity as pets. For breeding a deep nesting hollow, high above the ground, is preferred, with two or three eggs laid. Incubation is by both parents and takes about twenty-seven days. The babies fledge in about seventy days.

Breeding in captivity is not easy, but it can be done, so we decided to see if they would make a pair.

Honey arrived in a beautiful, large, special parrot cage on wheels. Since it was now winter and not so hot outside, we put the two cages side by side on the porch. It was immediately obvious that Houdini was quite excited by the new arrival. He clucked and chuckled, groomed himself endlessly and executed graceful aerobatics on his perch. Then he'd sidle up to the other cage and press against the bars to try and get as close as possible to Honey, who acted as if he did not exist. I let the situation continue for a few days to make sure they knew each other well before I put them together.

Although CC did not have any useful advice about how to handle the introduction, I waited for the weekend before trying anything.

'I will need another pair of gloved hands, if it does not work.' I told him.

'Why would it not work?' answered CC optimistically. 'It's obvious he's nuts about her.'

We carted the cages back inside before we opened Houdini's cage. I let him hop onto my arm and talked to him quietly as CC slid open the door of Honey's cage. The bird was so mesmerised by his prospective mate that he temporarily forgot his hatred of CC. Honey sat on her perch with a vacant look on her face. Slowly I lifted Houdini towards the open cage. He hopped in quietly, all his normal bravura disappeared. So far, so good.

CC closed the sliding door and we stood back watching.

Houdini tutted and whistled softly, and slowly made his way towards Honey. He stretched out his neck and took one of her shoulder feathers into his mouth to preen it.

Faster than lightning Honey turned on him, beak wide open, eyes blazing. The next thing we knew, Houdini cowered in the far corner of the cage with a badly cut and bleeding tongue, while Honey returned to her dozy state as if nothing had happened.

'Well,' said CC, 'I guess that means no cockatoo babies any time soon!'

I asked Nambi to recover Houdini and comfort him a bit before he went back into his own cage. He was a subdued bird for a few days, but he regained his confidence as soon as Honey and her blood splattered cage were removed from the scene.

The unfortunate matching experience had shown me that it would be nice for Houdini to have a special parrot cage, so that I could leave him outside under the almond tree. On my next leave to Holland, which happened to be a week or so later, I searched for and found a large cage with parrot-proof door locks. I bought it (at great expense), had it sent to Dubai (at great expense) and then Nambi and I put it together (with great effort). The door locks were so complicated that it took us quite a bit of practice before we knew how to work them.

I filled the food and water bowls and took Houdini to his new abode. He was quite happy, walking busily back and forth on the perches, turning a few summersaults, exploring the top upside down and perching near the door to study the lock.

'Good luck, mate', I told him, 'these locks are made for guys just like you.' And I wheeled him into the garden in the fresh air, assured that he was safely confined while I went to work.

It took Houdini about three hours to figure out the locking mechanism and to move his perch into the Indian almond tree above. There he proceeded to dismantle the tree of the majority of its leaves and nuts that were strewn all over the lawn when I returned for lunch. Houdini in the tree screeched a happy "welcome home" and pranced among the branches looking positively pleased with himself. I called Nambi who had not noticed anything.

'Now what do we do? After the feast he has had, he cannot be tempted back inside with almonds.'

Nambi looked very worried. The bird was not at all interested in either his friend, holding a cob of corn, the cats or me. He stayed in the top of the tree till it was "happy hour" and the Ring-necked Parakeets flew to their roosting place towards evening. Then he joined them and we never saw him again.

Of course we searched for him. I even put an ad in the newspaper: "Lost, Cockatoo" – followed by a description and when and where he had been lost. A day later I had a phonecall. A strong Pakistani accent told me: 'I am calling about your advert. I am cook looking for work.'

I had to suppress a giggle as I told him that I had advertised for a bird. Did he think I had lost a cook or two?

I missed Houdini more than I could have imagined. His incredible zest for life and his funny antics had given me so much enjoyment over the time that he was with us. It was many years later that I heard what had happened to him.

My friend Carien was visiting again from Holland. One morning she talked with the Englishman who lived in one of the neighbouring houses. I had never liked the man, though until then I would not have been able to say why. He flirted openly with Carien, looking sideways at me to watch my reaction. I could not care less and that seemed to irritate him. Suddenly he said: 'I know what happened to your cockatoo.'

Now he had my interest. 'What!?'

'That day when he escaped, he landed in the garden of friends of mine just down the road. They managed to catch him and kept him for a long time.'

'Why the hell did you not tell me! I loved that bird!'

'But I did not,' he replied, grinning maliciously. 'I hated all that noise he made, so I was happy that he was gone.'

I was furious. Houdini was noisy, but only for about half an hour twice a day, and not during times that anyone would try to sleep.

'Where are your friends now?'

'They left, but they gave the cockatoo to a sailor, and for all I know, he has been happy sailing the oceans since then.'

I could only hope so. Especially I hoped that whoever enjoyed his company now would be nice to him. For he was a special bird – and he knew it!

22

REPTILES

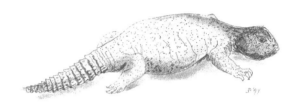

Never in my life had I thought of holding a reptile. I thought they were beautiful and interesting and I was not particularly scared of any, even snakes. But, like most people I thought them to be slippery and cold, usually quite dangerous and anything but lovable.

My attitude changed during a weekend outing to the island of Bahrain. CC and I were staying with a couple, Chris and Marion Cornes, who were members of the Natural History group there and they took us out on a tour of the island. On that Sunday afternoon I saw my first wild gazelle, my first Spiny-tailed agama and my first Yellow-spotted agama.

We spotted the gazelle from a distance as it walked slowly along a low ridge etched against the pale blue sky. It looked like a dainty dancer walking a tightrope as it tiptoed carefully over the rocks. In contrast, the first "Spiny" (called *dhub* in Arabic) I saw was a very flat specimen on the road. Our Bahraini friends told us how the locals would aim to hit the reptiles as they lay on the tarmac basking in the sun. Some sport!

Fortunately the colony of the Spiny-tailed agamas was quite large and we stopped to investigate an area with a lot of burrows. It would be difficult to spot these burrows from a car, as they were usually hidden at the foot of a bush or clump of grass or under small limestone overhangs, their opening perfectly half-moon shaped.

'Do you know how you can tell the burrow of a reptile from that of a mammal,' CC asked. Of course I had no idea.

'Reptiles make half-moon shaped burrows because their front legs are attached to the side of their shoulders, while in mammals, the front legs are in front, below the shoulders. A reptile that is digging sends the sand sideways making a horizontal opening, while a mammal throws it backwards between his legs, making a vertical or round hole.'

I noticed a tiny horizontal slit underneath a bush.

'How about this one?'

'That one is the burrow of a spider or a scorpion – basically they dig in a similar way as reptiles.'

The *dhubs* were out to get warm in the sunshine. While they were warming up they were still quite sluggish.

'Look,' said Chris, 'when they are still cold they are slate-coloured, but when they start to warm up they become increasingly sulphuric yellow, only their heads remain dark.'

Chris and CC circled some still-grey Spinys and managed to catch one each, just to have a better look. The face of the lizard was pre-historic, with large soulful eyes and many thick folds around its scrawny neck. Its body was fat with wrinkled skin and the long tail was covered all around with spiked scales. That powerful tail was the only defence of this herbivorous animal. Given a chance they could inflict nasty wounds on anyone that came within range of the swishing tail.

'Here, hold this,' CC said and shoved the animal he was holding into my hands. 'Take the tail here at the base and hold your other hand loosely around its neck, then nothing can happen.'

I had no chance to protest and so I found myself holding a reptile for the first time in my life. It felt wonderful – like a soft leather bag that has been lying in the sun. The animal was quite docile and as I looked into its golden eyes, I had a curious feeling – a bond of some sort between this pre-historic animal and myself. From somewhere a thought came to me: *I am going to make a nature reserve for these animals some day.*

In the course of the next years I found out a lot about these gentle "dragons of the desert".

Spiny-tailed agamas (*Uromastix acanthinurus*) are the second largest of the reptiles of the Arabian desert (the Grey Monitor is the largest). The animal is truly pre-historic as it has inhabited Arabia continuously for twenty million years, without needing to change its appearance. The body of an adult measures about thirty-five centimetres while the tail is equally long. The skin lies in large folds around its neck and body, and the *dhub* can inflate this loose skin and blow itself up to almost double its volume to frighten an attacker. Combined with a loud hissing noise that it makes when threatened, it gives an impression of fierceness. But this is only show. In actual fact a *dhub* can only defend itself with a lash of its spiny tail. Its teeth are unusual in that they are so-called acrodont teeth. They are attached to the jaw without sockets, rather as if the jaw itself were serrated. This makes them strong to grind down the dry vegetation that it eats.

The lizard lives in a burrow, which it digs itself, spiralling down to a length of two to three meters. The best substrate for these burrows is the compacted sandy gravel between sand dunes. The spiny is solitary but lives in loose colonies of up to thirty or forty individuals. They lay eggs, two or three at a time. When the young hatch, they fend for themselves immediately. While adults are exclusively herbivorous, the young eat other animals (small lizards, insects) from time to time in order to augment the protein they need for growing. When they are warm enough to be active, they meander from plant to plant, munching small mouthfuls of vegetation. If danger threatens they try to make it back to their burrow as fast as possible.

Chris put his spiny down on the sand and asked me to put mine right next to it. The very second the two animals were released they came into action. One immediately demonstrated the use of the large folds on its neck and body, pumping air into them to increase its size. It hissed ferociously and whipped its tail back and forth. The other spun around and fled as fast as his short stubby legs could carry him. In fact it went so fast that the legs looked blurred as in a cartoon movie!

'So, they are not very social,' observed CC. 'It is a colony of solitary animals.'

We left the *dhubs* in peace and drove slowly along the empty road. Suddenly CC called out:

'Please stop!'

He got out of the car very carefully and quietly and started to move slowly towards a meter-high bush a few meters away in the field. In the top of the bush sat a small lizard with a most unusual coloration. His head was cornflower blue while his throat was dark indigo, turning into bright turquoise further down his body. All over he had elliptical yellow spots. The tail was bright orange, the colour and shape of a carrot. We watched in amazement as these colours very gradually became less pronounced at CC's approach. Whereas before he had been displaying his beauty to attract a female, now he was trying to fade into the background to escape the predator. Obviously he trusted his ability to hide for he did not run away but sat still and was caught quite easily. As soon as he was caught his colours became as bright as before - this time probably from excitement and fear.

We crowded around CC to have a closer look at this Agama flavimaculata – the Yellow-spotted or Blue-headed agama. Throughout my time in Arabia I saw many of these lizards and they were always very cooperative, sitting still for photos. My joke to fellow-naturalists was always that the tourist department of the government put these out for our entertainment and they were actually made of coloured papier-maché. Someone else aptly called them "psychedelic dinosaurs". They did not display very often and to see one in its full glory was a real treat.

Having once held a reptile I lost my abhorrence of them completely. It made me realise how important the "see-and-touch" teaching programmes in zoos and schools are. Once you have held a snake in your hands you are much less likely to react in fear and harm an innocent reptile that crosses your path.

Gerard had kept many snakes in the house that I now lived in. When I first knew him I had come to photograph his snakes, since I did not expect to ever meet any in the wild. Little did I know.

When Gerard returned to his home country, he left his huge

glass terrariums with me, and they stood around the house filled with old newspapers and other stuff, until I used one to house the dwarf hamsters.

One day when I arrived at work, there was a commotion in the waiting room. I walked over to see what was happening and the lab girl was almost hysterical.

'What's the matter?' I asked.

'A snake – a snake in the flowerpot!'

That can never be a big snake, I thought, *the pot is not very big.*

I peered below the foliage of the potted ficus. On the dark soil a reptile the size of a pencil lay curled trying to burrow into the soil. Its skin was ribbed and pinkish with blue and purple spots. I knew immediately what it was, as I had seen pictures of it. It was not a snake but an amphisbaenid, a legless lizard. This strange animal is adapted to living underground and therefore its legs have evolved into mere vestiges hidden under the skin. In Europe we have a similar animal called the blind or slow worm.

I picked it up and it immediately knotted itself around my finger with surprising force. I took it home and later acquired another few of these strange creatures, that occupied a small aquarium filled with loose sand and some pieces of tree bark, where I fed them baby mealworms. They were not particularly interesting pets or terrarium exhibits, since they never showed themselves. In order to check on them I had to dig them up and hold them, and then they would firmly encircle my finger. Later I read somewhere that they bite when handled. At the time I did not know that, otherwise I might have been more fearful in handling them. In any case, they never bit me, so either the report is false or I had some particularly gentle amphisbaenids!

The Amphisbaenid (*Diplometon zarudnyi*) lives underneath the surface of the sand, coming out only occasionally at night. Then it leaves a most unusual track – a series of unconnected curlicues, starting with a small pit that is made by the tail being pressed into the sand to give leverage. It eats mainly small grubs, ants and insects. Their skin is a mottled dark pink colour, and has transverse ribbing along all of the body.

By this time I had seen many different snakes during my desert walks I made with the dogs. The most common ones were the long, thin colubers, or racers. In the wadis there was a pretty checkered one called the wadi racer, while in the sands the sand racer occurred in various shades of beige. One day I found one under a saltbush and I bent over to see what it was. The tip of the tail was nearest to the path and I followed the line of the body with my eyes to the other end, which surprisingly was also a tail! I could not see that end properly so I picked up the tail that was nearest me and lifted the metre-long snake from the bush. It barely reacted and then I saw why: he was in the process of eating a rather large lizard – and the second tail that I had seen was that of the poor prey. As I put the snake back, I marvelled that I had dared to pick it up at all. I had become so used to reptiles that I had not even stopped to think.

One of my colleagues at the clinic said one day: 'We are going home to Australia for six weeks and my son is looking for someone to take care of his two pet snakes for a while. We have found a housesitter for the cat and the dogs, but he is scared of snakes. Would you know someone?'

Feeling particularly courageous that day I offered to take them. That weekend father and son came to deliver their terrarium. The inhabitants were two absolutely gorgeous corn snakes. Their basic skin colour was orange, with wide transverse red spots, outlined in brown and with thin red lines between the spots.

Corn snakes (*Elaphe guttata*) are commonly found in deciduous forests, rocky hillsides and farm areas over a broad swath of the United States. They have also been reported in Mexico and the Cayman Islands. They are most active at night or in the hours of dawn and dusk. While they are primarily ground-dwellers, some are semi-arboreal. Young wild Corn snakes start off feeding on small invertebrates, such as crickets, later feeding mostly on small rodents and birds, killing their prey by constriction. They lay eggs, becoming sexually mature at around two years of age. Hatchlings range in size from 22-36cm; adults are generally 76-152cm in length.

The snake owners gave me a frozen packet of dead mice. Each snake had to have three mice once a week

'While they are feeding,' said the boy's father, 'put this piece of carton between them because if one finishes before the other he may start eating the same mouse that the other snake is trying to eat, and then he won't stop but eat the whole snake too.'

I shuddered at the thought, but I was not concerned because I would not let that happen. The boy showed me how tame the snakes were, by letting them crawl all over his arms and shoulders. I handled them a bit too and was reassured that they would not be difficult to care for. And indeed, the cornies were OK. They were not very active, lazing about on the branches in their terrarium in graceful garlands of colour. When it came to feeding time, I first carefully placed the piece of carton diagonally in the terrarium before I dropped three defrosted mice into each half. An hour later the mice would be gone and the snakes would be nicely rounded in the middle.

One day someone called at the door as I was feeding the snakes. I had just dropped in the mice and walked away from the terrarium without realising that I had not put on the cover. I talked with my visitor for fifteen minutes or so and then returned to the small bathroom where the snakes were.

Snake, singular! One was gone.

I realised it must have climbed out of the terrarium so I looked around where it could be. The bathroom was two meters square and the only objects in it were the toilet, the washing machine and the small chest of drawers with the terrarium on top. I looked under and behind everything but could not find the snake.

A terrible thought crept into my mind: *Could the snake have gone to the other side of the aquarium and eaten his partner?* I looked at the remaining snake. Did he look fatter than usual? In a panic I called CC who scorned the whole idea of one snake eating the other.

Then I called Gerard, who after all was the snake expert. He said: 'Yes, I suppose it is possible. These corn snakes are infamous for that behaviour. But it would take time and you did not leave them alone that long, did you? So it is really more likely that he is hiding somewhere. He'll appear again next week when it is feeding time.'

I was not completely reassured, so I decided to take the fat snake to the vet-around-the-corner and get X-ray proof. But before we left I made a role of paper napkins to jam into the opening between the bathroom door and the floor. If the missing snake had not been eaten and was hiding I did not want it to escape from the bathroom, to be eaten by one of the dogs or cats or to frighten the cleaning lady to death.

At the vet's we stretched out the long reptile on the examination table and took the X-ray. The picture showed a nifty row of vertebrae with, lined up against it, the squashed remains of three mice – no other snake! Much relieved I went home again, put the snake back in its home and closed the lid.

I checked the bathroom every day, but saw no trace of the other snake, till the sixth day. Then he was suddenly there, sliding along the floor, on cue for dinner. I grabbed him quickly, not paying attention to where I took hold of him. He whipped around and bit me fiercely in the ball of my hand. I hung on and deposited him back into his terrarium, where he calmed down immediately and let go of my hand. I guess in the week of freedom without being handled he had forgotten that he was supposed to be a docile pet. But more likely it was my fault for grabbing him too quickly.

In any case, it put me off snakes for a while and I was glad to be rid of them when the family returned from their holiday. I gave the boy the X-ray as a welcome home present!

23

MONKEY BUSINESS

I had been away on a holiday and on my return Nambi told me we had a monkey. In what had been one of the wildcat cages I found an adult Rhesus macaque.

'How did that happen?' I asked him.

'Big English madam coming,' he explained. 'She find him, she bring him.' The big English madam had to be Monica, an acquaintance and patient of mine. I called her to ask about it.

'I was at Spinneys (the supermarket) and there on the parking lot was a taxi with this poor monkey tied to the roof, spread-eagled on his back. Some young guys were going to drive around with him like that. I became so furious that I frightened them into giving the monkey to me. But then I did not know what to do with him, so I thought of your cages and brought him around. I hope you don't mind.'

Of course I didn't mind that a poor creature had been saved from fear and horror. The monkey (that strangely enough I never named) was quite tame, greeting me with obvious approval as he jumped on my shoulder and started grooming my hair. I sat down on a big log that lay in the cage and enjoyed the late afternoon sunshine. The little furry paws in my hair felt nice, so I let him be. The problem arose when I had enough and wanted to get up. He clung to my head, grabbing fistfuls of hair, while his hind legs tightened their grip on my neck. In loud chattering noises he voiced his protest at the interruption of his preferred pastime. I had to call Nambi to bring a banana to distract him, before I could make my escape.

When I told CC about the grooming problem of our new housemate a little later, he yelled down the telephone: 'Don't do that ever again! Rhesus monkeys are very, very dangerous. When they are imprinted like that on people they see you as their mate. And in Rhesus philosophy female mates are subservient. If you do not obey his wishes, he may attack you.'

I laughed in disbelief – after all, the monkey was not very big.

'Don't be mistaken,' said CC, 'they are incredibly strong. I know of one keeper who hand-reared a male Rhesus macaque and was killed by him one day when the monkey disapproved of something. Never go into the cage without a big stick to defend yourself, and tell that to Nambi too. And stop that grooming thing!'

I was impressed, I had never heard him that angry or anxious. So I followed his advice, keeping my distance from the monkey from then on.

The Rhesus macaque (*Macaca mulatta*) is a primate species that is genetically and physiologically similar to humans. Rhesus monkeys are the most widely used nonhuman primate in biomedical research. They have given their name to the rhesus antigens found in their blood in 1940, which has enabled doctors to determine different blood groups in humans. Rhesus monkeys were also the first primates to be rocketed into space.

Their origin is in Afghanistan, India, Thailand and Southern China where they prefer forest habitats, including semi-desert, dry, deciduous, bamboo, and tropical woodland up to 3,000 metres. They are agile quadrupeds, as much at home in trees as on the ground and they are even skilled swimmers, having been observed crossing bodies of water up to one kilometre wide. When they are seen in the water they are usually searching for food, escaping from danger, regulating their body temperature, or playing. Swimming is a skill seen in infants as young as two days old. They live in multi-male, multi-female troops. Females lead the troop, although males are dominant.

Soon it was apparent that my monkey was rather unhappy on his own. I discovered that he loved ice cream lollypops which I made from low-fat yoghurt. But that distraction only lasted minutes. I gave him a children's bath to play in, which he thoroughly enjoyed till the novelty waned. Then I bought him a large teddy bear, almost his own size. He hugged the bear to his chest and groomed it till the fur started to disintegrate. And then he humped it. He humped it to pieces. It was clear what he needed – a mate.

It seemed easier to me to find him a group of Rhesus monkeys somewhere. But CC explained: 'The cruelty of keeping Rhesus macaques as pets is that a solitary animal can never be integrated into an existing family group again. The males in the group do not welcome intruders. They are so ferocious they will tear the newcomer apart, limb by limb, alive!'

So, failing a suitable family, we would have to make one of our own. I went to Reza Khan, then curator of the small Dubai zoo. This zoo often had to deal with confiscated wild animals – a real problem. While I was there he showed me two young lions, very stunted in their growth. The Arab owner had had their claws and teeth pulled when they were still cubs so the animals would be safe to have around the house. Without their teeth they had to have mashed food and without bones to chew they had obviously not been getting an adequate calcium supply. The two cats looked pitiful, subdued and somehow without dignity. I said to Reza: 'The only humane thing to do is to put them down.'

'I know,' he said, 'but I am not allowed to do that. I need to convince the authorities that it is not against the Islamic law to kill a sick animal.'

I was aware of this problem. Especially in the early days, when camels were still roaming the desert unconfined and road accidents were quite frequent. Many of these were fatal for both man and animal, but in some cases the camel survived and was left badly injured. It would be lying by the side of the road, and food and water would be provided by the owner. Often the injuries were so bad that the animal died after a few days, but no one put it out of its misery. In one case a camel had a broken pelvis and lay for weeks in the burning sun without a chance of healing properly. The expats of Dubai protested loudly in the newspapers and eventually the police was given permission to shoot badly injured animals.

The same unwritten law caused a rather more amusing incident. A friend of mine who had a pest control business told me about it. Most pests were insects, rats and mice, of course, but in one case the target was the increasing population of pigeons that lived on the highrise buildings of the city.

'Of course their droppings dirty balconies and sidewalks and the health ministry feared the spread of disease,' Alan told me, 'The pigeons were easily caught – they were crated and a few thousand were loaded onto large trucks. These trucks were driven deep into the sandy desert, some six hours away, to where the Rub' al-Khali starts. There they were set free.'

He chuckled.

'Guess what happened?! Obviously the authorities had never heard about the homing instinct of pigeons. The birds were all back at their usual perches before the trucks were even halfway on their return trip!'

At the zoo, Reza did have a female Rhesus macaque for me. We filled out a loan form, although both of us knew that the monkey would never return to the zoo. Then I took her home. For the first couple of days I kept the two in separate adjoining cages, so they could get used to one another. At a weight of six kilos and a height of 30cm the female was less than half the size of the male and obviously frightened of him. It was an anxious moment when I opened the door between the cages. The male immediately stormed across to the cowering screeching female and I feared the worst. However, the male jumped on a branch behind the female and put his arms around her in a tender embrace. Then he sat and groomed her for minutes, until she had calmed down and started to return the favour. The pair developed a reasonably happy relationship, but the strong and active male was often so boisterous that his mate would scream when he became too wild. What I had not noticed was that the male, obviously still bored with life in a cage, had started to untwist the wire that connected two stretches of wire mesh.

One early afternoon my neighbour Julie called me at the

clinic: 'Marijcke, I think you have to come home quickly. The police are here and want to shoot your monkey!'

I wasted no time asking her what had happened but quickly transferred my next scheduled patient to a colleague and raced home. There was a small crowd standing in my garden – two policemen, a few neighbours and an agitated Nambi. They were all watching the male monkey as he sat in the large Indian almond tree ripping off branches and throwing them down.

I pushed my way through to the front door to take my handbag inside, and as I strode into the house, I felt a light slap of a cold, small hand against my leg. I looked down and there was the monkey, grinning at me. He turned around immediately and raced back into his tree.

I asked the policemen to take everybody outside the gate while I took charge of the situation. I explained to them that the monkey was tame and would not hurt anyone. He would come back into his cage in the evening because he knew that his mate and food were there. At the moment he was not hungry, being full of almond fruits, and could not be tempted inside. But if I offered him his favourite food (a yoghurt ice cream) in the evening I would have him inside in a jiffy. The police agreed to wait till nightfall before taking any measures.

Together with Nambi I checked where the monkey had made his escape and repaired the opening. The female had not taken the opportunity to get out also. The big male sat on the corner of the roof of a neighbour's house, overlooking our garden. You could hear him chattering happily to himself.

'Nambi, I have to go back to work. Please keep an eye on the monkey and try to keep him in our garden. Put some toys out and the baby bath and keep the dog inside.'

When I came back late that afternoon, the monkey was still in the garden and showed no indication of wanting to come inside. The police drove up to the gate and asked me how it was going. I told them I would get the vet who would anaesthesize him so we could bring him back inside.

When the vet arrived he brought an ancient looking dart gun. 'You've done this before?' I asked him.

'Oh yes, it's not difficult with a large monkey like that!'

146

Famous last words.

The very second he fired the dart towards the monkey, the latter turned his back and the dart hit him exactly in the middle of his spine. Within seconds he fell off his branch where Nambi stood to catch him. We carried the unconscious macaque to his cage where he could recuperate. The female was kept in the adjoining cage for the time being.

When the male came to, he was paralysed from the waist down. It broke my heart to see him dragging himself around, unable to walk and jump. I waited for a few days to see if there was any improvement, but we had no such luck. Within days he had pressure sores on his legs. When CC came that weekend, we decided to end his misery. We collected some pills at the vet's clinic and CC mixed them with the yoghurt ice cream that the monkey liked so much. When I wanted to follow CC to the monkey's cage, he said to me: 'Don't come, you don't want to see this.'

He was right, my imagination was quite sufficient for this sad moment. We buried him under the banana tree. At least he had had a pleasant few years with me.

The female could fortunately be added to two young macaques that CC had at his zoo in Al Ain. Somehow I had never made a connection with her and I did not miss her at all.

Sometimes I wondered what a future archaeologist would make of the collection of bones in the banana corner of my garden: the bones of the wildcat kitten, marmoset, rhesus macaque, Russian dwarf hamster and various birds all rested there together.

24

JENNY AND THE
CLOUDED LEOPARDS

During the Thursdays when CC was with me in Dubai, we sometimes went to the *suqs* in Sharjah where there were several pet shops. CC was always on the lookout for rare animals that were for sale, and I wanted to check the conditions in which the animals were kept. Throughout the years I had built up quite a good relationship with the Sharjah authorities and if I reported a dealer who defied the existing rules and laws, there was a chance that something would be done about it. It was only a small chance for I am certain that bribes regularly exchanged hands. The suq inspectors of the department of animal husbandry were mainly from the Indian sub-continent and their salaries would be pitiful. They had no heart for the animals for which they carried responsibility and back home they had large families that needed support.

In the early years the animal suq was on a muddy bank of one of the creeks. The animal shelters were made of corrugated iron and in the summer they were like ovens. The cages were badly overcrowded and never cleaned. Fresh food lay on top of sodden lettuce, drenched with urine and mingled with the remains of whatever creature had not survived these conditions. I often spent hours supervising the cleaning of certain cages.

I was not alone in this activity. There was another Dutch lady who was generally feared by the animal dealers. Her name was Lydia and she had been in the Emirates for countless years working as a belly dancer. It seems an unlikely job for a person from Holland where most people are big, blond and blue-eyed, but Lydia must have had gypsy blood, because she had long black curls, coal-black eyes and a lissome body. I knew her as the animal campaigner first, but later when I saw her dance I realised she was also very good in her profession. As an animal rights campaigner she was brave and had a heart of gold. Often, she got so mad at the prevailing conditions that she created quite a rumpus and more than once she was given warnings by the police to calm down or be deported. In later years we sometimes worked together to change a particularly bad situation. Lydia had many local contacts who told her where things were bad, and I had the contacts with the higher government authorities that could do something about it. Together we were able to make some differences.

One afternoon in the early years (when I did not yet know anyone in Sharjah) CC stopped the car in front of a proper pet shop along the road. It was a small stone, air-conditioned building. As soon as we entered CC showed some consternation. Immediately to our left were three cages stacked one on top of the other. They were about four feet long, three feet high and two feet wide and completely made of wire bars, including the floors. The top one housed a beautiful dachshund that seemed a bit listless. The middle one held a sloth bear cub. Two medium-sized cats of a species that I did not know crouched in the bottom one.

'Those are clouded leopards,' muttered CC, 'one of the rarest cat species in the world. Don't show the salesman that you are interested!'

As we pretended to look at birds and tortoises, I kept glancing back at the stack of cages. The poor animals had difficulty moving on the barred floors, and the urine and faeces of the top animals fell through the bars to the lower cages. The leopards being of the cat family kept themselves reasonably clean but the bear's fur was matted with dirt.

Before we left we asked the prices of everything. The dealer wanted 20,000 dirhams (around $6,000) for the leopards and 8,000 dirhams for the bear. Once outside again I had to take a few deep breaths to settle my stomach and my anger.

'We've got to get those animals out of there!' I said to CC.

He shook his head: 'How can we? We cannot confiscate them and we'll never have enough money to buy them. Besides, buying them would only encourage the dealer to find more rare animals.'

'Of course you are right. But the most important thing right now is to save the lives of those clouded leopards. And I am going to do it. I don't know yet how, but it'll happen – you just wait and see.'

That evening he told me: 'Clouded leopards live in the jungles of Southeast Asia from Nepal and southern China all the way to Borneo. Their Latin name is *Neofelis nebulosa*. They have a beautiful coat with squarish patches. This provides excellent camouflage in their forest habitat.'

I had noticed the unusual pattern of their spots that were darker coloured on one side, giving them a three-dimensional effect, as if the patches were embossed. CC continued: 'They are the best climbers in the cat family, with special ankle joints that allow them to come down tree trunks face forward. Their short legs provide a low centre of gravity, they have powerful gripping paws and a one meter long tail for balance. Their prey includes birds, squirrels, monkeys, deer, and wild pigs. Males weigh only 20 kg, females are about half that size. They are solitary and mainly active at night, but really, we don't know much about their private lives.'

'You said they were rare and endangered. I assume it is loss of habitat again that threatens them? Do they do well in captivity?'

'They used to be notoriously difficult to breed, because the male would often kill the female. Eventually zoo experts started to introduce prospective mates to one another at ages of less than one year and that has resulted in some breeding successes. And yes, they are listed as an Appendix I endangered species by CITES, and vulnerable by IUCN. Not much is known about the number of clouded leopards that are still living in the wild, because the animals are so shy and secretive. In most range countries hunting them is forbidden, although this is rarely enforced. And the clearing of jungle for palm oil plantations is not forbidden, so their habitat is disappearing fast.'

Now it seemed even more important to find a better place for the little leopards.

I had been a member of the Natural History Groups of the Emirates since I arrived. There was a group in each of the three larger cities. The Abu Dhabi group was especially well connected to some of the VIP sheikhs of the royal family. As soon as I got home I started calling my acquaintances around the country. It took only two days. Via the chairman of the Abu Dhabi group I made contact with one of the sons of the President, who was involved in wildlife conservation. He was easily persuaded that the leopards needed better conditions than the pet shop was providing and of course he was rich.

CC sent a truck with cages down from the Al Ain zoo and I went to the pet shop where I bargained the price down by 20%. Then we loaded the two cubs into their cages and wished them a safe journey to their new abode. With CC in charge I knew they would get the best possible care.

Then I went home to do something about the sloth bear and the dachshund. It turned out that the latter had never had a walk in his eight months of captivity. I alerted the K9 organisation in Sharjah who managed to get him out – it took weeks before he was strong enough to walk properly.

My friends in Dubai pitched in when it came to the sloth bear. Donations dribbled in: in hundred and five hundred bills and when I had 5,000 dirhams together by the end of that week I went to the shop and bargained for the little bear. I had arranged that she could be kept at the Dubai zoo until we found a breeding group for her somewhere. One of the most generous donors went with me when we drove to Sharjah with the large cage in the back of my car. The cub was so small and intimidated that the transfer was easy. In the shady Dubai zoo, we let her out in a huge six metre square cage, right next door to the two maltreated lions. As I left I saw her, sitting with her matted fur as a dirty cloak around her, close to the dividing wire contemplating her new neighbours.

The Sloth bear (*Melursus ursinus*) is a nocturnal bear that lives in the lowland forests of the Indian subcontinent and Sri Lanka. Its body is covered in long, shaggy fur, ranging from auburn to black, with a distinctive "V"-shaped whitish mark on the chest, a whitish snout and black nose. The snout is long with bare lips and it lacks upper incisors, adaptations for its insect-based diet. The front feet are turned inwards and have non-retractable, curved ivory claws that are adapted for digging. The males are larger than the females; reaching a height of 1.8m and a weight of 140 kilograms. Poaching as well as loss and fragmentation of habitat are the primary threats to its survival in the wild. In spite of its name it does not move as slowly as a sloth. In fact, it is also known as the "dancing bear" of Indian road shows and circuses.

The next few months I corresponded with the contacts that CC set up for me. There was an established breeding group of sloth bears in the Artis zoo in Amsterdam. They had a surplus of Syrian brown bears, that Dubai zoo was eager to have. So before the year was out Jenny, the sloth bear cub, was exchanged for a group of seven Syrian bears.

About five years later I was staying with friends in Amsterdam who lived near Artis. I wandered through the zoo trying to find the sloth bears. When I had found the enclosure I looked for the zoo keeper in charge of the bears.

'Yes, Jenny is doing fine,' he said, 'but she has not bred yet. She is very small for her age.'

'I guess that is due to the fact that her growth was so stunted in those early months,' I said.

'That is probably right, but it certainly gives her no trouble right now. She is outside with her favourite companion. Go have a look.'

I walked around to the front of the bear pit. At that time Artis still had old-fashioned enclosures for some of the animals and the bear pit was one of them. The space that was available for the animals was fine, but CC had taught me that it is not good to have the public look down on the animals. First, this way you cannot really appreciate what the animals look like and second, it is psychologically wrong.

I leaned over the small wall and looked down to where Jenny was playing with another, much larger bear. Her coat was long and shiny, really beautiful. The two bears tumbled on the grass and chased each other around boulders and tree trunks. Then they flopped down in a patch of sunshine and Jenny rolled onto her back, showing the yellowish half moon patch on her chest. A young couple was standing next to me, watching. The girl said to her friend: 'I really hate seeing animals like that cooped up in such a small enclosure.'

I could not help smiling and said: 'Sorry to butt in, but I happen to know for a fact that that little bear there thinks this is heaven!'

And then I told them the story.

The clouded leopards fared less well, unfortunately.

When we moved them into CC's care we did not know that his days at the zoo were numbered. CC did not return to Al Ain after his summer holidays. Among some of my concerns at the time were my worries about the young leopards. They were not easy to take care of, and I knew that the present curators at that zoo did not have a clue. So I started the process of moving them to Europe. First I had to contact the sheikh who had paid for them and get his permission. I would have to be very diplomatic about that, because criticism of the Al Ain zoo would not be welcome. It took many months to get his approval for the move.

I called the curator who was in charge of the bears.

'How are the clouded leopards doing?' I asked him.

'What leopards?' This "curator" was a European who, in spite of twenty years at this zoo, could never remember the names of the species he was supposed to take care of. He would not have lasted long in any European zoo, even as an animal keeper.

'The small leopards. Remember, the ones that the sheikh placed in the zoo.'

'Ah, those. There is only one left now.'

'What?! What happened?'

'The male died just a few weeks ago.'

'Did you do an autopsy?'

It turned out that they did and I managed to speak to the Filipino vet.

'We found that he died of a fatty degeneration of his liver.'

'How could that happen?' I asked.

'Well, I suppose they gave them too much food.'

On my next day off I set out for the zoo. I was unable to have a look at the remaining clouded leopard. Being a nocturnal and shy animal she rarely showed herself in the daytime. But from the curator I gathered that she too was very fat. I implored him to put her on a slimming diet and then went to visit the present director, a local man who had absolutely no interest in zoos or animals. I showed him the letter from the sheikh, allowing me to arrange for the removal of the leopards to Europe and arranged a date two months later.

When I called CC he was as upset as I was about the death of the young male. He had a place for the female, though, and agreed to pick her up at Frankfurt airport, when we were ready to send her. He urged me to make sure that the travelling cage would be properly constructed. There was a foreign vet working temporarily at the zoo at that time. I asked him to supervise the construction of the travel crate, bypassing the employees of the zoo. I did not realise that this was a big mistake on my part. No one could have guessed what would happen as a result.

The big day arrived and with the vet in Al Ain supervising the loading of the crate, I decided to remain in Dubai to be present at the transfer of the crate from the truck to the airplane. A few hours before the departure of the plane the truck arrived. I peered inside the crate through the fine wire mesh and saw the small leopard cowering in the back. She had plenty of room and the crate seemed to be properly constructed. I handed over the stacks of paper that needed to accompany the transport – and watched as the crate was loaded on an airport vehicle and driven to the freight area to await the arrival of the plane. I was not concerned about the wait. It was night time and pleasantly cool. Lufthansa had an excellent reputation as animal carrier. There was nothing more I could do.

CC's phone call came at mid-morning.

He was furious.

'She arrived dead! What the hell did you do? How could this have happened?'

I sank onto the sofa, shattered. I don't cry easily, but this time

I sobbed so loudly that Sandy came to me, her head tilted in surprise. She jumped up and sat next to me, leaning against me to comfort me.

What could have happened? I would have to wait for the answer to this question until the result was known of the autopsy that CC was going to have done. And then I would have to let everyone know the sad news. It took a few days till CC's next call: 'She was poisoned. Her stomach and intestines were one bloody mess. In the stomach we found seven small pieces of undigested meat. They were small enough to have been pushed through the wire mesh. I should have a chemical analysis done but that is very expensive and it is obvious that it was a very erosive poison. She must have suffered immensely before she died.'

I knew that the poisoning must have taken place while the crate was still in the zoo. Neither the truck drivers nor the Lufthansa personnel would have had a motive or enough knowledge of poisons to do such a thing. It was not until more than a year later that I found out what had happened.

One of CC's Pakistani zoo keepers, who had been very fond of him (and by extension of me), told me that when the crate was loaded, the assistant director had sent everyone away and climbed on the truck apparently to inspect the crate.

I confronted the assistant director, who did not admit to anything, but raged at me for having ordered an outsider to supervise the construction of the crate.

'I could have done that' he said, 'I am very good. You did wrong and now your animal is dead!'

He laughed and I wanted to punch him in the face. But he got away with it, for I could not prove anything. Never in my life will I understand people who can harm animals for any reason – but causing an animal a slow and painful death because your pride has been hurt means that you must have no soul or conscience at all.

Fortunately, since that sad time, many changes for the better have occurred at that zoo.

25

BREAKING UP

CC was very unhappy in his job at the Al Ain zoo. He hated the country, the climate, the local people and their culture. He missed the contact with colleagues and he missed Europe. When the Berlin wall fell, he happened to be there on vacation. He celebrated all night and all day with millions of fellow Germans. When he told me about it his eyes misted with emotion. His Germany was whole again. Now he really wanted to go back.

One day he announced that he was going to Germany to apply for a job at a zoo in his former home town. His chances to get the job were quite good but he hesitated because the zoo was so insignificant and small.

'Never mind that,' I said, 'It gives you a chance to make it bigger and better!'

He made the quick trip to Europe, feigning a family emergency as an excuse for time off. When he came back, he said it would be quite a while until he received the result of his interview. I asked him: 'If you do get the job, do you want me to come with you?'

'That's up to you,' he replied.

'You know what I feel. I need to know what you feel!'

'Sure,' he said, 'Whatever.'

It was not exactly the answer I had hoped for, but nevertheless I started to practice German, took out a subscription for a newspaper of his hometown and prepared myself mentally for a move back to Europe.

1992 was called the "annus horribilis" by the English queen. I agreed with her wholeheartedly.

It did not start out so bad. The first few months in the Emirates passed very quickly, filled with hard work to save the leopards and the bear. We went on an early vacation in Europe, seeing the alpine spring flowers in southern Germany and "doing" the zoos.

We were enjoying a nice dinner on the last evening, when CC said: 'That was really a perfect vacation, perfect food, perfect weather, and perfect company!'

I felt good too.

CC was staying behind to see his family and to go to the zoo where he had applied for the job of director, to find out what was happening. If I had known that it was to be the last night with him, I would have chosen a nicer hotel than the rather dingy station hotel, where we stayed so that he could catch the early train to the East.

I returned to the Emirates and waited. No news came. I did not want to bug CC but I was really curious whether he had gotten the job. When the date on which he should have been back passed without a word from him, I finally called his brother. I knew that CC always stayed with him whenever he was in that area. Indeed CC was there and came to the phone.

'Hi, good to know you are still alive! What's happening?'

'I started work three weeks ago and will not be coming back.'

'Just like that? Why didn't you let me know earlier? You must have known I was waiting for news. And what is going to happen to your stuff in Al Ain – and your gratuity?' In the Emirates jobs did not come with pension plans, but for each year that you worked three weeks' salary was added to a gratuity that was paid out when the work contract was ended. If you absconded, as CC had just done, you lost that money. In his case if must have been close to $9,000, and I would have thought stingy CC would have done anything to get that money.

Not so. Apparently his dislike for anything to do with the Emirates was stronger than any of the bonds he had with the place, including with me. He was now living permanently with his family, where he had his food cooked and his laundry done and probably paid next to nothing towards his room and board.

I still did not realise what was happening. CC asked me to clear out his stuff from his house in Al Ain and to send his books to him in Germany. I spent a weekend packing his meagre belongings. He had never really furnished his house, so there was only a bedroom suite, a fridge and a cooker to be sold. That was the easy part.

His bedroom looked as if it had been burgled. Papers and pictures lay scattered on the floor. Among them were a number of pictures of me that he had asked for in the early days of our acquaintance. There were also some bank statements of his bank in Germany that showed a very healthy balance, far more than I had ever had.

I tried to sort out my feelings as I sorted out his stuff. He had obviously not intended to come back. I realised now that he must have known that he had been chosen for the job in Germany even before we went on vacation. Did he leave those pictures and bank statements for me to find in order to hurt me? What was I doing here? I should never have agreed to help him. Tears were streaming down my face while I put his books in boxes and carried them to the car. There were no more than three boxes to be dispatched – remains of an eight-year stay.

August came and a day before my forty-ninth birthday a letter arrived from CC. It did not contain good wishes for my birthday. Instead it said: "Don't bother to come to Germany. My brother does not like fat people."

I do not remember much of the rest of the letter, except the PS at the bottom.

"I have heard from Canada that the divorce from my wife is now a fact."

I had not even known that it was imminent. What was the use of letting me know this now, when he had just ended our relationship?

The next day a huge bouquet of flowers was delivered to my house – from CC. I binned them.

I was utterly devastated. Even though I knew the relationship was not perfect, I was not ready to be alone again. It did not help that my friends and family all said: "Good riddance to bad rubbish!"

Nobody seemed to realise that losing your partner this way was just as bad as losing him through death. In a way it was worse. When your partner dies, people sympathise and try to comfort. Now, no one did. No one even had any patience with the fact that I was so distressed.

Except Sandy.

Up till that time she had always slept in her basket in the hallway, but now she broke through my defenses and jumped on my bed to snuggle against me at night. When I cried, as I often did during those nights, she gently licked my hand. I knew that it was bad practice to have her sleep with me but I was grateful for the warm body stretched out against mine. At least she did not mind that I was fat!

A few weeks later my brother and his son were celebrating their birthdays together. I decided to make a quick trip to Holland to attend the family affair in an attempt to break through my sadness. When everyone had left after a noisy children's party, my nephew Casper and I were sitting on the sofa watching a video about insects that someone had given him. He sat vigorously sucking two fingers of his left hand, resting his other hand on my thigh. In an admiring tone of voice, he said:

'You know everything there is to know about nature, don't you?'

'Oh gosh, no!' I answered, 'there is so much – I only know a very little bit.'

He contemplated the answer for a moment. Then, as his free hand continued to stroke my thigh, he said:

'Fat legs don't matter, do they?'

Later I realised that my animals also did not mind what I looked like, but what counted was that I cared. So "Fat legs don't matter" became my new motto for life.

26

A NEW BEGINNING

There is the old cliché that says: "When one door closes, another opens." I would never have guessed it could be so true.

The first months after that memorable summer of '92 were sheer misery. I felt hurt, discarded, unwanted. The worst thoughts were: *For how long has our whole relationship been a sham? Where did the friendship go? Was there ever any?*

Just when I thought I was recovering, a parcel came from Germany – a Christmas gift from CC. It was a very large box, filled to the brim with German delicacies – marzipan, lebkuchen, chocolates, gingerbread. I looked at it, recalled CC's excuse for breaking up and called Nambi.

'Can you please take this and share it with your friends?'

It would have choked me to eat even one piece.

I had to find new things to get through the weekends and was grateful for the many opportunities that Dubai offered to pass the time. Almost every weekend I went hiking in the desert, sometimes with friends and always with Sandy. Now that she was fully grown, a beautiful sleek strong dog, she loved the long walks and rough climbs. I enjoyed seeing her run or stand on a hilltop looking at the valleys with her keen eyes. Once, as I knelt by a small stream to wash my face, she was suddenly on top of me, her paws over my shoulders, nudging my neck with a playful nose. She liked it when people came down to her level. I always had to be careful that she did not see a praying Muslim somewhere. She would have gone up to play with him, convinced that a person kneeling in the sand, bending up-and-down and waving his hands was inviting her to frolic.

I was at work when the door to a new life opened, although I did not realise what happened until much later.

'Hey Marijcke, look what we found this weekend!'

My friend Dee and I were perched on the straight-backed chairs just outside the kitchen door of the clinic where we worked, having our coffee break. Winter mornings were pleasant and cool in Dubai. Dee lived in Ras al Khaymah, the northern-most city of the UAE. It was still a genuine Arab town, wedged between the steep Ru'us al Jibal mountains and the azure waters of the Gulf. Dee and her friend John had been out hiking in the mountains as they did most weekends. This time she had something special to report.

She handed me a photograph. It showed the carcass of a freshly killed leopard, hanging against a rock face. Its beautiful skin, hanging down in folds, glowed in the sunshine. The picture moved me beyond words. It had already been a few years ago that four leopards had been killed in that area in a six months' period of time. I had assumed that those had been the last leopards in the Emirates. And now...

A thought came to me: *If there are still any leopards in these mountains, they must be kept safe, somehow.* For all I knew this had been the last leopard, but still I felt the need to try and do something to safeguard whatever might be left.

It had been Gerard who told me that there were leopards in the mountains along the eastern coasts of the Emirates and Oman. But we knew so little of what happened in those remote regions that we had assumed that the leopards had gone the way of most of the larger wildlife. Cheetahs had disappeared long ago, wolves and hyenas more recently. Caracals were still present and so were wildcats and foxes. That evening I wrote a small article for the English-language newspaper, inviting people to join me to start a campaign for wildlife conservation, specifically to save the remaining Arabian leopards. Two weeks later the clinic's waiting room saw the first meeting of what was going to be the Arabian Leopard Trust (ALT). The initial twenty people soon dwindled to a small group of volunteers, who were the backbone of the first wildlife conservation non-government organisation (NGO) in Arabia.

There were Rajive and Shudhira from India, he a business man, she a designer, who took on the production of fund-raising objects such as T-shirts, leopard-print textiles, toys, puzzles – a never-ending array of articles meant to raise awareness as well as funds. There was Moaz, originally from Syria, who was a mountaineer and soon became our link to the mountain people, the *jibali*. We provided him with a questionnaire and he spoke to the farmers and hunters in Arabic and tried to find out what lived and died in the mountains. There was Sue, a teacher, ideally suited to help develop teaching programs for the kids that we wanted to reach. There was I, who overcame shyness to knock on everyone's door for help, for attention, for money. I wrote articles for newspapers and magazines, begging letters to businesses, animal stories to sell and give away to kids.

Others came and went, some helping briefly, others staying longer, but this strong nucleus remained for several years, and then gradually was replaced by others with different talents and strengths.

Soon I was so busy with the new ALT that I had no more time for maudlin behaviour. The trust occupied all my spare time for the next ten years and led to many amazing adventures. Had CC still been around, I would not have had the time to do this. The door on CC had to be closed before I could let the leopards in.

27

BAS CHALAS

It was June and very hot, even at 8am. The huge mesquite tree spread welcome shade over the driveway. As I walked out the gate to go to work, a small dog crawled out from under the car. It was dirty white, still very young, though not a small puppy any more. It came over to me without fear and wagged its tail furiously.

'Where have you come from, little doggie?' I talked to him softly as I scratched his ears. They were hanging low with the weight of dozens of ticks. 'Poor thing, you must be thirsty.'

I walked back into the house and got a bowl of water, which I placed in the corner of the driveway, near some wood that was stacked against the wall. Then I drove off. As usual I was trying to harden my heart to the misery of the little dog. There were so many like him roaming the streets of the city, unwanted, uncared for and half wild. Over the years I had seen hundreds of dogs that needed a good home, but I could not take care of hundreds. I had Sandy, whom I loved so much that I really did not want another dog to come between us.

When I returned from work that day, the little dog was still there. This time it ran towards me greeting me like his long-lost and much-loved friend. It wagged its tail in a curious manner, not back and forth, but sweeping mad circles. I felt it could take off and start hovering any second. My work-tiredness vanished and I picked up the little guy and carried him into the garden.

'Let's get you cleaned and rid you of those nasty ticks.'

Sandy bounded out of the house, excited and curious. She did not seem put out at the arrival of another dog. I pulled the garden hose around the house to the shady back yard and shut the little gate to keep Sandy out. I asked Nambi, who was in the kitchen, to hand me some cooking oil and a roll of paper towels. I hated tackling ticks, but it needed to be done. With oil-soaked paper I rubbed the ticks till they suffocated and relaxed their bite, and then I twisted them free. It took quite a long time, for the dog was covered from head to toe with the nasty pests. Then I gave him a bath. He emerged from the suds a pure white and lovely smelling creature.

I did not want to keep him, but I thought I'd take care of him until I could find him a good home. He was extremely friendly and trusting. Sandy liked him right away and before long they were rolling about in the air-conditioned living room, having great fun.

I was reminded of a little poem in Dutch that says:

> *I wished I was two little dogs,*
> *Then I could play together.* (In Dutch it rhymes.)

The next day I took the dog, as yet unnamed, to the vet and had him checked out, dewormed and vaccinated. When I returned, Nambi came in and told me: 'Madam, little dog belonging to man there.' He pointed down the street. The house servants' grapevine had been working overtime again. Everything anyone did or experienced was spread around the neighbourhood within hours. The men and women from the Indian sub-continent who worked for the Europeans and the Arabs formed a strong guild. They took care of each other as much as possible. They carried their friends' mail and packages back home during their leaves. They complained or bragged about their employers. One girl in the street had an unpleasant man as boss who refused to let the girl use his post box for her mail, so Nambi had arranged with me that my post box could be used. Whenever I walked down the street with Sandy, friendly waves and soft voices greeted me. It did not surprise me that the owner of the dog had been traced so quickly all the way down the block.

I was glad I had not become attached to the little guy yet as I carried him down the street to his proper home. I wanted to have a word with the owner, both about the state in which I had found the dog and about the series of vaccinations that still had to be completed. The owner was not there but the house servant took receipt of the little white bundle and told me when I could see his boss. So I returned the next day. The Levantine Arab who lived in the house was not happy with my visit. As we stood talking on his doorstep, I heard a pitiful whine emerging from some bushes at the corner of the house. The little dog crept from between the branches, his tail curled tight between his legs. I looked at him with horror. The whole right side of his face was a bloody mess and he was obviously in great pain.

'What happened?' I asked the man.

'He had to be taught that he cannot run away!' said the idiot, without a trace of compunction. I almost yelled at him: 'And this is how you do that?'

Carefully I lifted the dog and examined his face. The cheek seemed more hollow on the right, was the bone broken? His eyeball was displaced, protruding from the socket like gruesome Halloween make-up. But this was no make-up, this was real. I turned to the owner and told him: 'I am taking this dog to the vet and if you want him back you'll have to come and see me first.'

The man merely shrugged and let me go with his dog.

The vet operated on the little dog and wired the broken jaw while putting the eyeball back in its proper place. He gave me eye drops that had to be instilled several times a day. Every time I did it, the little dog cried with pain. Sandy tried her best to prevent me from hurting her new friend, pushing her nose against my arm and trying to get between me and the puppy.

I called him Bas, because he looked like a dog of that name that our family had had many years ago. It also is the Arabic word for "enough". Later that became Bas Chalas, which is Arabic for "enough is enough", for I was adamant that there would be no more dogs after him.

Bas Chalas healed very quickly, being young and getting healthier by the day. His coat became long and shiny and his wispy tail grew into a proud plume with which he continually whisked the air. He followed me like a shadow whenever he could and rough-housed with Sandy the rest of the time. I marvelled that I had ever thought that it was proper to have only one dog. CC had often remarked: 'People always do the wrong thing: they get two cats, where cats like to live solitary, and then they get one dog, where dogs like to live in a pack with a leader. The animals adapt. The cats learn to tolerate their housemates, and the dogs substitute the human family for their pack, but having two dogs and one cat is much more natural.'

Catastrophe was not so happy with the rambunctious newcomer and took refuge once again in one of the glass terrariums, as she had done after Sandy arrived.

Although Sandy was without doubt the leader, she was very gentle in her authority. Every evening I had a bone for the dogs to chew and when they had finished with their own bone, they usually looked for the bone that their friend had discarded and chewed some more. One day Sandy had taken over the bone that Bas had left and was sitting on a garden chair, dreamily gnawing on it. Bas came back and decided he wanted his bone again. As I watched he walked over to Sandy, approaching very quietly and slowly, step by step. Then he stretched his neck, still very slowly and cautiously, gently took the bone from Sandy's mouth – and walked away with it. I could hardly believe my eyes. I had expected quite a brawl. Had sweet Sandy remembered that it was not her bone to begin with?

It is said that dogs do not see colours. In the case of Bas I was not so sure. He definitely liked red, fire-engine red. Anything of that colour was dragged away and hidden in or near his basket. Surprisingly he never chewed anything. So things just disappeared but did not get destroyed. Sometimes they were objects that belonged to visitors.

'Have you seen my red sneakers?'

'Go look in Bas' basket – they're probably there.'

And yes, tucked between the wicker and the cushion was the lost property.

On Valentine's day someone sent me a single red rose. I put it in a narrow-necked vase on the low sitting room table. A few hours later I found Bas standing in the middle of the room with the red rose carefully held in his mouth. I burst out laughing, he looked so cavalier. Of course that made him drop the rose before I could take a picture. He also had it in for the poinsettias which I always planted near the door of my house in the last months of the year. The first year Bas was with us they did not last long. He kept picking whole branches and walked around the garden looking ridiculous with the large red star covering half his face.

I soon discovered that two young dogs and a nice garden are not compatible. Bas was a digger. He dug holes so deep that only his bushy tail would still be above ground, lying like a bath rug on the sand. When the dogs played they would tear through the borders which soon looked like war zones. Once I saw Bas sprinting through my zinnias that were just in bud. He dove behind an oleander bush as I started yelling at him to get out of there. The oleander bush stood close to a wall that was covered with bright blue morning glory. When Bas emerged from behind the bush, he was festooned with garlands of morning glory, one blue flower dangling by his cheek and another perched rakishly above an ear. Who can stay mad at such a sight!

Every other year the K9 charity organised a dog show. Of the hundreds of events and activities that happened in Dubai all the time, I thought this one was the most fun. Besides the competitions there were demonstrations of trained police dogs and there was a market with hundreds of stalls with dog-related articles, artefacts and food.

On the spur of the moment I decided to enter the competitions with both dogs. Neither of them had ever walked on a leash. In fact, I did not even own a leash, so I grabbed the washing line from the back yard, cut it in two and took the dogs, neatly washed and brushed to the show.

In the morning the non-pedigree dogs were being judged. Most of the morning categories were just for fun. I had entered Sandy in the categories "The dog with the friendliest face" and "The dog that the judge most likes to take home", while Bas would perform in "Less than a year-olds" and "The dog with the waggiest tail". I felt sure that Bas with his strange circular wag would win that category!

Bas was on first in the puppy category. He walked proudly beside me on the washing line as if he had been trained for months. He was a bit excited and looked very alert and beautiful. I lifted him on the examination table and the judge looked him over carefully. We stood aside as the other dogs were examined and waited for the verdict to be announced.

'And the winner is…Bas Chalas!'

The big red rosette that was pinned to his collar was exactly to his taste!

Sandy was nervous of the crowds, the noise and the presence of so many other dogs. In the first category she would not show her face to the judge, and in the other one she spoiled her chances by squatting down right in front of the judge and producing a huge pooh in the middle of the show ring. The K9 helpers obligingly brought out the shovel as I slunk off with my badly behaved beloved.

When the time came for Bas to show off his waggy tail, he had lost interest and barely moved his bushy appendage despite my coaxing. Still, we already had a prize so it did not matter. And there was still another chance, for the overall winner from the morning would be chosen from among the winners of each category. While waiting for that time to come around I took Sandy back home – she was not really enjoying the crowds. I reflected that at least she was not upset because she did not win a prize as children would have been. The whole thing was way below her dignity!

When I returned with Bas we took our place in the winners' parade and marched around the ring a few more times. To my immense surprise Bas was pronounced the most beautiful bastard of Dubai. He had to sit on the highest platform, got an even bigger rosette and a silver cup not to mention a year's supply of dog food.

As I stood next to the judge for the photo-op, I told him about the state in which I had found Bas only six months before.

'I must say,' said the man in a posh British accent, 'you did a super job with him.'

Basje's erstwhile owner thought that too. He stopped me in the street one day and said:

'That dog has become beautiful. What food do you give him?'

'It is not a matter of food. A little care and love was all he needed. He is a super dog all by himself!'

The only thing wrong with Bas was his strongly developed hunting and killing instinct that emerged when he was fully grown. Anything furry or feathery was chased, quickly caught and dispatched, with the exclusion of those animals that belonged to my household. Catastrophe was a friend and joined in play at times. Bas never harmed her. But any other cat that happened to enter the garden was a goner. It was no longer possible to walk him off the leash around the neighbourhood where almost every house had a chicken coop, a rabbit hutch or one or more cats. If he spotted a possible prey he became deaf to commands and once he had caught something he would not let go until it was dead. He always won the fight with cats, because their claws could not rake his skin through his thick coat. Even my beating him with a shoe on his backside as hard as I could did not make him relinquish his prey.

Our desert walks together became impossible because there always were goats somewhere. And although most of them seemed feral, as soon as something happened to one of them an owner would pop out from behind the rocks and claim compensation.

I bought a muzzle and put it on when we went out on a trip. The hard plastic bands obstructed his vision and on coming down a hillside he misjudged a jump and sprained his hip. Although nothing was broken the haematoma was enormous, making his leg stand out sideways and preventing him from walking. For several days I had to carry him out and support him whenever he needed to relieve himself. So in the end Bas stayed home whenever we went on desert trips.

From time to time we had two dogs of a friend staying with us, Bali and Sarah. Bali was extra-ordinarily stupid – even her own boss said so. She loped and drooled and rolled on her backside, a happy dog but not a smart one. Sarah was Sandy's age and Bas fell in love the instant he met her. They became inseparable.

169

For years, even after we had left the Emirates, I could still get Bas excited by asking him: 'Where is Sarah?'

He would cock his head to one side, one ear up and one ear down, and if I kept asking, he'd start barking. Sarah and Bas made short shrift of my last chickens. I had inherited them from Gerard and did not care much for them, so I was not too distraught at that loss. Then one day the dogs got out of the garden and caught one of the chickens of my neighbour Julie. Fortunately she accepted my apologies, but I decided to keep the dogs locked in when I was not around and Nambi was working his afternoon job. Returning home from work, more often than not I would find the house a disaster area. Pillows had lost their stuffing, turning the room into a "snow" scene. Toilet paper had been unrolled and festooned the living room furniture. Apples from the fruit basket were spread around the floor, making it treacherous to walk there. And the dogs lay exhausted on their cushions and in their baskets.

Walks were needed to make them tired enough to prevent them wreaking havoc in the house. I decided that the beach was the safest place. The Dubai beaches in those days were gorgeous. At low tide you could walk for hours on the hard sand. The dogs ran and splashed through the water and Sandy and Sarah often went for a swim. Usually there were only a few people loafing in the sand or taking a dip in the gentle waves. The best thing of all was: there were no furry or feathery creatures there and I did not have to worry about any mischief. That is, until I saw Sarah running past me with a roast chicken in her mouth! She had stolen some swimmer's lunch!

Cowardly I walked away as fast I could, pretending the dogs did not belong to me.

Although Bas never occupied as great a part of my heart as Sandy did, he certainly brought a lot of fun to my life. He was never moody or mean, and as long as there was no potential prey around he was quite obedient. He was a very doggy dog and a great cuddler, who would go into trance whenever his chest was scratched.

'He has died and gone to heaven,' said Gerard on one of those occasions. Fourteen years later he had still not actually done that.

But a small part of him went after Sandy died: his most beautiful asset, the bushy tail, started losing hair a few weeks after her death and became a bare worm-shaped appendage. There was no sign of infection and he did not chew his tail, so only two possible causes were left: either it could be an old dog's equivalent of a bald head, or it was due to his mourning the loss of his great friend.

Basje died in my arms a week before his fifteenth birthday. I had discovered that the chronic cough that he had had for two years was not due to an allergy but to the fact that one of his lungs was completely obliterated with cancer. Since there was no cure and the cough made him very tired, I arranged for the vet to come and put him to sleep. As usual, the decision was tough, and the loss of him hit me harder than I had expected. Now he lies nose to nose with Sandy under the rosebush. Even now, every time before I get up from the kitchen table, I check quickly that I am not stepping on his tail...

28

PUTIH COMES AND
THE MARMOSETS LEAVE

It was Joe on the phone: 'I am moving back to the States and I have an old ferret that I do not want to take back there. Would you like to have her?'

I had heard that ferrets were great pets, but I did not have the slightest idea how to keep one. So I told Joe: 'Sure, as long as you tell me how to take care of her.'

A few days later Joe walked up the path with a cat carrier. The small creature inside was an albino that peered at me with short-sighted red eyes. I showed Joe the box that I had prepared for her. It was a large wooden crate on legs, standing in the shade of the mesquite tree near the kitchen door. The front and a half of the top were of wire, so there was plenty of ventilation. I had filled it partly with straw and it contained a night box as well as a litter box. For company she had the sand foxes that lived in the garage just across the narrow bit of the yard. Joe approved of the box but commented: 'Add a towel or a blanket to the straw – she likes to burrow into something like that. And make sure you attach the food, water and litter trays securely to the box, for she is inclined to tip things over.'

'What does she eat?' I asked.

'I usually feed her half a quail, complete with the smaller feathers and the intestines. Any chicken bone that is left from your dinner will give her a lot of pleasure. Don't ever give her sweets. She'll love them but they are very bad for her health. You must give her plenty of water, she dehydrates very quickly. She has been vaccinated against canine distemper and she needs her toenails clipped every two weeks or so. She is very tame and loves to play, but she is completely deaf.'

'How old is she?'

'I am not entirely sure but I have had her for seven years so she is already quite old. They rarely reach a double-digit age.'

Whenever I had time, and certainly every evening, I took the ferret out to let her run around the house and garden. I called her Putih, which is the Indonesian word for "white". She was a funny little creature. Whenever I picked her up she snuggled into my neck and I could sniff her strong animal smell. Her nipping was a sign of affection and never painful. The dogs found her fascinating and she played with Bas all the time. They were a lovely pair, my two white pets. From the very beginning of her stay with me, she was easy to keep, due to her age and her near-sightedness. She did not destroy any belongings or get lost in furniture as young ferrets do. She was amazingly clean, using the litter in her box and the cat litter when inside the house. She spent most of the day sleeping so she was never bothered with the fact that I was away at work for the largest part of the day. Evenings were our play time.

I found out the very first evening that she loved playing with my hand. I wriggled my fingers right in front of her nose, so she would notice them. She gave a little shriek and jumped sideways, shaking her head, then rushed forward to nip at my fingers. Then, perhaps amazed at her own courage, she danced away, jumping with all fours as if she were on a pogo stick, curving her lithe body to keep my hand in sight, uttering small happy noises. This behaviour is called the ferret's war dance. She kept it up for ten minutes or so, and then lost interest and started to explore her new surroundings.

The ferret (*Mustela putorius furo*) belongs to the family

Mustelidae which includes weasels, minks, otters, badgers and skunks. Ferrets cannot survive in the wild. It is unknown exactly when ferrets were first domesticated, but ferret remains have been dated to 1500 BC. The ancient Greeks kept pet ferrets. They were most likely bred from the European Polecat or possibly from the Steppe polecat.

For hundreds of years the main use of ferrets was for hunting, or ferreting. With their long, lean build and curious nature, ferrets are very well equipped for getting down holes and chasing rabbits out of their burrows.

The ferret, as its ancestor the Polecat, is a hypercarnivore, which means that it cannot digest plant material. However, it eats every last scrap of its prey animals. The ferret's jaw has a lock with a special hinge to prevent dislocation while cracking bones.

A few years later Putih moved with me to Sharjah. There she lived in a small sandy yard at the back of the house, together with a hedgehog. When it got hot that first summer I moved Putih, who was now totally blind as well as deaf, into the guest shower room. I had to alert guests not to step on the towel that lay crumpled on the floor, as that was where the ferret lived. In spite of her handicaps, the little creature managed to take long walks into the huge tract of desert that was the garden and surprisingly she always found her way back to the bathroom.

One day she developed severe diarrhoea. Because she was so old, I decided to let nature take its course. We might not even make it to the vet in time and it was better for her to be comfortable. At one point during that anxious afternoon I wanted to refresh the faeces-soaked towel underneath her. As I picked her up she whipped her head around and bit into my thumb. Her teeth penetrated to the bone and she would not let go. I yelled for Nambi to come and help me, and together we prised open her jaw as gently as we could. A few minutes later she died. My thumb stayed sore for quite a while after we had buried her under a frangipani bush. During all her time with me she had always been a real sweetie, so it was not difficult to forgive her for that last slip of the jaw!

Around the time of Putih's arrival I decided that I should make a better provision for the group of marmosets I still had. I was always aware that my life in the Emirates was insecure. Having been booted out of the country once already and being quite a public figure now due to my nature conservation activities, I knew that my life could change in just a minute. A seemingly trivial event, an inopportune word could cause a cancellation of my visa and I would have to pack up and leave. I did not want my precious little monkeys to be left behind into the bad or indifferent care of strangers. So, after some hesitation, I called CC. I did not like to call him, for whenever we talked he said something that would leave me hurt or angry, but he did have a zoo, a place for my marmosets, and he would give them the very best of care.

After he agreed to take the group, I set out to make some proper crates. I could only transport pairs together, so I needed at least four carriers. A few months earlier, the old breeding male had died of old age. I found him one morning, motionless, hunched over his food bowl. When I picked him up there was still a trace of warmth in his slender body. I buried my face in his fur and inhaled the characteristic fresh hay smell. He had lived with me for ten years and he was not young when he arrived, so he must have lived well beyond his expected life span of twelve years. His mate had died a few years earlier as had their first pair of young, Jip and Janneke, so I needed to transport only relatively young pairs. Two of these were breeding pairs, the others were siblings.

The boxes had to be made just right: of sturdy wood, with ventilation holes drilled all around, a thick slat of wood attached to the outside on all sides, so that nothing could be placed flush against the crate and obstruct the ventilation holes. The door had to have an observation window, covered on the inside with mosquito netting, preventing anyone from sticking a finger inside. On the inside the edges of the mosquito netting had to be carefully hidden underneath slats of wood so that the monkeys could not pry it loose. Water bottles of the sort that are used for hamsters, closed tubes with a sucking nipple, were attached upside down on the inside of each box. For the 12 hours of the journey they did not need any food. A sturdy handle was screwed into the top. The door would be closed with a padlock and a spare key would be put together with the CITES papers and export/import permits inside a ziplock plastic bag taped to the top of each box.

The medical papers that the animals needed for their transport should have been based on veterinary examinations. Fortunately the vet-around-the-corner knew my household so well that he did not insist on seeing each individual animal. He knew that there were no sick animals in the group. He also helped by not charging for providing the necessary papers.

I went to the Ministry of Agriculture and Fisheries to meet Dr Osman, the Sudanese veterinary responsible for issuing CITES papers. I was lucky to have found Dr Osman, because he was very helpful and always interested in what I was doing. I had come to him several times already over the years, when animals had to be sent to Europe for one reason or another. Together we completed the numerous forms and documents that were necessary before I could even buy a ticket with the airline. Airlines like KLM and Lufthansa were quite exacting when it came to animal transports, but I was sure that this did not apply to many other airlines, for the trade in and transport of endangered species were always lively in the UAE. From time to time Dr Osman even called to ask for help when he had confiscated an animal that he could not identify or when he did not know on which CITES list a particular animal was mentioned. In short, we had become rather good friends over the years.

'Good morning, Doktora!,' he called out when I entered his dingy office on the fourth floor of the ministry building.

'Sit down, sit down. Do you want coffee?'

He flapped a languid hand at the servant boy who ran off and reappeared a few minutes later with a tiny cup of green coloured cardamom brew that had nothing to do with coffee. I had learned to love the drink, which gave quite an invigorating kick.

'How are you, Dr Osman? Well, I hope. And how is your family?' As we sipped our thimbles of *qahwa* we discussed the family, the weather, politics and some recent events in the animal trade. Finally he asked: 'Are you sending animals again?'

'Yes, this time it is even a small group of animals,' I explained, describing the marmosets. I handed him the medical papers and told him that all but two of the present animals had been born in captivity at my home. As usual, he did not make any difficulties about the lack of provenance of the two outsiders and told me to come back in a couple of days to pick up the duly stamped and signed papers.

A week later the day had come for the marmosets to leave.

That was the day the marmosets chose to escape en masse. When Nambi opened the outside cage in the morning to set out the food trays, two of the males shot past him, scrambling along the outside of the cage to the top where they jumped onto the overhanging branches of the mesquite tree that shaded the yard. This had happened before and the monkeys always came back when they got hungry, so I was not too bothered about it. Instead I was worrying about when to start catching the troupe. I could not start too early because then they would have to be in the confinement of the box too long. But if I left it to the last minute I ran the risk of not catching them all on time. I decided I needed expert help and called Gerard. We arranged a time in the early evening, for I had to report to the Lufthansa freight office around 10pm.

Some commotion in the kitchen had Nambi running to fetch me. 'Madam, more monkeys out now!'

What the hell was happening?

Somehow the door of the night cage had slipped loose, something that had never happened before. It had given the chance to another three monkeys to escape first into the kitchen and then via the open window to the outside cage and the big beautiful tree. It was getting quite crowded up there. The marmosets were having a ball. Happily squeaking and twittering, they chased each other along the thick branches and trampolined on the thinner ones. Their white ear tufts stood out proudly, signifying their alertness. Their long tails streamed behind them as they ran. They were happy!

Inside the larger cage one lonely marmoset looked on. Next door in the erstwhile pigeon cage the separated pair was getting quite excited. Was I going to be able to quench this palace revolution on time? I could not help laughing at the situation. Served me right for contemplating such a far-reaching move!

Luckily hunger pangs and raisins did what my cajoling could not do. The errant marmosets returned to the big cage long before nightfall. Gerard arrived together with his visiting father-in-law. I appreciated that they had interrupted a family get-together to help me out.

We started with the separated pair. As a precaution I closed the door of the bathroom where their night cage was. We blocked the exit to the outside aviary. Then Gerard carefully opened the cage door and grabbed one of the monkeys. She started screaming at the top of her voice. Her mate ran along Gerard's arm and jumped onto the sink, looking desperately for an escape route. While Gerard and I were busy putting the female into the box, the male, excited by his mate's screams, richochet'd around the bathroom, splattering urine all over the place.

Finally we could turn our attention to him. I threw a large bath towel over him, so that Gerard could grab him and control his movements while he tried stuffing him into the box. Obviously he had to open the door a crack to do this and the second he did so the female squeezed out and added her part to the Great Escape.

Eventually we managed to box this first pair. I looked at my watch with anxiety. Were we going to be able to do the rest on time? Gerard and his father-in-law were discussing strategy in the kitchen in their own language. I could only just follow what they said.

'If we leave them here, we can catch one or two but the others will escape to the outside cage.'

'Is it not easier to chase them outside and prevent them from coming back in?'

'Yes' said Gerard, 'I think that could work.'

So Gerard took the boxes to the outside cage and removed the potted plants where the marmosets used to play hide and seek. Then he made sure the door was properly locked, for the last thing we wanted was a nocturnal excursion of marmosets into the mesquite tree. When he called that all was safe, I disturbed the little guys from the night box where they had already settled down and gently persuaded them to walk along the chickenwire tube that led to the outside cage via the opening of the ventilation

178

fan. As soon as all the marmosets had gone outside I blocked the opening with a pillow, while Gerard and Nambi stood quietly in a corner. Then they plucked one marmoset after the other from the wire of the cage and put them in their boxes.

'Phew, I never thought we'd make it,' I sighed.

'It is not finished yet,' said Gerard, who had detected some shortcomings of the transport boxes. He sent Nambi for the tool kit and proceeded to hammer some nails in the door of each box.

'I don't think that is allowed, Gerard,' I said, 'The airline insists that their vets must be able to open the boxes.'

'Well, they can – it is just going to cost them a bit more effort,' he said, adding:

'Better safe than sorry. These creatures are like quicksilver. You don't want any scooting around airports! In any case, I am sure no one will even look or notice!'

And that turned out to be true. While the helpers returned home, Nambi and I took the boxes to the airport and successfully delivered them into the hands of the Lufthansa agent. After a sleepless night of worry and a long day of waiting, the phone call from Chemnitz came: "They are all here and everything is fine."

A few years later I saw them in their new abode and they had obviously settled down well!

29

MORE BIRDS

I was halfway up the rock outcrop of Qarn Nizwa. It was still cool, early in the day, and dewdrops glittered on the grasses that jutted from the rock crevices. I looked across the sea of sand that surrounded the hill. The sand was a dark ochre yellow here and it undulated without interruption for as far as you could see. Far in the distance the flare of the Dubai oil field kept its lonely watch. The sky arched above with aquamarine transparency, not a cloud in sight. Perched on a rock, I let the silence wash over me and took deep breaths of unpolluted air. What a nice change from the noise, dirt and fumes of the city.

I was looking for a little plant that I had once found here. I wanted to photograph its seed pod. I had seen someone else's picture and was intrigued: the pod was a three-cornered lidded box in which flat round seeds were stacked in three separate piles. This should be the time the pods would have replaced the insignificant greenish flowers that grew in pairs on an upright stem.

I had discovered the plant some years earlier on another rocky outcrop 200 kilometres south of here. If I had not been such an amateur, I would have made a proper description of the plant and

I would have been immortalised as the author of *Dipcadi biflora*. Instead, I had argued with my botanist friends in the UK who wanted to include it in the species *Dipcadi serotina*, which had bending stems with up to six flowers. While we were arguing, a botanist in Oman found the same plant. She went through the right procedures and soon had her name attached to the plant's name as its author. I just had not known that I had discovered a plant that was new to science.

I climbed a little higher, negotiating huge boulders and trying to stay upright on the loose scree. As I rounded a meter-high rock a huge shape exploded from a low cave behind it. Even though it was a silent explosion, I recoiled with the suddenness of it. An owl with a meter-wide wingspan sailed soundlessly between the branches of a low acacia and out over the rocky hillside. With thumping heart I peered into the cave. In the soft sand that covered the bottom lay three large eggs. I took a picture and retreated quickly, as I did not want to disturb the breeding. Back in the car I waited for an hour till the adult bird returned to sit on the nest again. Fortunately the air was warm and the eggs could not have cooled down too much.

The next day I happened to talk to Gerard: 'Boy, that was some scare. I have never had such a large bird fly practically into my face. I had no idea there was a nest there.'

'That must have been a Desert Eagle Owl,' said Gerard, 'You must show me where it is, then Mike and I can film it for our picture.'

'Are you sure that that will not disturb the breeding?'

'We'll be careful.'

Gerard and his cinematographer friend Mike were making a film about desert wildlife. I had already guided them to the place in the deep desert where the sand foxes had their burrow. Another time we had spent many happy hours standing in fast-flowing streams filming toads and dragonflies. Mike and I had started working together soon after my first book on desert plants had appeared. We had been at it for several years now and some parts of the movie had already been shown on television. I knew the two men had endless patience and would take every precaution not to disturb the wildlife they were filming. I showed

Gerard where the Desert Eagle Owl's nest was and they took shots of the eggs and later of the hatched baby owls. When they had fletched Gerard took a very young owl that he had found on the suq to the nest and posed the tame bird in such a way that Mike could take close-ups of the young owl eating a gerbil.

I was learning a lot about wildlife movies. Many supposed wildlife scenes were set up in controlled conditions by animal handlers like Gerard. My sand foxes had starred in a film made by Oxford Films about wildlife in Oman. There was no way you could tell they were not genuine shots of foxes in the wild. Gerard was very clever at setting up the backgrounds.

The young feathered movie star was called Robert and after the filming was completed he needed a home. Nambi built a large narrow cage along the wall of the shaded back yard. The back-yard was becoming quite a maze of pens, cages and enclosures. Robert would have some ten meters to test his wings while he grew up. Right now he was still a fuzzy faced, wide-eyed young-ster. His favourite perch was just opposite my bedroom window with only a meter between the wall of the house and the wire of his cage. Every morning, when I pushed the curtain aside, Robert's huge golden eyes would stare at me and he would greet me with a mournful 'uuu-huu'. I would uuu-huu straight back and start the day with a smile. Somehow the young owl moved me. He looked so innocent and forlorn with his unblinking round eyes and fuzzy down still poking between his brand-new feathers. He did not like people very much and though he tolerated Nambi and me as his caretakers, he always hid when visitors came into the yard.

I had a phone-call from Ulli, the German professor who was the director of the microbiology lab: 'Marijcke, have you heard about the botulism outbreak at the Creek?'

'No, what's happening?'

'For some reason the botulism bacilli that are normally in the mud are multiplying like mad and infecting many birds. Most die in a few days of general paralysis.'

'The poor things. What can we do about it?'

'Nothing much, unfortunately. When local conditions change,

182

it will pass, but in the meantime we are losing many birds. There is no antitoxin for birds yet.'

Although botulism is very dangerous for people too, we were not concerned about people getting affected, for the area that Ulli was talking about was a nature reserve that was frequently patrolled. It consisted of mudflats and mangrove stands and was not very conducive to human activities. *Clostridium botulinum* is the name of a group of bacteria commonly found in soil. The bacteria form spores which allow them to survive in a dormant state until exposed to conditions that can support their growth, usually low-oxygen conditions.

In birds the symptoms of botulism include double vision, difficulty swallowing, and muscle weakness. These are all symptoms of the muscle paralysis caused by the bacterial toxin. If untreated, these symptoms may progress to general paralysis. Death is quick when the toxin paralyses the respiratory muscles. The birds that recovered from the initial infection faced a lingering death of starvation as the still weak muscles prevented them from swallowing.

A few days after Ulli's phone call one of the Natural History Group members brought me a Marsh harrier (*Circus aeruginosus*) that he had found. The raptor was a young female, judging by the large creamy patch on her head. She was emaciated and floppy, but the fire in her eyes showed that she had not lost her urge to live. The vet-around-the-corner told me that in time the paralysis would heal and a complete cure was possible if the bird could be kept alive. I decided to see if I could save her by feeding her nutritious fluids. In order to find out about how to do this I went to see a friend who took care of the sheikh's falcons. I assumed he would know about other raptors too.

'Peter, what can you tell me about marsh harriers?'

Peter looked a bit surprised.

'Why? Are you thinking of keeping one?'

'Well, I already have one, and it is more a matter of keeping her alive.'

'What can I tell you? It is an ancient species, dating back to about 3,000 years ago. It hunts a wide variety of prey, mostly water birds and frogs, but also small mammals. It is a slow flier and can remain airborne at speeds of less than twenty miles per hour. It flies at a height of only a few metres, always taking advantage of cover, sometimes hovering or performing impressive aerobatics before dropping.'

'Is it a threatened species?'

'No, it occurs in many countries of Europe and the Middle East and is a quite successful breeder. It's one of the few raptors that are all right so far.'

'The one I have has botulism. She seems very determined to live, so I am going to help her a bit.'

'You've got to make a mash of quails and squirt it into the back of her throat. Good luck. You're in for an interesting time!'

So I put the big food processor to work and devised a revolting brew of mashed quails in chicken consommé. This I drew up in a large syringe and then Nambi and I would start the feeding. Nambi held the bird tightly in leather-gloved hands, while I opened her beak and carefully squirted some soup into her throat. It did not take our bird long to catch on what was happening. She ceased to resist and opened her beak of her own accord when she saw the syringe coming. Consequently she recovered very fast and soon was hopping around her cage with vociferous joy.

Next was a trial of small pieces of meat. A few days later, when it seemed that she could swallow those without a problem, I gave her a whole quail, which she pulled apart and ate as she was supposed to do. She was now flapping her wings vigorously all the time, so I figured it was time to let her try her luck in the wild again. Colin, the Bird man, came with me when we took her to the fishponds at the back of the sheikh's palace. When we opened the carrier cage, she hopped into the tall grass by the roadside, sat there for some minutes gazing at us, then turned her head, spread her wings and flew off, arching high above the palace walls.

That was the easy patient.

In the same period of time other birds were brought to my door. A small snipe was too far gone to be saved. But the Purple heron was well enough to stand upright and just needed some careful feeding. It was huge, one meter tall when its snake-like neck was not stretched. It was also beautiful, with purplish brown feathers and orange toes and legs. I never knew whether mine was male or female as there is no apparent difference between the two.

Purple Herons (*Ardea purpurea*) are resident and breed in areas from the tropics to mid-temperate countries. While they tend to roost in coastal areas (mangroves, marshes, estuaries), they prefer to feed in freshwater wetlands. Their slim bills are large and strong enough to kill even large snakes. Their long necks give them a far and powerful reach. They nest in small colonies, often with other heron species. Preferred nest sites are dense reed beds and thick vegetation where they pull down the reeds to make a platform. The males find and bring nesting materials to the females, who do the actual construction of the nest. Both parents feed and look after the young.

We followed the same feeding procedure as with the harrier, except that the soup this time was a noisome sardine broth. Nambi would enfold the bird in a large bath towel while I squirted liquid down its throat. This was not quite without danger for the bird tended to lash out with its powerful beak and since it aimed for my eyes I was glad I wore glasses. In fact, after the first feed I donned goggles for extra protection.

Sometimes, after an especially nerve-racking, sweaty procedure, I'd hand Nambi a cold beer as we flopped on the garden bench.

'We are a good team, Nambi.'

He smiled agreement.

'Very nice bird, madam, but little danger!'

The Purple heron eventually regained its strength and soon was able to pick up whole sardines, which it threw up in the air to catch them with outstretched neck, manipulating the fishes until they were head down in its beak before swallowing them. We took it to a large marshy area far away from the contaminated "top of the Creek" mangroves and set it free.

I had less luck with a flamingo that was brought in close to death. It was a beautiful gentle bird – one of the hundreds that lived in the nature reserve at the top of the Creek. The flocks that gathered there had never yet bred there and they were a bit paler than they should have been, because there were not enough crustaceans in the mud to provide the dye needed for their normally darker pink colour. They were provided with additional food by the people that were employed for the nature reserve but obviously still did not get the additional element they needed. Many of them must have been affected by the botulism outbreak, but only this one ended up in my care.

The Greater flamingo (*Phoenicopterus ruber*) is the largest of the flamingos, standing over five feet tall. The males are usually taller than the females. Their long legs and necks allow them to feed in deep water. The feet are webbed, enabling them to stand on mud and to swim, which they do well considering the length of their legs. The webs help when they stamp their feet to stir up organisms out of the substrate. The flamingo's beak is light-coloured at the base and has a black tip. It is a unique shape, with a forty-five-degree angle in the middle. Standing in shallow water with their head down, they filter the water through the sieve-like lamellae of their beaks. The thick fleshy tongue acts as a plunger to suck the water and food into the mouth, and then forcing only the water back out. They prefer to be in large numbers which assures group safety when in the vulnerable feeding position. They will not breed unless in large numbers. Normally a twelve-inch mud nest is built in the water near the shore. The nest is about five to eighteen inches high and one white egg is laid. Both parents will care for this egg, and after an incubation period of about one month, a grey downy chick with a straight pink bill will be born. It will remain dependent on the parents to feed it for four to six weeks. The parents will only feed their own chick even after the chicks get off the nest and mix together. The juvenile birds do not reach full size for up to two years and the adult plumage is acquired after two to four years. Late maturation is often coupled with considerable longevity and these birds often live twenty-five to sixth years.

The vet-around-the corner taught me how to feed a flamingo. This had to be done via a long tube that had to be inserted into the throat all the way down to the bird's stomach. It was a difficult process, tiring for me as well as for the bird. The feeding in itself was successful for the bird regained its strength and was

186

soon standing upright. But it refused to eat by itself, no matter how many juicy shrimps and crabs I floated in a large tub in front of it. Then I remembered that CC had once told me that flamingos are very unhappy unless they are in a flock of at least a dozen. In one zoo we had once visited, a rather ingenious solution had been found for the problem of a paucity of birds – mirrors had been placed around the flamingo pool, giving the birds the impression there were more of them than there actually were. With just one bird in my aviary, I would need at least a dozen mirrors and I doubted if that would solve the problem. So I called an acquaintance who worked at the Emirates Golf Course.

'Hey Bert,' I said when he came to the phone, 'don't you have some flamingos in one of your ponds?'

'Yes,' he said, 'Why?'

'I need a home for a rescued bird that refuses to eat because he needs some mates around him to feel secure. Could he possibly join your lot? The vet assures me that he is healthy now and does not pose a threat to other birds.'

'Fine – bring him on over.'

So we bundled the bird in a large towel and with Nambi holding him I drove out to the golf course, where a happy flamingo lost no time joining its new flock.

30

ARABIAN LEOPARD TRUST ACTIVITIES

Soon after we started the Arabian Leopard Trust, we realised that we knew absolutely nothing about leopards. So I decided to take my vacation in South Africa where I could visit a few leopard experts.

It was to be my first vacation without CC and I was slightly apprehensive about the whole venture. Our vacations had always been such fun. I need not have worried. It turned out that I had learned CC's lessons well: I observed better than ever before, spent days by myself in various wildlife parks and enjoyed watching many of the beautiful beasts of the bush. Practically the only animal that I did not manage to see was the leopard.

Via one of the leopard organisations I came into contact with Chris and Mathilde Stuart and stayed at their remote farm for a few days. Chris was a zoologist, British by birth, and Tilde was a medical doctor from Austria. Both had made South Africa their home and wildlife conservation their mission. They wrote guide-books for nature reserves and mammals, illustrated with their own excellent photographs. I invited them to come to the Emirates to help us find leopards.

The days before their arrival shortly after Christmas 1993 were hectic with the many preparations we needed to make. With the help of our field worker Moaz we had picked an area in the Hajar mountains where leopards were said to have been sighted.

Somehow I managed to get the help of the local police to take the researchers and all their equipment to that remote site by helicopter. Many people and companies pitched in with donations in kind and in time to make the expedition a success. This and the many events that were to follow have all been described in detail in a book called *Working for Wildlife* that we produced ten years later.

Two weeks after we had dropped the couple off at Wadi Ziqt, I decided to pay them a visit. I had friends from Holland staying with me and we decided to visit the site by driving up the wadi with my battered old Nissan Patrol. Luckily Moaz was available to do the driving, for it was an extremely rough and challenging trip through the boulder-strewn dry riverbed. The last hour we had to walk, burdened with backpacks full of fresh food and additional equipment. We clambered over the rocks into the narrowing canyon. The sediment of aeons had been scoured out by the force of the water till it now towered twenty meters on both sides of us. At a fork in the wadi two side rivers enclosed a triangular high plateau. The Stuarts' camp was on top.

They were quite happy to see us.

'So this is what you call desert, is it?' were Chris' first words. He was referring to the fact that since the helicopter had dropped them off it had rained for days. They had been unable to leave the shelter of the tent, and after four days of torrential downpours even that shelter had no longer kept them dry.

'But what an experience,' said Tilde, 'You should have seen the waterfalls all around, the river on two sides in full spate. The noise was incredible. The ground was shaking with the crashes of huge rocks being swept downstream.'

'I am sure there are not many people apart from the locals who have ever witnessed that,' I agreed, 'I would have liked to see it! But since the rains stopped, did you find anything interesting yet?'

'Yes,' said Chris, 'we have been catching foxes – like the ones you have in your garage, except that they are chocolate brown.'

'Sand foxes? That is not possible,' I exclaimed, 'they do not occur here. They must have been red foxes.'

'Oh no, definitely not red foxes – they were the same size as the sand foxes but darker coloured and with an amazingly thick plumed tail.' The description of the tail twigged my memory. Some time ago I had read an article about the discovery of a new species of fox in Oman – the Royal fox or Blanford's fox (*Vulpes cana*). Chris had not heard of it, but when we later compared the Stuarts' pictures with those of the fox found in Oman, they were identical.

We had found a new species of mammal for the Emirates and established an extension of its range in Arabia. The Stuarts also found out that the Blanford's fox, being an opportunistic feeder, lived exclusively on the fruits of the ubiquitous *sidr* tree during its fruiting season.

The Stuarts stayed two months and apart from the fox they also caught and photographed an Egyptian Spiny mouse (*Acomys cahirinus*) – until then only a roadkill had been recorded in the Emirates.

Even more exciting was that they spotted a female Arabian tahr with young near a waterhole. The latter animal is a mountain ungulate that looks much like a goat but is an entirely separate species – *Hemitragus jayakari*. They were thought to have been extinct in the Emirates, their last record having been thirteen years earlier on Jebel Hafeet 200 kilometres to the south.

The Arabian tahr is a small ungulate indigenous to Arabia (Oman and the UAE). It is a territorial animal, usually found singly or in small family groups with one adult male. Males mark their territory by scratching "scrapes" in the ground with their hooves and marking them with urine and dung. Tahr are able to run across steep slopes, escaping predators by climbing up seemingly inaccessible cliff faces. When alarmed, they stamp their hooves and emit a shrill whistle. Their diet is similar to that of goats, and single tahr can be found staying close to herds of feral goats. Like goats they need to have almost daily access to water.

The male tahr has a very coarse and shaggy coat in winter, with a long black mane running from the neck to the tail and distinctive ruffs at the legs. Both males and females have short curved horns. Gestation period is about 140 days and usually a single kid is born.

In the wild they have become rare due to being hunted and to habitat competition with goats. In Oman a nature reserve has been created for tahr in the southern Hajar mountains.

The ALT expedition had been a success in that it had given an indication about the status of wildlife in the mountains: the situation was extremely worrying. No leopard sign had been found in the first research area, and only one pugmark in another wadi. In spite of their diligent searches during weeks of mountain trekking the Stuarts had hardly seen any wildlife: no gazelles - therefore no wild prey for carnivores; no raptors, a sure sign of lack of prey. The Stuarts called their report *A Minute to Midnight* and urged the government to seriously consider protection of all remaining wildlife and the establishment of nature reserves.

In the meantime the committee members of the ALT had tackled another one of the goals of our trust. Early on we had formulated four targets:

- to raise public awareness about the presence of wildlife in the Emirates and the difficulties it was facing
- to bring together those wild Arabian animals that were already in captivity so that they might breed
- to do research in the country about the present state of wildlife and to determine which areas might be suitable for nature reserves
- to establish nature reserves where some of the remaining wildlife might be safe.

Everything we did contributed to the fulfilment of the first target. The Stuarts' expedition had made a start with the third target, and now we were facing a challenge that resorted under the second target. We had only been meeting for a few months when news reached us that an Arabian leopard was being exhibited on the market of Sana'a in Yemen. The newspaper there had reported on the dismal conditions in which this young leopard spent his days. In his cage there was barely room to move, it was filthy with his excrement and leftover food, he was being tormented daily by his keeper so that he would roar to please the people who had paid money to see him. On a pole nearby the shrivelled head of his mother was stuck over a sign that invited people to pay some money because it was expensive to feed the leopard. Yemen expats were outraged about this situation but the leopard remained where it was.

I had once seen an Arabian leopard that was caged in the garden of one of the important Dubai sheikhs. I had tried in vain to persuade the owner to send the lone leopard to Oman where the breeding centre of the Sultan kept another three adults. The only excuse for keeping leopards in captivity should be to breed them and increase their number.

Now we discussed the captive leopard in Yemen. If we could acquire this leopard, we could not only improve his unhappy life, but we would also have a leopard to show to people, so that they could become interested. On the other hand, buying the leopard from its present owner might encourage him and others to catch more leopards. Since an adult leopard is hard to catch and keep, they would aim for a mother with young, and then kill off the mother. None of us wanted that. It was a dilemma, but the need to have a flagship animal for our campaign won in the end. Horrifying pictures of the leopard in its small cage, brought back from Yemen by a visiting oil man, clinched the argument.

I started to correspond with the Yemen expats and tried to set up meetings with various government departments that would need to be on our side before we could buy and transport the leopard. In fact, I hoped to convince the authorities to confiscate the leopard, since in theory the hunting of wildlife was forbidden in Yemen. We had settled on a date for a Yemen visit. The day before I was to leave, we sent a sturdy crate, borrowed from Dubai zoo, to Sana'a.

The next morning the civil war between the North and South of Yemen broke out.

As daily rockets fell on the market area where the leopard was being kept, we practically gave up hope to ever set eyes on this leopard. It took a year before things had settled down and Yemen was one country again. And miraculously, the leopard had survived!

I flew to Yemen shortly after to attend a conference at the university and to try and see what I could do to liberate the leopard that was still in his dismal cage in the suq. Assisted by several nature-loving locals and expats in Sana'a I managed somehow to get permission to buy the animal and export it to the Emirates.

Gerard, who had had the Arabian leopard on his mind for many years, was sent out to collect the leopard. In May 1994 Nimrod Felix, a.k.a. Arnold, arrived in the temporary quarters we had built for him at Gerard's place. Within days he settled in and seemed happy – happy enough to come to the wire and be tickled underneath his huge paws, as he rolled on his back and grunted with pleasure. We were proven right in acquiring the cat, when one day an Arab friend of Gerard came for a visit. This yuppy Arab, usually only interested in racing boats and fast cars, took one long look at the leopard and said to Gerard: 'Do you mean to tell me that *this* animal lives in *my* mountains?' and his eyes misted with emotion!

The ALT had spent the waiting year raising funds, organising research expeditions in the mountains, and making contacts with people all over the world that could help or advise. I had already acquired a number of animals that needed protection – wildcats, sand foxes, an owl, hedgehogs, a falcon, a mountain gazelle – the gardens of Gerard and me were getting crowded.

One of the achievements of the year was making contact with the Oman Breeding Centre and being given a young female leopard on breeding loan for Arnold.

Another lucky break for the ALT was that the Sheikh of one of the Emirates, the Ruler of Sharjah, had become vitally interested in all we were doing. And that would have far-reaching consequences, both for the Arabian leopards and for me personally.

31

MALAIKA

By now it was well-known throughout the country that the Arabian Leopard Trust was trying to acquire and put together any wild-caught local animals. Many of the well-to-do Arabs had collections of exotic animals, and from time to time we managed to lay our hands on one of them. A baby gazelle was donated by one sheikh and walked around in Gerard's garden, providing some excitement for the caged leopard that also lived there. The vet-around-the-corner was hand-rearing a caracal cub that belonged to a Dubai sheikh and managed to persuade the owner to give it to us for the breeding program.

That is how Malaika ended up in my garden.

She was still very small, just weaned, when she arrived in a cat-carrier. I put her into one of the former wildcat cages, opened the carrier box and left the cage, closing the door behind me. Then I talked to her softly. Nothing happened. She was obviously scared. Just at that moment Gerard arrived unexpectedly.

'Look what I just got, Gerard,' I welcomed him.

'What is it?'

'A caracal cub – but she is too shy to come out.'

Gerard entered the cage and murmured something that I could not understand. Immediately there was movement in the catbox and a beautiful small cat emerged. She looked at Gerard and cautiously approached him. Then she rubbed her head and shoulders against his legs. He bent over to scratch her behind the ears and she started to look very content.

I always marvelled at Gerard's way with animals. Even though he was an accredited hunter (or maybe because of it) he really understood animals and they seemed to trust him. That is, most animals did, but for some reason Sandy did not. In time her dislike of him would be explained but when the caracal arrived I had no inkling of it yet.

The caracal needed to be named. In order to raise some public awareness we held a competition in a number of schools. ALT-volunteers gave slideshows about local wildlife, with special mention of caracals, and asked the kids to propose a name for our new arrival. The winner was "Malaikat-al-layl" – "Queen-of-the-night".

Caracals (*Caracal caracal schmitzi*) are the desert counterpart of the European lynx and the American bobcat. They occur both in the mountains and on the sandy gravel plains of the desert and have very large home ranges. The territory of the male overlaps that of several females. They can go for long stretches of time without water, getting their fluids from their prey. They live on small mammals and reptiles as well as birds, which they are able to knock down from flight. In ancient times caracals were used to hunt birds in this manner. Reproduction takes place all year around, with litters being larger in times of plenty after good rains. Usually three or four cubs are born after a gestation time of around seventy-five days. Cubs are weaned at three months but stay with the mother for up to one year.

Malaika was beautiful. Her fur was russet all over, slightly darker on top. Her triangular face was strongly marked with black tearlines that ran from the inside corner of the eyes to the tip of the black nose. Her whiskers emerged from rows of black spots on both sides of her upper lips. The area around the mouth and below the chin was creamy white. Her golden eyes were slanted and ringed in black. To emphasise the mascara effect, there were white lines just below the eyes and a white triangle ran from the inner corner of the eye upwards to a black spot just above the eyes. Most beautiful of all were her large triangular ears that ended in tufts of long black hair. They were in constant motion, cupped forward when she was intent on something, swivelling back and forth when she was listening, pressed backward when she was scared.

Local legend mentioned that caracals use their ears to attract prey. They hide behind a rock with just their ears sticking out. When they wiggle their ears, curious gazelles or goats come to investigate, thinking they are seeing a tuft of grass. Another story says that the caracal will lie on its back, waving its feet in the air. Again curiosity will kill... but not the cat. This alleged habit of the caracal has earned it the name of *khanwayt* in Oman, which means "the suffocater". That is only one of the twelve names that the Omani have for this animal. Another local name is *anaq al ardh* which means "the earth embracer". In the Emirates people refer to the cat mostly as *al hamr* which describes the reddish colour of her fur.

Malaika soon lost her teenage plumpness as her legs became longer and her body lengthened and thinned into sleek predator efficiency. Her powerful feet stayed large in proportion to the rest of her body and had retractable claws. She had a deep scar on her neck, where she had been tied with a piece of wire during the first weeks of her life. Possibly because of this ill treatment she remained very shy. Even the lady at the vet's office who had hand-reared her had to keep her wrapped in a towel while feeding to avoid being badly scratched. This towel was Malaika's favourite toy – it served as a security blanket under which she slept and she carried it around and into her climbing tree, draping it over the branches and then jumping at it from below.

She became quite used to me and we played together for long times with me waving long twigs or stems of grass and she hiding, pouncing and running mad circles. At other times she would lie totally relaxed on her favourite tree perch when I was present. But even when she looked most content, I never heard her purr. One of her favourite games was to ambush Nambi when he was cleaning her cage, jumping on his broom and trying to take it away from him.

Once Mike came to film her. The microphone on his camera

was covered with a large furry sound-muffler that immediately aroused her interest. As Mike tried to film her in action she kept trying to swipe the muffler and all he could film were close-ups of her huge paws. Finally with a deft left hook she caught her "prey". We did get it back, but it was not easy.

Since our aim was to breed the captive animals I started to look for a mate for Malaika. The Wildlife Research Centre in Taif in Saudi Arabia agreed to give us a male on breeding loan. After several delays a fierce-looking male arrived, which we put in the adjacent cat cage. He was quite different in character to Malaika, giving the impression that he was always somewhat annoyed with life. Where Malaika's ears were in constant motion, his were aimed aggressively forward and completely immobile. In several books it is mentioned that caracals communicate with their ears. If that was true, then Mephisto (as I had called him) must have been tongue-tied.

The two cats were left in their adjacent cages for several months in order to get them acquainted. During this time Malaika had not shown any signs yet of being on heat. She was two years old by now and should be sexually mature. I discussed the matter with Gerard.

'Of course it would be better to wait till she is on heat,' he said. 'But as long as you are careful, you can just open the door between their cages and see how they get along. Be sure to stand ready with the garden hose to separate them if the male shows any signs of aggression.'

It was a nerve-racking exercise. When the door opened, Mephisto padded across into the other cage, where Malaika crouched behind a tree trunk. They sniffed each other warily and I heard some soft growls, but I could see no sign of aggression. Mephisto took over Malaika's cage and displaced her from her favourite perch.

Apart from the easy and successful breeding of the wildcats I had no experience in breeding wild animals. If I had been more experienced I might have been alerted to the fact that the caracals were not bonding properly. They stayed more or less in separate cages, even though the door was open, and ignored each other. Later I learned this is not a good sign, but by then it was too late.

That winter was a very wet one, the wettest in more than thirty years. It was very difficult to keep the animals comfortable even though they had roofs over their cages. The drains were constantly clogged with litter from the wind-blown trees and the damp never had a chance to dry out. Everything smelled like mould and everyone longed for the return of sun and heat.

One night in February I woke with a start. It was pitch dark, my alarm clock showed 3am. I knew instantly something terrible had happened, even though I had not consciously heard anything. I leapt out of bed and ran to the bathroom window from where I could see the caracal cages. Through sheets of rain I could distinguish the two cats near Malaika's den. I saw Mephisto crouched over the prone figure of Malaika. They did not move or make a sound. Was this a mating ritual? I did not know what to do but the feeling that something was wrong overwhelmed me.

As I rushed out into the wet night I put on the outside lights and banged on Nambi's door in passing.

'Nambi, wake up, something is wrong with the cats!'

When I reached the cage, Mephisto had moved closer to the den and he was dragging Malaika by the scruff of her neck. She lay limp and there was something about the angle between her head and her body that confirmed my worst fear.

Nambi came running, his hands at his waist still knotting his sarong. Armed with his broom he came into the cage after me and carefully closed the door. Then he chased Mephisto away while I quickly grabbed Malaika and carried her out. She did not move or breathe. Inside, I laid her on the kitchen counter and examined her. She had no mark anywhere on her body but her neck was broken. I felt utterly miserable. Her beautiful spirit was gone. I put her in a plastic bag and into the freezer, so I could have Gerard do an autopsy later on. The next day I called him and told him what had happened. He promised to come by and pick her up. When he arrived I burst out in tears and told him what had worried me all day.

'I keep thinking that maybe she was not dead, that I did not look at her carefully enough in the middle of the night and that I killed her by putting her in the plastic bag and freezing her.'

Gerard answered: 'I'll know that soon enough!'

Later that evening he called: 'You can stop worrying. She really has a broken neck.'

That put my mind to rest, but it did not relieve the sadness.

When I reported the accident later to the American studbook keeper of caracals, she sighed: 'It happens again and again. Caracals are really difficult to breed, just like Clouded leopards. If they do not bond properly in the first few hours, you can forget it. It means they are not compatible. It is likely that your female was too young and timid to defend herself during a mating attempt that was too aggressive. In another breeding centre in your area a male bit off the female's leg during mating recently.'

I had never warmed to Mephisto and after Malaika's death I had difficulty behaving rationally. My brain told me that he could not be blamed for her death. If he was trying to mate, he only did what was natural to him. Or else, he could have been irritated by the incessant rain and cuffed her too fiercely when she had made friendly overtures. My heart, however, remembered the way he had wanted to drag her into the den.

As it turned out, he survived her by only a few months. Again, his death should be blamed on me. For some reason I had not taken Malaika's security towel out of the cage after her death. I just did not think of it. While I was away on vacation Mephisto stopped eating. The keeper that Gerard had sent over to take care of the animal had not reported it and so the reason for his lack of appetite was not checked and he died. On autopsy he was found to have his intestines blocked by pieces of towel material. He had obviously chewed on the towel in boredom and frustration and no one had noticed. Again I felt miserable and guilty. The animals had to suffer because we made mistakes.

An almost life-size photograph of Malaika hangs on my bedroom wall and often I gaze at it, admiring her beauty. She should have been at the zenith of her life now, having enjoyed motherhood several times. Only when her expected lifespan of seventeen years has passed, will I be able to look at her picture without sadness.

32

MOVE TO SHARJAH

In the early nineties, someone told me about a colony of Spiny-tailed agamas on both sides of Intersection 8 of the Sharjah-Dhaid highway. When I checked it out, I found a large colony of these interesting reptiles that I had first encountered in Bahrain. From then on I often went down there to observe the little dragons going about their business among the sparse vegetation of the sandy flats.

One day I found horrible snares lying at the entrances of half a dozen burrows. Local and Asian expat people were catching them to eat – they tasted like chicken, they told me.

I found out that the land where the *dhubs* lived belonged to the Dr Sheikh Sultan bin Mohammad al Qassimi, Ruler of Sharjah and Member of the Supreme Council of the Emirates. I wrote him a letter asking him if he could make the area a nature reserve to protect the animals:

> …I understand that the *dhub* has played an important role in the traditions of the Emirati people. Would it not be important to preserve this animal in order to be able to show future generations what it looks like and how it lives? I believe that many visitors to the Emirates would also be interested to see this 'gentle dragon of the desert'. The easily accessible colony at Intersection

Number 8 could become a major tourist attraction, if it could be preserved by fencing it off and giving access only to authorised people...

A few days after sending off the letter I was sitting in my office when the receptionist rang and said the sheikh of Sharjah was on the telephone. I was nervous when I picked up the telephone. The only sheikh I had talked to till then was the young man who was the sponsor of our clinic, but this was one of the seven Rulers!

'Marika,' said a cheerful friendly voice, 'How are you, Marika?'

'Very well, sir, and how are you?'

'Good, good. I got your letter, Marika. Tell me, what do you want me to do?'

I explained that I thought that just a fence would be enough protection for the *dhubs*.

'I shall build a wall,' said the sheikh.

I hastened to explain that the *dhubs* should have a chance to foray out if there was a drought and food would become scarce inside.

'We will feed them with salad,' said the sheikh.

'But then they are captive and that is not the idea of a nature reserve. You will then also need a keeper to take care of them.'

'That is fine. I want to make a desert park anyway,' said the sheikh. And he told me about his dream for a desert park where the people of his emirate could enjoy a protected area of desert filled with local animals and plants.

'And we will make a fountain and we will put the *whirral* there,' said the sheikh.

The *whirral* was the largest reptile of the desert, the Desert monitor. I doubted that it would enjoy living on a fountain but who was I to argue with a Ruler!

Sheikh Sultan lived up to his words and fenced off one square kilometre of the area. I was amazed to see how large one square kilometre was. Then one day as I drove past, I saw a construction site in the corner of the area that was closest to Intersection 8, one of the overpasses of the Sharjah-Dhaid highway. It turned out that a Natural History Museum was being built there. I became involved with the design of some of the displays, providing photographs and facts for the botanical sections to the UK designers, while Gerard did the taxidermy for the zoological displays. The geology department of the Natural History Museum in Cardiff, Wales, worked on a state-of-the-art geological history of the emirate of Sharjah, filling many large rooms with fantastic fossils and rocks, brought from all over the world. An Egyptian professor of botany was employed to create a wild-flower garden at the back of the building.

In the meantime the Arabian Leopard Trust was trying to raise funds to create a breeding centre for the animals that we already had in captivity. We were so active that we were in the newspapers and on TV continuously. Apparently this did not go unnoticed. One day one of the British architects employed by Sheikh Sultan called me and said:

'Are you sitting down?'

'What is going on, Peter?' I asked rather apprehensively.

'This morning we were discussing your leopards and His Highness suggested that in order to breed these animals needed a quiet place. Then he said to me: "Let's give Marika a mountain." He has chosen an area of seven square kilometres of land in the mountains in the eastern part of the emirate for the ALT to use. I am looking at it now on the map. It is a beautiful piece of land!'

I recalled how large the one square kilometre near Intersection 8 was and knew that we would have plenty of space for a breeding centre and maybe even for a nature reserve for the smaller animals. We would, however, need to fence it, build breeding cages, and provide keepers, food, equipment. In earlier discussions the manager of the breeding centre in Oman had warned me that I could not start a breeding facility unless I had an on-going source of income to finance its running.

I was daunted by the challenge, but never doubted that a solution would be provided.

An excited ALT committee went to look at the site the next weekend. It was quite remote, several kilometres away from any village or paved road, and it had a few permanent water holes. The mountains were not very high, but with plenty of vegetation (for the desert, that is) and many nice caves for foxes and caracals.

We started persuading people to donate metres of fencing in exchange for having their names mentioned on special signs in the future breeding centre. We held a huge day-long event on the site in one of the valleys, with musical entertainment moderated by one of the best known DJ's of Dubai radio. The boy scouts of America helped me to set out a walking trail across the hills and made signs to point out existing plants, geological formations and introduced skulls, snake skins and bird's nests. There were market stalls full of fund-raising items as well as food and drinks.

The day before the event I was standing on the top of one of the hills with Sue, one of the ALT committee members, when we saw a cloud of dust in the distance

'What is that?' I asked. Sue answered:

'That must be the toilet-portacabin that Seamus promised to lend us.' A huge crane and truck soon materialised, bumping along the rocky trail. I wondered at the long trip it had made to us out here in the boondocks. First it had to drive along 50 km of highway, then on a dirt track, winding through a stone quarry, dipping in and out of dry wadi beds, snaking around the base of a mountain, and finally across a trackless gravel plain. With a lot of effort the portacabin was placed on a relatively level area of that plain. As a finishing touch a green carpet was rolled out on the steps leading to the "gents" and a red one leading to the "ladies".

The event was a great success. Besides being lots of fun, it raised 16,000 dirhams, around $4,570. But in spite of all our hard work, it soon became apparent that there was no way we could raise enough funds for a breeding facility. We were all volunteers with limited free time. We spent every weekend manning tables at fairs, selling our special products and metres of fencing, but the income was nothing compared to what we would need to establish a breeding centre. So far we had only had the expatriate community contributing to our cause financially. Contributions in kind, such as the indigenous animals for the breeding programme and the hundreds of quails that were needed monthly to feed them, were provided by rich local people. At committee meetings we wondered what we could do.

Then I had another phone call from the sheikh – and an invitation to visit him in his summer home in Kent, in England, to discuss my being employed as the director of his desert park. I had never met him yet and was very curious as well as a bit apprehensive about the forthcoming interview. I need not have worried. His Highness was a wonderfully kind and humorous man, full of life and dreams. He said: 'I shall take another square kilometre of desert next to the museum and there I will build the breeding centre that you need. And I shall also build you a house in the desert.'

I asked for and was permitted to continue campaigning for the Arabian Leopard Trust, with the possibility of having fund- and awareness-raising events at the desert park. It did not take too much persuasion for me take the job. I agreed to become the next director of the Sharjah Desert Park after my notice period for the clinic had expired. The sheikh looked at me with a hint of a smile and said: 'And then the sand foxes will be mine after all!'

Many people were involved in the creation of the Sharjah Desert Park, but it began with some Spiny-tailed lizards, a meddlesome Dutch doctor and a generous sheikh with a vision.

33

CHARLIE, THE TWENTY-THREE-TOED HEDGEHOG

'Madam, hatchoo baby dead!' My houseboy Nambi handed me a scrap of pink skin with a few white spines – all that was left of a baby hedgehog. I did not even know we had babies. Nambi said there was another baby still alive with the mother.

There were several hedgehogs sharing the four by five metre aviary with budgies, bulbuls and tortoises. All had come to me rescued from one place or another or – in the case of the mother hedgehog – from the danger of being run over in traffic on a local highway.

I walked around the cage to see if I could determine what had killed the baby. Since most of the tiny animal had been eaten, it had to be a predator attack. Was it a rat, or was it one of the other hedgehogs?

I decided to put the remaining baby with its mother in another, safer place. The only box that was available was smaller than the aviary, but that could not be helped. We put it in the backyard in the shade of the large mesquite tree and placed the mother and child inside. They did not have much running space but at least nothing could happen to them now. Or so I thought.

In the late afternoon I went to check on the pair. To my horror I found the mother dead in a corner of the cage. Abundant scratch marks along the side of the box indicated that she had been frantic to get out. In the heat of a June day, she must have overheated and succumbed to heat stroke. The tiny baby lay close by her side. I picked it up. It was very still, but after a few minutes in my warm hands it stirred and sniffed the air. It was probably only five or six days old, a tiny pink creature. Its head was almost half the size of the whole animal, with a long pointed snout and tightly closed eyes. On its back a few soft white spines gave little protection to its vulnerable body. It was terribly smelly from having been so close to its dead mother for several hours.

I had no idea how to raise such a tiny baby. Since adult hedgehogs like canned cat food, I reasoned that maybe babies would like the substitute milk that kittens thrive on. I still had a few boxes of the powder in the freezer, left over from the raising of the wildcat kittens. I mixed some of the powder and filled the smallest feeding bottle I could find. When I offered the tiny nipple to the baby, it reacted immediately. To my surprise its mouth was huge. This baby needed a larger nipple for it to suck properly. Luckily I had one so I changed the nipples and tried again. The small creature did not hesitate for one moment but started to suckle frantically, emptying the bottle in no time at all.

That was one hurdle overcome successfully. Now for a warm place. I arranged an electric heating pad in a box with towels and put the hedgehog in. It slept throughout the day, only waking up for the two-hourly feeds. For the night I had to find a place that would be safe from the dogs' curiosity, so after the midnight feed I put the contents of the box inside the washbasin of the spare bathroom and closed the door. In the morning I woke up early, expecting to find a very hungry baby, but between the layers of the towel in the washbasin no baby hedgehog could be found. I had completely forgotten that hedgehogs are active at night. I also had underestimated the stamina of the little guy.

I searched the small bathroom, anxious that it might have been injured by the fall from the washbasin. Although the room only contained one chest of drawers and one washing machine besides the toilet, I could not find the hedgehog anywhere. I moved the furniture to look underneath – nothing. Then a dreadful thought struck me: could it have fallen into the washing machine drain? I removed the hose from the drain and yes, down in the depths I could see movement. My arm did not reach far enough, so I fetched a soup ladle from the kitchen and fished out a sopping wet hedgehog. Thanks to the fact that I had used the washing machine the day before, it was also a very clean-smelling hedgehog now. I had no idea how long the little creature had been in the drain, but his Olympic feat earned him the name Mark Spitz, after the seven-times gold-medal swimming champion of that time. Even though that name was so well earned, it did not stick. A few weeks later a friend watched me feed the baby and called him "Charlie" (because he waddled like Charlie Chaplin) - and he remained Charlie for the rest of his life.

Charlie developed very slowly. His eyes stayed closed for almost two weeks. Since I did not dare to leave him alone in the house with the dogs, I carried him with me. At first, when he was so small and cooled off so quickly, I put him between my breasts underneath my T-shirt. I remember walking through one of Dubai's shopping malls with Charlie in my bra. It felt a bit prickly, but Charlie loved it. He made happy little noises and settled down to sleep quickly after each meal. Due to the feeds with the cat milk substitute he made very few droppings, and a small piece of tissue placed underneath him took care of those. When he grew a bit larger I kept him on an electric pad in a cat carrier and in this way I took him to work at the museum and even to meetings with the municipal authorities. Thanks to the strict feeding routine he was a content, very active hedgehog. In my office I used to let him out of the cat cage, and he ran around like a little wind-up toy.

Very strangely, he had six toes on his right front foot and seven on the left. His back feet were normal.

One day I had some guests to dinner. When it was time to feed Charlie, I did so as we were still sitting around the table. After he emptied his bottle he ran around on the table and found the cork of the wine bottle that we had emptied. He pushed the cork around with his nose, becoming more and more excited by the novel game – or possibly by the nice smell. When the cork rolled away, we flicked it back to him and to our amusement he caught on to the idea and nosed the cork straight back towards our hands. It was an exhausted little hedgehog that went to sleep when the guests left.

Soon he was so active that he could no longer be contained in a cat carrier. In order not to lose him in the house, I let him run around inside the bath tub. This was also necessary because he was getting solids now and as a result he produced copious quantities of very smelly droppings. One day I had left the door to the bathroom open. I was in another room and saw Sandy walk by with her mouth wide open, holding a spiny ball between her jaws. I shouted: 'Sandy, drop that ball!'

This she did immediately, leaving a slightly dazed but otherwise unhurt hedgehog on the floor. I was always amazed that Sandy, who could gnaw big bones into oblivion, never harmed any household pet. She wanted to play with them, but did so very gently. Still, she might have made a mistake so it was better not to let her get used to this practice.

Charlie was a Brandt's hedgehog, one of the three species of wild hedgehogs that occur in the Emirates. He was all black, lacking the white edge around the face that Ethiopian hedgehogs have. Brandt's hedgehogs are more common in the mountainous areas, whereas Ethiopian hedgehogs prefer the sandy coastal plains. Not much is known about the private lives of wild hedgehogs in the desert.

Probably the person who could tell us most about them was a man called Rashid who lived on a high pass in the northern Ru'us al Jibal mountains. Some ALT members, Robert and Ali, visited him with some friends one day towards sunset. As the sun went down, Rashid started to say his evening prayers. While the visitors sat quietly waiting for him to finish, they suddenly noticed half a dozen black hedgehogs approaching the area where they sat, outside Rashid's hut. They milled around a bit, until Rashid had finished his prayers.

'They are waiting for their food,' he told Robert.

'What do you give them?'

'Dates and water and goat milk,' he replied.

'Do they come every night?' They seemed perfectly tame.

'Yes, not only these, many more come.'

'How many?'

'Oh, about 400,' said Rashid, off-hand.

'Every night?'

'Yes, every night.' It was hard to believe.

While the first group was still eating, more hedgehogs appeared. Throughout the evening groups of up to ten hedgehogs would appear at intervals, gorging themselves on Rashid's offerings. Even when the men left and drove down the zigzagging mountain road, they encountered groups of hedgehogs, all making their way to their benefactor's hut. It seemed quite impossible that these hedgehogs, which are solitary by nature, would trek together in groups. But they did.

Desert hedgehogs move differently from European hedgehogs. While the latter shuffle around with their bodies close to the ground, desert hedgehogs walk fast, on extended legs but on flat feet. It is obviously an adaptation for having to walk on the hot desert sand or rocks. It gives them the peculiar Charlie Chaplin gait that had given Charlie his name.

One specific characteristic of Brandt's hedgehogs, described by the mammal expert Dr Harrison, is a type of behaviour that I observed also. During a camping trip, I heard a small sound outside my tent and when I got up to investigate its source I saw a Brandt's hedgehog running away. I overtook him and he immediately rolled up tightly. However, when I reached down to pick him up he threw his whole body several centimetres into the air, hurting my hand.

This reflex movement is a quite adequate defence mechanism to ward off most predators, who would not really like having their sensitive noses pierced by spines. There is evidence, however, that leopards and caracals have learned to deal with this, as empty hedgehog skins are sometimes found in areas where the big cats occur.

Some months later when I moved to a newly built house on the grounds of the Desert Park, I had a five-by-ten-metre yard between two wings of the house, closed off by a wall from the rest of the garden. This is where I made homes for Putih, the ferret, and Charlie, the hedgehog. The ferret, who was blind and deaf due to old age, did not harm the hedgehog. I built shady places with piles of palm tree fronds, and "houses" with bricks and pieces of wood. A few pieces of PVC drains stuck into the sand here and there provided more hidey-holes and entertainment. There was not much vegetation, but I watered whatever came up as possible shade and interesting features for the two creatures.

During the autumn and winter both were very happy there. Charlie learned to climb the four steps to the kitchen door and would sit waiting for his food or even for just a bit of play and TLC. He was a very gregarious little hedgehog and would have spent all day with me if I had let him. Whenever I could I'd let him come out and play, but he was full of fleas, which even repeated treatments did nothing to eliminate. So most of the time we played outside. When it started to get hot, I'd stretch out on the cold floor of the air-conditioned kitchen and played with Charlie as he was sitting on the top step. He loved being tickled underneath his chin, where the hair was short and very soft.

That summer was scorching. For a full six weeks the temperature did not fall below forty degrees centigrade (104° F), even at night. I brought the ferret inside, since she was not a desert animal and already so old. But I considered Charlie as a native of the desert capable of coping with the heat. I turned out to be wrong. One day Charlie was a bit listless and the next day he did not come for his food. I searched the yard and found him, dead, in a hole he had dug about a foot under the surface. It was obviously not deep enough, for like his mother he had succumbed to the heat. I felt guilty that I had not acted immediately when he was listless the day before. Later I learned that in the Breeding Centre next door half a dozen hedgehogs had died in that same week.

We all learned an important lesson: there are limits to the adaptations of even those animals that are desert-born and bred.

34

FROM DOCTOR TO MUSEUM DIRECTOR

Icelebrated the good-bye to medical life with a "never-on-call-again goat-grab" on top of a sand dune just outside Dubai. The Lebanese restaurant that catered the food also provided tables for the buffet. I heard the delivery men complain loudly as they struggled uphill through loose sand with the huge round platter that held an entire roasted lamb, stuffed with rice and nuts. Dozens of *mezzah* dishes surrounded this masterpiece: *tabouleh* and *fattoush* salads, *hummus* and *moutabal* dips, *falafels* and *sambousis*, *kibbe* and the typical green and bright crimson pickles.

Most of my colleagues from the clinic as well as many of my Dubai friends attended. Some had brought musical instruments, others piles of wood for a few huge camp fires. As some strong men helped haul crates of beer and other booze to the top of the dune, one of them asked: 'Is this legal?'

'I guess not,' I answered, 'but I doubt if any policeman will come to check out a campfire this far out in the dunes.'

For the time being I would have to commute from Dubai to

Sharjah every day, for the building of my house on site had not yet started. It was an hour's commute each way and that winter was, as I mentioned before, the wettest since the nineteen sixties.

The bad weather started with a spectacular storm on 4 December, at the very moment I wanted to pick up my new company car, a 4WD Nissan Patrol. A friend was taking me to the Ruler's office in the centre of Sharjah. As we drove eastwards from Dubai the darkest sky I had ever seen closed in on us. The instant we drew up at the gatehouse of the office, the skies opened. I got soaked even as I sprinted across the sidewalk and into the gatehouse. Howling wind followed me inside and it took three men to close the door behind me. The window fogged up with a dozen steaming bodies crammed in the small space but I cleared a peephole and watched as the roundabout was transformed into a raging torrent on which tables, sheets of corrugated metal and even bicycles swept by. After half an hour of sheer violence the rain became an ordinary downpour and I decided to take my chances trying to reach the office building across fifty meters of front yard.

When I arrived, wet as a drowned cat, in the stately marble hall of the office, an awesome sight awaited me. There was a waterfall cascading down the curving staircase and the hall was completely flooded. When I had struggled upstream to the first floor I saw the reason for the flood. Torrents of water came through the gap below the balcony doors. Obviously the balcony slanted inwards and had no drains, gutter or threshold. Builders in the Emirates often don't make provisions for rain. It hardly ever rains. Roofs are flat and rarely waterproof, entrances to buildings are often below street level and everywhere in the cities the drains in the sidewalks are permanently closed with hinged lids to prevent litter and sand going down them. Then when rain does come, people forget to open the lids and the streets are flooded.

A few oriental carpets floated in the middle of the first floor hall. Several men stood alongside the wall looking at the unusual event.

'Why don't you roll up those carpets and place them against the opening under the door? It will prevent more water coming in.'

The men looked at me without comprehension.

'That is what we do in Holland,' I explained, 'We call it building dykes!'

I probably did not get the descriptions for dykes right in Arabic, for no action was taken. Or maybe they just did not believe me.

An hour later I was making my way through flooded streets in my brand-new car. Towards the outskirts of town the floods became gradually less but then, just beyond the airport, I saw something very strange. I blinked several times, not quite believing what I saw. The dunes, usually a golden yellow were almost entirely white. Scarves of mist furled and unfurled above the whiteness, and a few bewildered camels stood like phantoms in swirling fog. This strange fog was caused by the steam produced by hailstones, the size of tennis balls, lying on hot sand.

Below the bridges of the overpasses dozens of cars were parked in tangled groups – those were the lucky ones. The ones that did not make it to shelter stood at the roadside with broken windshields and dented roofs. If I had left ten minutes earlier my new car would have been a battered write-off. I stopped to walk into the white desert and gathered up a few of the hailstones. When I arrived at the museum ten minutes later they had not yet diminished in size and we kept them in the freezer compartment of the restaurant fridge for some days to show people what they were like. The hailstorm had been small and quite localised - at the museum no one knew how the desert had been transformed just a few kilometres away.

As I approached the one square kilometre area that was now my domain I dwelled on the pleasant idea of being boss. Although my new office was still a mess, having been used as store room for the builders, before long, I imagined, it would be a well-furnished and efficient place of work, with a wide view of sand dunes stretching to the horizon. I would have personnel and together we would perform miracles of education and research. What a wonderful feeling.

Still pervaded with the warm glow of excited contentment I drew up to the police post at the entrance gate. The police guard stepped out of his hut and asked me what I wanted.

'I am the boss of this place,' I said pleasantly.

The man looked at my still sodden appearance and said slowly: 'That is what all the Indians say!'

I was dumbfounded. Then I started to giggle. What a wonderfully weird come-down from my perch of foolish pride!

Police guards at gates were an omnipresent feature of life in the Emirates. I did not like to have such an obvious police presence at a museum that should be user-friendly, but it was one of the many "Arabic" things I would have to get used to.

In the two months between the opening of the museum and my arrival the place had been run by four local ladies, appointed as my "assistants" by the sheikh. When he told me about them he said: 'You have to take good care of them, for they are like daughters to me.' Now I needed to get acquainted with them.They were all graduates from the UAE University in Al Ain. Two were geologists, one was a botanist and one lady had done business administration. The latter was a very intelligent and ambitious girl who caused a lot of trouble with her meddling and superior attitude. I had to reprimand her several times for treating the lower staff without respect and she soon started to turn her dislike of me into damaging gossip. Within six months she tried to take over my job. While I was on a short vacation she went to the sheikh, reporting that I had misappropriated museum money and was anyway completely incompetent. I was told later that the sheikh heard her out, and then transferred her to another museum. I was very relieved that he had given me a vote of confidence and also to be rid of the difficult girl.

The three ladies that were left were quite nice but not academically gifted. The botanist was very pretty and only interested in women's magazines and make-up. Halfway through my time as director she got engaged and from then on received a hefty bonus on her salary that was not revoked when the engagement was broken off – one of the mysteries of local financing. The two geologists were close friends but only one had the ability to think for herself. They did everything together as if joined at the hip: send faxes, make photocopies, supervise the other staff. It took me a long time before I realised why it was so impossible for them to act alone.

In general ladies in the Gulf States are rarely alone. They grow up in close families. If they are well-to-do they live on compounds with several houses. In rich families, the women live apart from the men. They eat and sleep together. On their rare outings they all squeeze into one big car, and, covered with their black *abayas* and head scarves, they go shopping or to the doctor. In the coastal cities the younger generation did not wear the *burqa* or face mask any more, but their hair was always covered. My ladies always made sure that no outsider would ever see more than a wisp of hair straying from below their decorous headscarves.

Besides the gaggle of girls that were my assistants, I had sixteen people as lower staff in the museum. Ten hostesses accompanied visiting school groups, two drivers travelled the fifteen kilometres between the museum and the city to pick up and drop off the staff and to run errands. Two electricians had a busy time doing the maintenance on the exhibits. A young Indian boy ran the souvenir shop that raised funds for the ALT and a very young refugee from Sri Lanka took care of the grounds around the museum. I had no responsibility for the restaurant staff and fortunately for many years there never was a problem with any of them.

All these people were from various places in the region: Sudan, Somalia, Egypt, Jordan, Lebanon, Syria, Pakistan, India and Sri Lanka. It took two years before all the internecine wars between the various nationals had been fought. Everyone seemed to look down upon someone, or to have grievances against another. There were times I had to separate screaming, scratching, hair-pulling furies. But in the end, after some of the worst offenders were dismissed or transferred, we had peace and friendships started to develop.

My direct boss was the mayor of Sharjah, Abdullatif. He was a highly educated and efficient Sudanese whom I liked very much. Unfortunately for us he emigrated to Canada two years later but in those first two years he showed me the ropes and never hesitated to reprimand me in a very gentle manner when I had offended an Arabic sensitivity or to explain to me the intricacies of local court life.

My tasks as manager were sometimes rather strange. I was not allowed to hire or fire, only to make suggestions, and though I was told to submit an annual budget, I was never given the final version and therefore had no idea where cuts were made. I had a small amount of cash to spend when needed, but any expenditure over 1,000 dirhams (about $280) had to be approved by the financial department first. Getting an approval could cost up to three weeks and therefore I needed to plan things far ahead. Often you had to submit three quotes for the same article from different companies.

I spent many long hours at the marble palace that housed the accountants of the financial department – the director and his staff worked in a different building across town, which did not exactly make for efficiency. In the early days the accountants did not have computers. It was interesting to see them work with old-fashioned ledgers and adding machines. Sometimes I had the feeling they would have liked to use the abacus – as some merchants in the old suq still did!

Once a month I was given a big pile of cash – the salaries for all my staff. With it came a huge spread sheet with everyone's names and rows of information specific to their function and the amount of their pay. Each had to sign behind their name. I absolutely hated doing the rounds with this list and getting everyone's signature, but I wanted to be sure that matters were handled discretely. I performed miracles of dexterity trying to cover parts of the sheet because I found it embarrassing that people could tell in one glance how much everyone earned. I protested the system so long and loudly that eventually the money came in separate envelopes.

There were times when I wanted to make changes, for instance because the company that did the maintenance on the air-conditioning charged too much, or the company that serviced the elevators did a lousy job. More often than not I would be told I could not make the change and only after very persistent questioning about the reason was I given a reluctant answer: 'You cannot change it because that company belongs to the sheikh!''

No one ever mentioned which sheikh and I could only guess.

We had hundreds of visitors every day. Everyone was in awe of the state-of-the-art displays and exhibits. In the beginning, when the museum was unique in the country, VIP's from other emirates would visit. One such person from Dubai once remarked: 'There is only one thing wrong with your museum.'

'Oh, what's that?'

'That it is not in Dubai!'

Later Dubai and the other emirates also upgraded their museums but Sharjah was always far ahead with its innovative exhibits. In fact, Sharjah was named the Cultural Capital of the Arab World by UNESCO in 1998. Dr Sheikh Sultan was really pleased to get that award. He told me once that often he felt that his peers did not understand why he was doing so much for culture, but he hoped that future generations would appreciate his efforts. He held PhD's in History from Exeter University (1985) and in Political Geography of the Gulf from Durham University (1999), as well as numerous honourary degrees and distinctions. Yet, he always remained a humble, easily accessible man, who exuded friendliness and humour. He was (and is) truly a royal person.

In that first year Gerard had been allowed to build a few temporary cages on the museum grounds to house the various animals the ALT was already taking care of. The leopard remained in the custom-built cage in Gerard's garden, but the foxes, wildcats, birds and two wolves that had also been with Gerard all found new homes in the desert.

The wolves were housed in a special space adjoining the restaurant, where a wall of darkened glass gave a good view on the exhibit. One day one of the staff ran into my office and shouted: 'Doctora, doctora, the wolf is out!'

Apparently the keeper had opened the inner door to the cage, without first shutting the outer door. His hands were full of cleaning equipment and one of the wolves had slipped out between his legs. Fortunately it was not a visitor's day. I immediately rang the police post at the gate to make sure they kept the gates closed and then I called Gerard, who promised to come with his dart gun. Since it would take him almost an hour from his house to us, I had to keep an eye on the wolf. I wanted to check that there were no gaps anywhere in the fence around the one square kilometre terrain, so I took my 4WD vehicle and drove slowly along the fence in the direction in which the wolf had run. Rain was pelting down, making it easy to drive on the hardened sand, but difficult to see. Suddenly I distinguished a grey shape just beyond the fence. I got out of the car, unfolding my umbrella and approached the fence. On the other side, the wolf was happily playing with an empty water bottle – throwing it up in the air and then pouncing on it where it fell. It was rather lovely to see her out in the open like this. When she noticed me she walked towards me and stood up against the fence, sniffing carefully. It dawned on me that I was in a totally bizarre scene: in the middle of the desert, in pouring rain, holding a blue umbrella and standing nose to nose with a wild wolf!

After a few moments the wolf had had enough of our silent communication and walked off to the dunes in the centre of the field. I returned to the museum and walked into the same dunes, still holding my umbrella. When Gerard arrived he found me talking to the wolf that stood at ease some meters away. I felt really sorry that he had to dart her. When she lost consciousness her body looked curiously flat on the wet sand. Gerard turned on me and snarled: 'What the hell did you think you were doing? That animal is dangerous! Only last month she tried to kill me when I was cleaning her cage. She jumped me from behind and if I had not had the water hose….'

I did not reply. I had not felt threatened by the animal at any time. How could I explain that the wolf and I had liked each other?

The wet winter passed and the desert turned into lush pastures. Waving grass stood tall on the gravel plains and the valleys between the dunes were covered with carpets of wild flowers. I tried to get out into the desert as often as I could, expecting to find new plants. However, I discovered that the rains had resulted in a thousand times more specimens of the usual species. Often they were growing in unexpected places. The tiny violet that had taken me years of searching to find on riverbanks now grew in abundance on mountain tops. It was truly a demonstration of the adaptation of nature, how seeds are spread over the countryside in great quantities each year and how long these seeds can lie dormant under adverse conditions.

I did not have much time to traipse around the desert, for at the desert park site the building of both my house and the

Breeding Centre for Endangered Arabian Animals had started. I had suggested Gerard as the best person to design and run this breeding centre. In the beginning, like me, he had some trouble adapting to the Arabic way of working and I had to smooth things over when he had a few run-ins that could have cost him the job. The breeding centre he designed was brilliant. And large. Row upon row of cages – large, medium and small, for all the various creatures, a housing complex for the staff, an office and breeding facility for food animals, aviaries, ponds, it was all there.

'You'll never get this approved,' I said to him, 'Why did you make it so large?'

'Because I know that I'll never get money to enlarge it when we run out of space. I've got to get the funds now, when the enthusiasm is there and people want to get on with things.'

He was wise, for all that space filled up in only a few years.

In the spring of 1996 my friend Minie called and asked if I was going to the Queen's birthday reception given by the Dutch consul in Dubai. Minie and I spent a lot of our free time together, mainly to explore the mountains and wadis in search of plants and wildlife. She lived quite far away and said she wanted to go to the reception, but only if I was going too.

'Sure Minie, let's go together. It is always quite a nice do and you don't often come to one. You'll enjoy it.'

'I hope so,' she said, 'sometimes you have to be a bit social.'

The reception was given at the Sheraton hotel ballroom. When I arrived the room was already full of people. I think many of us came just because there was always a genuine market stall with the salted raw herring that every Dutchman loves. The room was packed, the noise of animated conversation almost deafening, with everyone, even Minie, having a good time. Through the crowd a staff member of the hotel approached me and shouted in my ear: 'There is a telephone call for you – your father!'

As I followed the guy to the hotel lobby, I was suddenly apprehensive. Why would my father call me at this time of the day? And how did he know I was here? His voice was cheerful as he said to me: 'I wanted to be the first to congratulate a colleague.'

'What are you talking about?' I was completely bewildered.

'Oh shoot,' he said, 'I think I have jumped the gun. Go back to your party, quickly, I'll call later.' And he closed the line without further explanation.

I stood there thinking: *Colleague? What does he mean?*

And suddenly it dawned on me. The Queen's birthday is the time when various honours are bestowed on citizens. In Holland it is called the "rain of ribbons". Many years ago my father had been made a Knight in the Order of Orange Nassau, honoured for his social work for mentally and physically handicapped people for whom he had created jobs in his factory. Was there a "ribbon" for me today? The thought had barely materialised, when the ambassador called for silence. Even though I had the one-minute warning, I was so overwhelmed that I cannot recall much of what followed. The medal was pinned on my suit and a scroll was read mentioning the reason for the award. Flowers came from Minie who had not only known about it but was, together with a few other Dutch friends, the instigator of the event. I knew the procedure well because several years before I had done the same for her. I thought she deserved her medal much more, since she had worked as a pioneering midwife in a remote area since the 1960's. So now we were all "knights of the realm" – my father, Minie and I.

The next day I informed my boss Abdullatif and he promised to let the sheikh know. I thought it was better if he heard it from me before reading it in the newspaper.

When a few days later the sheikh visited the museum with a VIP, he did not mention the event. I found it a bit strange, for he was usually very thoughtful and enthusiastic. Later I wondered whether possibly he was not sure what to make of the new concept – a knighthood for a woman.

35

THE HOUSE IN THE DESERT

Exactly a year after I had started work at the museum, the house that was being built for me was finished. It had been built according to my own design – my dream house. It was situated on a flat area between low sand dunes, on the second square kilometre that had been fenced off for the breeding centre and other yet-to-come facilities. There was no garden yet, and the swimming pool was still no more than a wish, but the house and its location were all I could wish for.

For Nambi a portacabin had been placed on one side of the house and for him this was a change for the better, too! He now had two rooms and a proper bathroom.

The dogs, Catastrophe and I moved in first – Nambi had to remain in Dubai for a few more days to look after the birds, until the aviary that Gerard was building as a housewarming gift was finished. The tortoises had a huge fenced off tract of desert behind the house. Putih the ferret and Charlie the hedgehog had a small courtyard all to themselves.

I sublet the house in Dubai to the ALT as an office for the secretary and store room for ALT wares. The two ALT drivers and Moaz, our field worker, also lived there. After some time I noticed that each of these men had their girlfriends living with them – a strictly illegal situation, that sometimes resulted in harsh punishments like prison time, deportation, and whipping or stoning (if one of the lovers was married). Since the house was still in my name I did not like the risk involved and wrote the men a letter telling them the girls had to move out unless they were their wives. If the CID found out I could be held liable for 'giving opportunity' and sent to prison. Tuan, our best driver and ALT helper since the very beginning, came to me, letter in hand.

'Madam, you don't have to worry about the CID.'

'Why not?'

'Because I am a CID informer, madam, and I would never let anything happen to you.'

I stared at him in disbelief. All these years we had had a CID informer in our midst! I was aware that all clubs and organisations were infiltrated with these spies for the government, but somehow I had never thought that our always helpful, cheerful, loyal Tuan could be one of them. I had not realised we had been enjoying extra protection!

I decided to give a house-warming Christmas party for twenty or so of my friends. The track that led the 125 metres from the gate to the house was loose sand, easily negotiated by 4WDs, but not everyone had such a car. So I paid a visit to the contractor who was building the breeding centre next door and asked him if he could possibly give me truckload of water on Christmas day so that the track would be firm for the visitors that evening.

'No problem, madam,' he said, tipping back his chair with his feet on the chipped desk, the image of the energetic supervisor.

On Christmas morning a sand storm whipped over the desert. It did not last long but was the harbinger of torrential rain. While I tried to cook several ducks in the electric oven the electricity cut out. I stood in forced idleness looking out the window at the storm, when a huge water truck entered the gate and started sprinkling the already sodden track. More water was the last thing I needed, but the workmen had been given an order and orders are always carried out. Luckily the weather calmed down and the drive dried out before the guests arrived. The electricity came back on so I had even managed to get the food ready on time. The dogs also had their friends Sarah and Bali visiting, and

Bas Chalas was so excited that he lifted his leg against the only tree in several square kilometres – the Christmas tree.

We watched the sunset from the flat roof of the new house, looking across miles of undulating dunes in all directions. To the left in the foreground were the beginnings of the breeding centre and zoo, with the museum and the children's farm beyond. When it got chilly we built a huge bonfire on the sand in front of the terrace and ate and drank and talked – not bad for Christmas in the desert.

I loved living in the desert. Every morning at dawn I got up and went out in sleep-T and shorts to give the dogs their morning walk. Often the dew lay heavy on plants and grasses and spider webs, transforming everything to jewellery. I explored the surroundings and observed the signs of nocturnal activity of the various desert creatures. The soft sand showed their tracks for just a few hours before the wind blew them away.

There were countless tracks of gerbils congregating around a bush with seeds they liked. The sand was trampled into a foot-wide path leading from their burrows to the bush – a gerbil highway.

A perfectly sinuous track wound up and down the face of a small dune. Where it met the prints of a small lizard, there were signs of a struggle – the Sand boa had made a catch.

Between dune ridges there were flat plains where the Spiny-tailed lizards lived. For three years I observed them daily, so that I got to know their every move and act. It was not as exciting as Jane Goodall's observations of chimpanzees, for the lizards were not known for the intensity of their activities. Also, I was not a scientist doing research, but still I enjoyed knowing that "old grandpa had been out and about again", judging from the foot-prints around his huge burrow, and that babies had hatched in another burrow, when I found torn rubbery eggshells. I deter-mined how far the lizards forayed by measuring the distance from their droppings to their burrow. I worried what happened to the lizards when their plain was inundated with rain water. I assumed the two to three metre spiralling entrance to the burrow must have varying levels to prevent water from entering the den. Since the water soaked quickly into the sand, the air trapped inside would be sufficient for a while.

My mother had died a few days after I had been offered the Sharjah job and since that time my father had been lonely and, in a way, miserable. I wanted to call my father every day, fearing that he would not be around very much longer. I needed a telephone at the desert house for there was no reception for my mobile.

I paid numerous visits to the telephone company, eventually gaining access to the top man and explaining to him my need to stay in touch with my ailing father. Family sob stories work well in the Emirates and finally two official looking gentlemen came to survey the situation. Lines would have to be laid all the way from the museum and down from the road to the house. I cautioned them that the water pipes were located right along the fence between my terrain and the breeding centre. The work men came and the first thing they did was to bulldoze the water pipes. I considered calling the house "Lakeview".

In due time the pipes were repaired and the telephone lines were laid. I was told I needed to wait for the connection. Minutes after the workers had left, Nambi came in, visibly perturbed.

'Madam, all melons gone!'

Nambi and I had been trying to grow melons in a patch next to the house. He had cleverly placed the seeds in the hollow dug out around each newly planted tree, where a sprinkling system provided daily water. Soon leafy vines had spread across the sand and yellow flowers had turned into fruits. I followed him outside where only the previous afternoon several juicy melons had lain ripening on the hot sand. Now only chewed rinds remained. I looked at Nambi's crestfallen face and joked: 'Well, you always tell me to share what I have with other people. I guess we have done our good deed for this season!'

Going inside I decided to try the telephone. I managed to call the museum – a Sharjah number – but on dialling a Dubai number I only heard cyber static. Luckily the telephone company director also had a Sharjah number, so I called him.

'Madam, you have to be patient! It takes time!'

'Time for what? Do the lines need warming up or something?' Clearly, I did not have a clue what it takes to make a new connection. Several hours later, the phone rang. It was the director. It was also three o'clock in the morning. 'You can call to Holland now, doctora, and I hope your father gets well soon!'

It was nice to be able to call home every day. I enjoyed talking to my father because he had sensible advice to give regarding the many new predicaments I was experiencing. After all he had been a manager all his life and one of his mottos was "Never do the work of ten people if you can put ten people to work." Another one was: "Tough is possible, too."

That saying soon became my own motto for the going was tough and soon to get tougher.

A few weeks later I had a call from someone who needed to find a home for several tortoises.

'I am moving to an apartment and I have sixteen tortoises of various species. Someone told me that you have both tortoises and space. Would you be able to take them?'

The tortoise pen was huge, so an expansion of my "herd" would be fine. One of the new tortoises was a fifteen year old Spur-thighed tortoise, undoubtedly born in the Al Ain zoo. She was already forty centimetres high and wide and heavier than I could carry. Immediately she started digging a huge burrow in a corner of the pen. Soon some of the smaller tortoises moved in with her. To my surprise this did not cause any problems. She was obviously not very territorial. We had tried to create shade by putting several boxes and piles of building wood here and there while the young bushes were still growing. The smallest tortoises usually crouched beneath the rim of the huge shallow water dish where evaporation of the water brought the temperature down by several degrees. I marked those tortoises that were of the same species and similar size with coloured nail varnish numbers to keep track of them. I tried to pick up each one of them at least once a week to check its weight. Each morning Nambi walked out of the kitchen balancing a huge platter on one hand like a trained waiter. The dish was piled high with lettuce, cut tomatoes, carrots, cucumber and nasturtium flowers and leaves if we had them. They loved strawberries, but those were rare and too expensive. It remains a mystery to me how a desert species could have developed a taste for strawberries.

To my surprise the desert was populated with many species of

birds that were easily observed from the house or during the walks. I particularly liked the Arabian babblers, called "the seven sisters" by the Arabs, because they move around in groups of six to ten birds. They sat on the fences, babbling, flipping their mobile tails straight up into the air. Both Indian Rollers and Grey shrikes perched on the fences regularly.

I watched the Rollers do their courtship display. The male would fly high up into the sky, then fold his wings to plummet straight down to earth, only unfolding them at the last minute, just below where a female was perched in a bush. Then he would spread his wings to show off their brilliant blue and turquoise plumage for her to admire.

Bee-eaters were also colourful. The only species around the house was the Little Green Bee-eater. They often sat on the backs of the terrace chairs, seeking shade and panting with the heat. Their backs were greenish-brown, while their bellies were moss green. Their faces were turquoise, with a bold black eye-stripe. After they had caught an insect, they would slap the prey onto their perch, in order to kill them before swallowing them. You have to be smart when you live on bees with stings!

It took me a while to figure out which bird it was that kept me awake at night, making plaintive calls for hours on end. I knew it was not an owl, although they were present too, as guests had told me. I, being severely night blind, could not see them. I asked Colin, the Bird man, about the strange caller.

'That must be Red-Wattled Lapwing,' he said. 'Does the call go like "did-he-do-it"?'

'Yes, exactly.' I laughed at the phrase which imitated the call perfectly.

Another mystery solved.

The lapwings were not only active at night. I used to see them strutting about between the low salt bushes on their tall legs, holding their boldly patterned black and white heads high, or showing off the large white V on their wings as they flew off. For a wetland bird it was surprisingly at home in the desert!

One mystery that I never solved was presented by a snake. On several occasions I found the perfect imprint of a complete snake in the sand. A sand viper had wiggled its whole body below the surface of the sand to lie in ambush for any passing prey. That I understood – I had seen it on films. But how had the snake been able to leave the spot without disturbing or even smudging the print? When I asked Gerard about it, he said: 'Are you sure the snake wasn't still under the sand?'

I had taken photographs and showed them to him - a complete body-print, folded tightly, with even the last thin tip of the tail showing.

'No, I guess not. I cannot imagine how it did that.'

The sand was perfect for studying tracks. The long sand racer snakes often left prints in which on close inspection you could see each individual scale of the skin, while the spines of the dhub's tail could also be distinguished in prints. One small print was omnipresent and for a long time I did not know what made it. It consisted of two parallel rows of tiny ninety-degree angles facing outward. They ran for long distances between hummocks and disappeared into tiny horizontal crevices between the roots of plants.

A friend of mine had acquired a "black light" and came to try it out in the dunes behind the house. On a dark night we went out wearing high boots and socks, for the desert presents a few dangers such as snakes and scorpions. It was the latter that we had come to find. Their carapace shows up in ultraviolet light and this makes it easy to spot them. At first we saw nothing at all. We needed to stop moving for the scorpions would be able to detect us from the vibrations caused by our footsteps and hide as long as we kept moving. My friend swept the light back and forth in circles as we stood quietly between the dunes.

'There,' he breathed softly, 'see, between those two clumps of grass.' In the eerie violet light a pale white form moved, like a ghost in appearance, but with a very scorpion-like scuttle. Soon we picked out another, and then another. They were everywhere, running fast between the bits of vegetation, hunting their prey of insects, lizards and rodents. It dawned on me that they were the ones that left the strange geometric pattern on the sands.

One evening some friends were having dinner with me on the terrace. Suddenly one of them jumped up and cried: 'A camel spider!'

A saucer-sized creature with a bloated cream-coloured body and eight long hairy legs, waving two enormous "antennae" ran across the terrace and scurried up the wall. Quickly I fetched a container, into which we coaxed the creature. Camel spiders have a quite undeserved bad reputation. They belong to the Solifugae – an order of non-spider arachnids that "flee from the sun". In the daytime they hide in dark places, and when they are disturbed, they look for any shade they can reach. If it is you lifting the stone they were hiding under, they will see your shadow and run for it. This habit has caused them to be called aggressive, which in fact they are not. Why would a small creature like that attack a giant? It would be a waste of energy and venom, if, indeed, there is any. Camel spiders are generally considered to be non-venomous. They kill their prey by the powerful bite of their awesome mandibles.

Our visiting arachnid was sitting in a clear plastic container and I was able to look at it more closely. It certainly would never win any prizes for beauty. Its appearance was rather fearsome

and it measured some fifteen centimetres in length including the legs. The eyes were located on top of the head, which was large and ended in two sharply pointed, separate mouthparts. To the sides of the pointed mandibles were what looked like another pair of legs, longer than the others. They were in constant motion and are called pedipalps – a kind of antennae with which the animal senses its surroundings.

I lifted the container to inspect the animal's underside. Along the proximal third of its hairy hind legs and running along the inner sides were small overlapping paddle-like structures. My animal encyclopaedia provided an explanation: these were so-called malleoli, a vibration sensitive organ, used by the camel spider to detect prey as well as predators.

As I was studying this interesting feature, I tipped the container a bit, and quick as a flash, the camel spider raced up the sloping side and onto my bare arm. I let out a most unscientific shriek and dropped the container. The camel spider had already jumped off my shoulder and ran into the house. One of my friends, Peter, who worked at the breeding centre and wanted to have this creature for his exhibits, followed it and tried to block its way. The camel spider must have looked up and detected some very welcome shade. It ran up Peter's leg into his shorts. Peter paled visibly and squeaked: 'Please excuse me,' stepping quickly into the kitchen and closing the door. A minute later he came out with the camel spider safely confined in a covered dish. During all this commotion the camel spider had not bitten either me or Peter. In spite of the horror stories about this creature propagated by US soldiers in Iraq, it is really harmless.

Neither as a doctor nor as desert park director have I heard of anyone being bitten by a camel spider.

I have seen several species of camel spiders in the Emirates, but one that really amused me was a very small one that I found between the rocks of a dry wadi. It had drawn my attention because of its unusual coloration. It was covered in silky hair that was russet on the body and purple on the legs. Its body was only one cm long and half of that was taken up by the ferocious-looking mouthparts. As I crouched low to take a picture of it with my macro lens, the tiny creature folded its pedipalps over the top of its head, covering its eyes! The picture did not come out very well because of camera shake - a result of my laughing at the ridiculous sight.

I was still living at the desert house when there was a partial sun eclipse visible from the Emirates. I had prepared myself with a perforated piece of carton, with which I projected the sun with the moon sliding across its face onto the wall of the house. That way I could observe the progress of the event without looking into the sun itself. Gradually the light became dimmer – a mid-day dusk. Birds stopped twittering. Insects ceased to fly. The desert became quiet. I had not realised how much background noise the insects made.

The diversity and numbers of insects in the desert was astounding. I had a visit from a Belgian ophthalmologist who studied moths as a hobby. He had spent all his vacations of a decade in the Emirates catching and classifying moths and had identified over 350 species, many of them new to science. One evening, when he visited me at the desert house, he placed his black light on a white sheet on the terrace. After half an hour we went to see what had gathered in the circle of ultraviolet light. Besides half a dozen species of moths there were huge ant-lion flies, many species of mosquito-like insects (real mosquitoes were rare) and a remarkable number of bugs of all shapes and sizes.

In the spring the young plants and grasses were infested with caterpillars with voracious appetites. The stork's bill plant was host to the caterpillars of silver-striped hawkmoths. These could be recognised easily by the horns on their hind part. Another horned caterpillar could be found on oleander bushes. When close to pupating it was large and fat, grass-green with yellow slashes along its sides between the rows of small black dots that represented its respiratory system. When I touched its head with a blade of grass, it reared up, bending its head down to reveal two large blue "eyes" that were hidden between the folds of its skin. It was a very effective defence mechanism, for the sudden movement coupled with the appearance of huge staring eyes was scary even to me, leave alone an unsuspecting hungry bird!

The caterpillar of the Plain Tiger butterfly had a different defence mechanism – or really two. When it was still very small the caterpillar was an irregularly shaped narrow strip, black at both ends and white in the middle. It was the perfect image of a bird dropping and therefore not perceived as possible food. These caterpillars fed on plants that exude poisonous white latex, and this made them unpalatable to birds. Their strong orange, black and white coloration, which was the same as the butterfly's, advertised this bad news to would-be predators.

Another frequent visitor to my desert patch appeared when the first citrus trees that I had planted started to flower. It was the Lime Swallowtail, a large, strikingly patterned butterfly. Its caterpillar liked to feed on plants of the carrot family. It had a defence mechanism similar to that of the oleander hawkmoth caterpillar, but instead of showing "eyes" when it reared up, it projected two white frills from between the folds of its skin. These frills squirted concentrated carrot juice! The smell was overwhelming and it would be quite painful to the mucous membranes of an attacking bird.

All these miracles of nature were not unique to the desert, but I became more aware of them because I lived so close to nature there. Nambi and I were quite alone for the first two years before the staff of the breeding centre moved in next door. We had no neighbours except the sleepy policemen on guard near the museum, over a kilometre away. I think Nambi was probably lonelier than I because he used to like to walk around to his friends in the old neighbourhood and pass the time of day after work was done. Here, in the lonely desert, he started a kitchen garden, working like a slave on his little plots of vegetables and developing intricate watering systems for his flowers and fruits.

In our second year I arranged for Nambi's oldest son Thiruppa to come to the Emirates and work for me. He had just turned eighteen and had never been outside his village. He did not speak a word of English when he arrived, and he was painfully shy. In the first weeks he would cringe if I merely greeted him. Nambi introduced him to a few Sri Lankan boys who worked at the museum and soon Thiruppa became more self-assured. I enrolled him in English classes in Sharjah and started him on driving lessons as well. If he could master English and driving there would always be a job for him somewhere in the Emirates and he would be able to support his parents and siblings back in Tamil Nadu. In between courses he helped his father with the house and garden work and eventually was employed by Gerard at the breeding centre as a cleaning boy and animal keeper.

36

DESERT PARK ADVENTURES

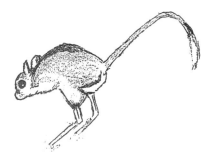

After the first tough year at the desert park came a period of relative calm and enjoyment. The breeding centre was being built
to Gerard's specifications and soon the animals that the ALT had
been taking care of were moved to their new premises. I was particularly concerned about the little sand foxes. When Mazzel and Tov
were moved to temporary cages near the museum, I noticed that
something strange had happened to Mazzel's tail. It was kinked in
a ninety-degree angle at the base, sticking out sideways instead of
sweeping behind him. I asked Gerard if he had been injured during
the move, but nothing untoward had happened. A few days later, on
a visitor-free Monday, I was walking across the museum grounds
with the dogs and when Sandy approached the foxes' cage, pandemonium broke out. Mazzel was running frantically back and forth
inside the cage, yipping and barking and even screaming with joy.
His tail flowed behind him in a long straight plume. His little body
squirmed close to the ground and he squirted pee like a spring rain.
This was truly a happy fox. Apparently the sight and smell of Sandy
had triggered this joy.

The next day the kink in his tail was back. It was obvious that it was stress that caused the problem. Gerard's keepers reported that museum visitors who walked on the grounds came close to the cages and taunted the animals inside. So we built a high fence covered with *barasti* around the whole complex to keep the visitors away from the cages that, being temporary, were not big enough for the animals to hide from tormentors.

When the proper cages of the breeding centre were finished all the animals had plenty of room and complete peace. But Mazzel never lost the kink from his tail for the rest of his life!

There was to be an official opening of the breeding centre at the time of the visit of the secretary general of UNESCO, who came to bestow the title Cultural Capital of the Arab World on Sharjah. To commemorate the important event an obelisk had been erected on top of a high dune right across the road from the Desert Park. The VIP would first dedicate the memorial obelisk and then perform the opening of the Breeding Centre for Endangered Arabian Wildlife. Four days before the event was to take place, the sheikh came for a final inspection. As he struggled through the loose sand between the cages, he decided that this was not acceptable.

'We need grass here! I want grass everywhere! It has to be there before the UNESCO man comes!'

When the Director of Parks and Gardens protested that he could not get grass to grow in four days, the sheikh said: 'You can do it. Just give me grass!'

A few weeks earlier an enormous complex of buildings constituting the brand new Sharjah University campus had been inaugurated. The size of this campus was astounding, as it harboured the co-educational American University of Sharjah as well as the more traditional Sharjah University and the Higher Colleges of Technology.

When the first main driveway was being constructed I had thought it to be the runway for a new airport. It stretched for a couple of kilometres through an area of levelled dunes in the middle of nowhere, miles outside the city. At the end of this wide avenue a domed white building arose, dominating a huge square, with tall buildings on two sides and a marble fountain in the middle. This was the American University complex. Then four smaller versions of the building appeared, two on each side of the main avenue, housing the two other educational institutes, for boys on the right and for girls on the left. There were so many white domes gleaming in the sun, that it caused one of my friends to comment: 'The Taj Mahal has had a litter of puppies in the desert!'

This enormous complex had been beautifully landscaped with palm trees, lawns and flower beds.

The planting of date palms was interesting to observe. They were transplanted from the nurseries as fully grown trees. The leaves were tied together very tightly as the trees were uprooted, loaded like logs on lorries and replanted by means of cranes. This was possible because the roots were shallow and the hole that received the tree needed to be only two metres across. Massive amounts of water were deposited every few days into the wide ditch that was left around the base of the tree. While the original palm fronds turned brown and looked dead, in due time new green fronds started peeping out of the tied bundle at the top. At that point the leaves were untied and the dead ones removed. From then on the palm tree kept producing new leaves with amazing speed. Within a few months a bare piece of desert had been turned into a shady oasis.

This lush landscape provided the Director of Parks and Gardens with a solution for the problem we were facing at the breeding centre. He ordered his men to cut the lawns surrounding the university into strips, which were rolled up, transported the ten kilometres to our site, and unrolled between the cages. As we stood contemplating the result – cool green paths where only sand had been a few hours earlier, the gardening chief turned to me and said sternly: 'I need to have this back immediately after the opening!'

Fortunately for us some political problem in the region caused the UNESCO VIP to postpone his visit by several months. By this time new grass had been grown at the university site and we were allowed to keep our lush lanes.

Opposite the Desert Park was a large tract of undisturbed desert with miles and miles of undulating sand stretching south.

Ten days before Christmas 1997 there was an airplane crash in that area. There were only two people who noticed it happening.

One was Thiruppa, Nambi's son. He was sweeping the paths in the Children's Farm when he saw the plane make its nosedive. Since his experience with airplanes was limited to his one flight from India to the Emirates he did not think it was worth reporting. Apparently he thought that some planes land on airports, others somewhere in the sand!

The other person who was a witness to the accident was an old bedu who happened to be saying his sunset prayers on top of a dune, when the plane crashed right in front of him! This man did realise that such a landing was not normal procedure but he had no car or telephone to alert the authorities. Still, something had to be done for he could hear people crying for help. So he climbed on his camel and trudged the seven kilometres up and down dunes and across sandy plains to the police post at the entrance of the Desert Park. The two policemen on duty did not believe him. They decided to investigate the incident before reporting it, as they did not want to make fools of themselves. However, they did not have a vehicle at their disposal so one of them climbed on the camel with the camel's owner and together they travelled all the way back to the accident site. When they arrived there, the cries for help had stopped and a deadly silence reigned. The light was failing fast as they ambled back to the police post to sound the alarm. The rest of the evening pandemonium reigned – police cars and ambulances shrieked back and forth, floodlights lit up the desert and barriers were set up to keep the people away that started to gather even this far out of town. Miraculously one person, the flight engineer, survived the crash. From his report the course of the event was pieced together.

Apparently the plane that came from Tajikistan was on its way to Sharjah, already at low approach altitude. The pilot had mistakenly asked Dubai airport for permission to land. Dubai told him that he needed to switch to the controllers of Sharjah airport and as he was doing so the plane went out of control and crashed. Because at that very second the plane was not being monitored by either airport, no one had noticed it disappearing from the screens. Eighty-five people perished.

That evening Thiruppa told me what he had seen. He had not mentioned it to anyone yet!

Not long afterwards Thiruppa himself was the star of a drama. I had decided to invest in a swimming pool. I lived too far from the city to join a pool or health club there, and the daily walks with the dogs did not provide enough exercise, especially when it was hot in the summer. I designed the pool long and narrow so that I could do longer laps. With some nice land-scaping around it, it soon became my favourite place to spend my time off work. I swam early in the morning before work and then again in the late afternoon when I returned from the museum. Especially in the morning it was important to check the pool for anything that might have fallen in. My knowledge of desert inhabitants increased by the day. Sometimes the creatures could be scooped out alive and set out to dry, but most had already drowned. The museum collection of bugs and beetles grew daily.

I was greatly puzzled when one morning I found a toad trying to climb up the steep sides of the pool. Where could he have come from? The nearest toad habitat was at least fifty kilometres away. I checked with the breeding centre but they had no amphibians as yet. So I gave them the toad to be the first of their collection. That evening I saw a heron flying low over the garden. Had he dropped a meal and was he searching for it? It was the one and only heron I ever saw there!

On one of the early morning swims I was doing a back stroke when from the corner of my eye I saw something moving. I turned my head sideways and saw a large Sawscale viper swim-ming straight at me. His triangular head being at my eye-level he looked particularly threatening. He was large for a viper, almost two feet long and as thick as a sturdy broomstick. A bite from those articulated fangs would be painful and could be lethal if not treated immediately.

I am sure I broke some Olympic records trying to get out of the pool! I had not seen the snake when I checked the pool so it must have been hiding in the filter space. I fished it out with a net and deposited it on the far side of the fence that surrounded my grounds. A few days later he was back, again swimming up and down the pool. Again I fished him out and saved his life. Instead of being grateful the snake came back again and bit Thiruppa as the latter walked in the garden.

Although the bites of these snakes can be quite dangerous, not every bite injects venom into the victim. Since Thiruppa's wound seemed to consist of only one fang puncture, I thought it might have been a glancing strike, so I decided to wait and see how things would develop. I got out my first aid vacuum extractor and applied it to the tiny wound. Several attempts to extract some venom were not very successful, but it was difficult to know whether it was because there was not much venom, or whether the wound was too small for the extractor to be effective. To reduce circulation I ordered him to sit still with the leg lower than the heart and placed ice around it. After an hour there was some swelling and this was an indication to visit the hospital.

The hospital staff in Sharjah turned out to be well-instructed on how to deal with snake bites. The nurse told me off for having waited and whisked Thiruppa off for some blood tests. They kept him overnight and repeated the tests frequently to see if there were any haemorrhagic effects of the bite. When his clotting remained normal they decided that no venom had been injected and sent him home. Even so Thiruppa's leg remained swollen and painful for many weeks and I treated him for a long time with ibuprofen.

A nicer creature that I saved from a drowning death was a small gecko. I fished him out and placed him on the tiled edge of the pool. As he sat drying out, I observed how he licked his eye to clean it. I had read about this but never seen it before. I quickly grabbed my camera from the house and slid into the pool to get an eye-level shot of the little lizard. He posed beautifully and I had a frame-filling view of his right side with the knobbly head and its gold-flecked eye. I stood perfectly still in chest-high water, barely breathing, waiting for the lens-cleansing action. There it was: its long tongue flipping upward – to the offside eye. Again and again he tended to that eye, while the one that was in my viewfinder got no attention. The lizard moved a fraction and a small blade of grass now obscured part of the eye. As I shifted my lens a fraction, the tongue shot out once more and now it did the job I had been waiting for. I managed one shot with the out-of-focus blade of grass blurring the action. Then the lizard decided his ablutions were completed and he jumped into some bushes, disappearing from sight.

The breeding centre that was adjacent to my grounds started filling up with animals. Nearest to my fence were the leopard cages and a large pen with ostriches. Arnold, the leopard saved from Yemen, and his mate Lucy were the first ones to move in. The two leopards had mated several times and Lucy had had several litters of cubs that she either destroyed or ignored after birth and consequently we still had no leopard offspring. We hoped that in their roomy quarters and with dedicated keepers, they would do better.

Arnold must have had very keen hearing, for whenever I came home late at night and lifted the latch of the gate, his roar would greet me. It felt strange and rather wonderful to have this animal as my watchdog.

A day or so after the ostriches arrived, I was walking with the dogs along the fence to inspect the water pipes. A hedge had been planted along the fence but it was still low and sparse, and we had a free view of the stately birds. Bas, my inveterate chicken-murderer, stood transfixed with awe for a moment. I could see what he was thinking: 'Wow, *big* chicken!"

Then he took off like a rocket and crashed into the fence that was partly hidden by the vegetation. He bounced back and shook his head, and then started chasing the birds up and down their pen. I was glad that he could not reach them, for he would have lost that battle. The ostriches were a mean lot that did not like to be disturbed. A short while later they badly injured a careless keeper with their powerful feet.

37

TROUBLE IN PARADISE

The year 1998 was not a good one. A new man was appointed by the sheikh to be my boss. He was a young, well-educated local man, whom I had known for several years when he worked in a project in Abu Dhabi. Farid had studied ecology at both American and German universities and was now studying for his Master's degree at Al Ain University. I had not been impressed when I read his thesis about a local mangrove forest. It was superficial, sloppy work, but since he was not supposed to be doing much field work as Director of the newly created Wildlife Conservation Department, I thought he was probably the best person we could get for the job. I hoped that he would relieve me of some the tedious administrative tasks and facilitate the contact with the local authorities.

Early in the year Gerard took me out to dinner one evening and told me that his marriage was over. I had been to his wedding in Europe, a grand affair in a beautiful old monastery. It was sad to hear that this couple was breaking up. Gerard was extremely bitter about it, and gradually his bitterness turned into hatred towards all women, and for some reason, especially me.

In the course of the next two years Gerard became a different person from the one I had known for fifteen years. He picked quarrels for very unimportant reasons, became quite paranoid and was always so tense that I felt he could snap any minute. At first I ascribed his nervous condition to the failure of his marriage.

Time will heal the wound, I thought, but in his case the nervous anxiety became worse with time. The project of designing the breeding centre, supervising the building, recruiting and training the (mostly South-African) staff and running the breeding centre and later the zoo was too big for one person to handle. And Gerard was not a team player. He wanted to be in control, always and everywhere. Sadly he chose the wrong way to do it. Somewhere along the line I lost my good friend.

Before long the situation at the desert park became extremely difficult if not to say ridiculous. As manager of the entire project, I should have been Gerard's boss. Of course, I had never acted like that, trusting that we would work in mutual respect and understanding, helping each other where we could. Obviously there was a rule that kept visits to the breeding centre to a minimum as we did not want the animals to be unnecessarily stressed by disturbances. Suddenly that rule forbade me access too.

Gerard and the new boss got on very well. When I introduced the two to each other, I had seen a spark of instant recognition fly between the two, and I had experienced a distinct feeling of uneasiness, a foreboding of evil.

I forgot all about the problems at work when my father died on the day before Easter. By chance, I was in Holland when it happened. I had to extend what was meant as a long weekend to a two week compassionate leave and I was very grateful that I could be with him during his last days. Both my brother and I sat with him that last night as he struggled to breathe. It was a moving experience which shattered me.

My father had a great ability to empathise. The day I left for the Emirates with my three cats, he took me aside. 'I just want to warn you. Where you are going now the people are not very nice to animals. You must be prepared for the possibility that you may lose one of your cats.' Coming from a man who did not like animals, this was amazing. From him I learned to be practical and to take disappointments in my stride, to be honourable and compassionate. I was going to miss him terribly.

A few months later I was sitting in my office when the mail

was delivered. It included an official looking letter from Holland. I could barely believe the content. I was being invited to Holland to receive another knighthood, this time the Order of the Golden Ark, a special award for people who have contributed to the conservation of nature. It was awarded every few years by a special foundation of Prince Bernhard, the father of the present Queen. I did not know anyone who ever had two knighthoods. I felt sure that there must have been a lack of communication between the offices of the Queen and her father, for certainly what I did was not worthy of two distinctions.

The ceremony was to be held in October at the royal palace in Holland and I was allowed to bring four guests. I decided that I would like one of those guests to be a representative of the Sharjah government, because after all, if it had not been for the Ruler of Sharjah there would have been no Breeding Centre for Endangered Arabian animals. The sheikh appointed Farid to accompany me. Besides attending the ceremony we would have time to visit a few zoos and animal exhibitions in Europe to provide us with ideas for the new zoo that was going to be built next to the breeding centre.

The seventeen recipients of the Golden Ark awards and their guests were treated to a day of festivities, including a visit to one of the best zoos in Holland and a luncheon in their famous jungle house. All of us had to give a short presentation about our work. Listening to the others talk of the difficulties, deprivations and dangers they faced in their work in far-off places, I felt again that I was out of place. I had done some hard work, that was true, but the greatest danger I faced was "termination and deportation" if I made a mistake. My life was easy and even posh. I felt a fake and stumbled through my presentation in utter embarrassment. The prince, however, was extremely gracious when he pinned on our medals.

'Ah finally,' he said as he stuck the pin through my lapel, 'this is about time!.' He was referring to us meeting, not to my being knighted, I think. My father and the Prince had been business acquaintances for decades and during their regular meetings my father had often bragged about my ventures and he had sent copies of all my books to the Prince.

At eighty-seven years of age PB (as he was affectionately

242

called by many) spent two hours on his feet, talking to most people in their own language and cracking jokes. To Farid he said: 'Do you know that this lady,' and he pointed at me, 'is the only woman I know who has refused to take money from me?!'

It was true. Sometime earlier his foundation had offered an amount of money for the ALT, but I had written to say that, since the UAE was an affluent country, I should be able to raise what we needed from among our well-to-do residents and that maybe the money of the foundation should go to poor countries where the conservationists had no resources.

I had intended the official presence of Farid to be a sharing of the honour of the knighthood. That turned out to be a miscalculation. After some time it became clear to me that my boss was telling everyone that I had wanted to flaunt my importance. He became more and more difficult to work with. Phone calls were not answered, faxes ignored, meetings cancelled or indefinitely postponed. I was being stonewalled. And the more I was being ignored and isolated, the more Gerard became Farid's friend and confidant. I was miserable but unable to do anything about it. I could have gone to the sheikh and complained, but I knew Farid would deny everything. Also, I had found out that he was related to the sheikh's wife and therefore had a lot of *wasta* – the special type of power that runs Arab society.

Around this time one of Gerard's staff, a Dutchman who ignored his rule about non-communication, told me that finally one leopard cub had survived and was now three weeks old. He was being hand-reared, and when he had seemed lonely they had provided him with a baby mongoose for company.

I felt terribly sad that Gerard had kept this from me. I went home and spent the next four days in bed with a high fever. It was an odd malady for I had no other symptoms. Then I noticed that I experienced an insatiable thirst and needed frequent bathroom visits. I got out my medical kit and dip-sticked my urine. The pink-coloured square immediately turned deep purple, indicating a high amount of sugar.

I had diabetes!

It was at this very low point in my life that something special happened.

38

THE DOG THAT SMELLED LIKE ALYSSUM

A TRIBUTE TO DESERT SALUKIS

He stood there suddenly among the bushes of the desert. I had passed that spot only three minutes before without seeing him. It seemed as if he had dropped from the sky – a very thin saluki dog with friendly eyes. Sandy and Bas ran up to him and sniffed him all over. They were not in the least aggressive – unusual for Bas who was a rather macho male and this was a male too.

He followed us at a safe distance to the house where I had a closer look at him. There was a piece of rope around his neck, which he had obviously chewed through to escape. Whoever had owned him must not have taken good care of him, because he was as thin as a rake and so weak that he could barely stand. I put some food and water out immediately, but he was wary and did not eat right away. He also did not leave. He hung around the house and after a while curled up under a bush and fell asleep.

Thiruppa approached him quietly and managed to remove the rope from around his neck.

In the next few days he started to eat and gradually became a little bit less fearful. He had long hairs on his ears that were matted into thick knots. His tail looked like a piece of rope. I did not like him much in the beginning. He was too thin, too timid, too foreign. It was definitely not love at first sight. The love grew slowly, deepening whenever I looked into those incredible almond-shaped honey eyes. He did not have the sharp intellect of Sandy or the cuddliness of Bas Chalas, but there was something about him that made me think of royalty. His neck and nose were incredibly long and coupled with the dignified expression of his eyes it made him seem a bit superior.

Gradually he started to come into the house. The first time it happened I was concerned because of my sixteen-year-old cat Catastrophe. When I brought Sandy into the house she had been so insulted that she took refuge in the hamster terrarium where she was safe from the attention of the boisterous puppy. I was not sure how she would deal with a new dog in her old age.

I need not have worried. One morning the dog stepped very quietly from the terrace into the bedroom and stood just beyond the threshold looking around. The cat saw him and without hesitation walked over to him, sat down on her haunches and reached up to touch his neck with both her paws. She butted her head against his and softly said: 'prr, prr.' I could not believe my eyes. With great relief I told the dog: 'Now that Catastrophe likes you, you can stay!'

The royal dog of Egypt, the Saluki may be as old as the oldest known civilisation. Their bodies were often found mummified like the bodies of the Pharaohs, and their pictures appear in ancient Egyptian tombs dating from 2100 BC. This breed is thought of by Muslims as a sacred gift of Allah, so the dogs were never sold but only offered as a gift of friendship or homage.

The Saluki is a brilliant desert sight hunter capable of incredible speed and agility over rough terrain with feet that have thick hairs between the toes for protection. It was used to course gazelle, the fastest of the antelopes. Salukis have also been used to hunt fox, jackal, and hare.

The desert Saluki has a slim, greyhound-like body with long silky feathering on the ears and tail, and an elegant, flexible neck. It stands quit tall with males reaching seventy centimetres, and weighing up to thirty kilos. The head is narrow and well-proportioned, tapering gradually toward the nose. The ears are long and hanging. It has sturdy jaws and large eyes that are either light or dark brown with a sweet, dignified expression. Its body is very elongated, with oblique muscular shoulders. It has an unusual gait: when at top speed all four of its legs are in the air at the same time. Salukis with a patch of white in the middle of the forehead are thought by Bedouin tribes to have "the kiss of Alla" and are regarded as special.

From the very first day, Bas was friendly with the newcomer. In fact, I needed to explain to him that the newcomer was the same sex as he! Since we used to have a children's TV programme in Holland called *Bassie en Adriaan*, the new dog was named Adrian. But that was only his first name. He was markedly bow-legged, with the toes turned out like neat little cushions. They looked like the legs on a Chippendale table or chair, so he was known as Adrian Chippendale. Shortly after he arrived I went to France and bought a farm in a place called Fougirard so his full name became Adrian Chippendale à Fougirard, which fitted his aristocratic nose.

We all went on walks first thing in the morning. Adrian always needed more exercise than the half hour that the rest of us liked to do, so he often stayed behind in the dunes and came home several hours later. That was a bit of a worry, for I was always concerned that the bedu from whom he had escaped would see him and catch him again, or worse, shoot him.

He had to learn many things that the other dogs already knew. There was the dog flap. No matter how many times I showed him what it was for, he looked at it with great suspicion. The problem was that it was designed for medium sized dogs, and Adrian stood almost a meter tall at the shoulder. Getting through it was a major feat of contortion for him. But he learned very suddenly on the evening when I gave him a bone for the first time. He had no idea what to do with a bone. Still, it smelled wonderful and when Bas tried to take the uneaten bone away from him, they got into a fight. Adrian was quickly overpowered by macho Bas, fled into the kitchen and dove straight through the dog flap. After that it was not a problem any more.

Like all the pets, he soon developed a routine. He would spend most of the day on the single bed in the guestroom. When he lay flat on his side, he would cover almost the whole bed, with his legs still dangling over the side. He could not sit very comfortably on his belly, because he was so narrowly built. His breastbone was like a keel. If he sat on his haunches he had to lean backwards, because his front legs were so long. It looked strange – like a canine pyramid. He preferred to curl up in a corner of the sofa, and when he did that, he folded his long legs beneath him and all that was left was a long-nosed dachshund.

He started to gain some weight – mostly muscle. His coat became glossy and his hair started to grow. The five centimetres long hairs on his ears were soon fifteen centimetres long, his tail grew a huge plume and his legs developed beautiful feathering. He was a brindled saluki – the real desert-bred saluki, seldom seen in Europe. A year later, when I entered him in the dog show, he did not win a prize because the British judges were not acquainted with this type of saluki. But among the Arabs that saw him there was not one who did not admire and covet him.

His eyes were almond shaped, the colour of honey, and he always looked pensive, even slightly sad. He never barked or showed aggression. The only problem I ever had with him was that he was not house-trained. He marked his territory, even after I had him neutered. He always used the same places, and I soon learned to put some protective plastic on the corners of those pieces of furniture. But that was his only vice, and it was understandable, since his "home" had always been the open desert.

The vet estimated that he was about a year and a half old when he arrived. When he had recovered from his near-starvation, he grew in strength and speed. To see him run in the desert was a wonderful experience. We used to walk on mornings when the dew lay like diamonds on the grass and fine mist floated between the dunes. When the sun rose and its rays raked the dune tops Adrian, standing there, was haloed in gold.

His most amazing attribute, however, was the way he smelled.

It was not so apparent when he first came, but after a few weeks of good food and care, he started to smell like flowery talcum powder. Later I learned that these salukis, as well as the larger Afghan hounds, have a specific gland just below the bone at the back of the skull that produces a sweet smelling substance. This is one of the reasons that the Arabs, who love all kinds of perfume, are so partial to salukis.

Once when I was having breakfast on the terrace Adrian stood beside me and suddenly jumped up on the table, seemingly without any effort, as if he had springs in his feet. One second he was standing on the floor, the next he stood on top of the table.

I looked at him in surprise and said: 'Hey, you're not supposed to do that!'

Immediately he jumped off and never tried it again.

The house in the desert had a long wide corridor. Early in the morning I would wear an Omani bedouin dress as a housedress. Its back panel was ten centimetres longer than the front panel, the idea being that this would wipe out your footprints if you walked slowly on the sand. Then your husband would not know where you had gone.

I was taller than most local ladies, so the back flap did not reach the floor and since I never walk slowly, the dress would billow out behind me as I strode down the long corridor. Adrian thought this was very funny. He used to catch the edge of the dress and follow me down the hall like a slip-bearer. Catastrophe would walk in front with her quivering tail held high, Bas was next and Sandy followed. Often I wished there was someone who could film us in this procession!

Soon Adrian learned to come to me for cuddles. When I watched TV on my queen-sized bed, old Sandy would always be on my left side, against my legs; Bas would be on the floor at the foot of the bed and Adrian chose the spot on my right side. He would stretch out very close to me and lower himself down with a grunt of satisfaction. He was a very sensuous dog. He loved being stroked and would nudge my hand for more when I stopped.

He would have preferred to stay the night also, but that was impossible. His body gave off an enormous amount of heat. Having him next to you was better than having a hot water bottle, but not very comfortable on summer nights in the desert. His high metabolism combined with his hour-long runs meant that he could put away an enormous amount of food. He ate very slowly, not at all like most dogs. Whenever I gave him food or drink, he would first look at me with those large golden eyes, as if to thank me, before he would lower his head to eat the food. I always joked that he had had an oriental upbringing, because after every meal he would come to where I was working at my desk, put his head on the desk next to my papers and let out a very satisfied burp. I had never met a burping dog before!

All three dogs were good friends, but there was a problem. Three dogs don't play together. Two play and one is left out. Since the two boys were best matched, it was mostly they who played together. Sandy was left out and used to howl with frustration. The only time when the two older dogs were active together and Adrian was left out was when it was time for swimming. Bas was a true water rat and Sandy liked it too, but Adrian was frightened to death of water. I tried to introduce him to the pool once, carrying him down the steps to the water. But he quaked with fear so I felt sorry for him. It was a good thing that he smelled so good naturally that he never needed a bath.

Then came the day I lost my job and my house. I had to move from the desert back to the city. The old house I still had in the city was very small. The kitchen was so small that when the animals all gathered around for their food, there was no room to turn! The garden was reasonably large but not large enough for both dogs and flowers. Bas and Adrian would run madly around the single tree churning up the grass and whiz through the flowerbeds. Before long a vegetation-free figure eight was the main feature of the garden. In order to save some of the greenery I had to put up chicken-wire fences around all the beds, which rather detracted from whatever beauty was left.

Every morning we drove to a large field on the outskirts of town, where some hares still lived. Within the first week Adrian brought me a hare he had caught. It was so obviously a gift, that I could not scold him. For a long time afterwards I thought it must have been a weak or sick hare, for he never caught another one, although the three dogs chased many.

Then one day I was sitting in the car with the dogs running outside, when they flushed a hare. I watched from the high viewpoint inside the jeep as the dogs chased it. Adrian loped after the hare with his five-metre strides and easily overtook it. A little distance in front of the hare he turned around and did a canine equivalent of "boo", causing the hare to jink ninety degrees. That gave Adrian the chance to chase after him again. I saw him do it three or four times before he got tired of it and let the hare get away. The only other time a hare was caught was when one tried to take refuge in a pile of rubble and was dug out by Basje before I could get there to pull him away. Seeing the poor hare being torn into pieces by Sandy and Bas, my two gentle pets, was not a pretty sight. Adrian did not seem to be interested at all in the killing spree.

Adrian still never wanted to come back with us after the half hour walk. He just was not tired yet. It was impossible to catch him if he did not want to be caught and it was equally impossible to hang around in the heat waiting for him to be ready to come back. So one day I decided that I would take the other two dogs home, have a cup of tea and glance through the paper, and then go back to the field to pick him up. He was sitting on a pile of sand in the middle of the field and as soon as he saw the car, he came racing towards me, jumped into the car happily and spent some quality time with me all to himself on the way back home. That became the pattern.

I did not feel very happy about leaving him by himself in the field for an extra hour, because I was always concerned for his safety. The field was next to a nature reserve that was being patrolled by police and they had the right to capture any unaccompanied dog. Adrian did have a collar with a very obvious red municipal tag. That would be enough protection against being shot but not against being taken to the municipal dog pound, if the police took exception.

Leaving him there was a calculated risk, but to restrict the dog's need for exercise also felt wrong. I tried walking him on the leash, but as Adrian walked faster than I could run, it was just not feasible. I tried every trick in the book to lure him into the car when I wanted him to come, but he ignored me completely. At least, I thought, no one else will be able to catch him either! But that was where I was wrong.

One day in October he was not there when I came to pick him up. I searched the whole field for a full hour, but could not find him. I left and came back after another hour and there he was, sitting as usual on his sand-pile, happy to see me, but without his collar. which I always kept loose on purpose. I immediately got him a new collar and tag. But two weeks later it happened again and this time he did not come back at all.

Even though I had always taken into account the possibility of losing him, I was not prepared for the enormity of this loss. I had fallen totally in love with this dog. I searched for him for weeks, handed out flyers, put ads in the papers, checked out dozens of sightings and became more and more depressed. One day someone who knew dogs called me and said she had seen him near the camel camps behind the horse racing stables. Through the flyers I had become acquainted with a Bahraini saluki breeder, a man as nice and gentle as his dogs! He told me that the camel camps were a very likely place for a saluki to take refuge, since they love the smells and sounds of the camels. I checked out the area at least a dozen times, shouting his name until I was hoarse, handing out my flyers to all the camel keepers and jockeys. Many people told me they saw him regularly, but I never managed to find him.

Sometimes I wondered why he never came back to the field. The camel camps were less than five kilometres away from where we still walked every day. I would have thought he could have found me again. People told me the lure of the desert was probably too much for him. He loved his freedom and the suburban garden life was not for him, but in my heart I knew that Adrian was as happy with me as I was with him and that he would never run away voluntarily. I just hoped that whoever had him would treat him decently.

After three months I stopped searching, because I was becoming too depressed.

Three seasons passed.

I came back in September from my summer holiday and took the dogs for their daily walk to the field. As soon as I had parked the car in the middle of the field a police jeep drove up to me. The policemen told me that this area was now incorporated into the nature reserve and that cars and dogs were no longer allowed there. I coaxed the dogs back into the car, but since they still needed to do their business, I let them out again at the edge of the field near the road. As I walked down the sidewalk, I saw Sandy scratch at something and pick up a bone. Thinking she might have uncovered a dead goat, I ran over to her and told her to drop the bone. She came away and as I turned to resume the walk something caught my eye: a plumed tail! A tail that I recognised! I took a closer look and saw a collar and bright red tag!

It was Adrian, or what was left of him. He was lying at the foot of the pile of sand where he used to sit and wait for me. His death must have been instantaneous, as he seemed to have rolled off the hill, so someone must have shot him. The murderer had buried him by pushing part of the sand pile over him – he obviously knew my routine and expected me to come back to look for the dog. I had checked the area several times when Adrian disappeared. Now I recalled that I had smelled a dead animal there, but I had not been able to find anything. It had not occurred to me that someone would have buried him. For eleven months I had daily driven within a foot of where he was buried! I would never have walked in this particular area if the police had not driven me off the field. It took an inveterate carrion-eater like Sandy to find my beloved saluki.

Tears streaming down my face, I gathered what was left of beautiful Adrian. Mendelssohn's violin concerto was playing on the car radio as I collected his bones. I can never listen to that music any more without remembering that sad moment! Later a few friends and I went camping in a beautiful spot in the desert and we buried him in the high dunes, again with Mendelssohn's sweet tones accompanying our task. The children in our party spelled out the letters R.I.P. in rocks on the surface of the sand. Adrian was back in the desert where he belonged.

From the relationship with Adrian I learned that it can be worthwhile to let love grow slowly. I always felt that the love he showed was not a rescued pet's devotion but something much greater. He accepted me as an equal. I wished I could have been as gracious and gentle as he was. Our time together was much too short but I knew that in those eighteen months we had mutually given and received a special gift of love.

I still miss him often. I miss that happy grunt when he lay down next to me. I long to feel his sleek body, with the skin taut as a drum across his ribs, the soft long-haired ears. I want to sniff again that beautiful smell. I sow alyssum in my garden every year, just to be able to sniff his perfume again.

I now think he was an angel that came to be with me for a while during a very difficult time of my life. I remember thinking that first day when I saw him that it was as if he had dropped from the sky. He disappeared as quickly and definitely. I feel privileged to have known him and to have had his love for a while. I just hope he is happily playing with hares, wherever he is!

39

A YEAR OF CHANGE

Just before Christmas my father's estate was settled and I found that I had inherited a small amount of money. I set it aside for a house in France. My father and I had talked about it often during his last year. I contacted a real estate agent, who started to fax me available houses in my price range, warning me that there was not much to be had for such a piddling sum. In February I took a week off and travelled to France.

The real estate agent took me around four possible houses. The first was too big, the second too small and the third did not have enough land. At that point I thought I would need a large area to be able to give Adrian his runs. I did not yet know that Adrian would never make it to France. When we went to see the last house we drove quite far into the countryside. The narrow roads wound up and down hills covered with vineyards and orchards. Sprawling farms with square tower dovecots dotted the landscape. Then we drove through a pine forest with filemot bracken lining the road, and finally we turned into a lane that ran downhill into a small valley to a seven-house hamlet. As soon as I glimpsed the house lying beside a curving grass track, I knew this was it.

It was raining hard, the sky was black, the house neglected

and dirty, the driveway slippery with mud – and yet I knew. An old couple lived there now, and the lady of the house showed me around. I liked the spaces, the proportions of the rooms, the meter-thick walls and the huge barns. The house had a good roof and sound foundations. The bathroom was new and functional - I only found out later that the drains emptied into an open hole in the ground.

The next day I went back and was shown over some of the land – there was a fresh water spring with an old stone washing place at the foot of a huge whispering poplar. The land that came with the house was bordered on two sides by small permanent streams. There were meadows and rather wild forests on hillsides, a huge garden and a sizable orchard. Since it was winter I had no idea what the garden would look like later. Had I known how high the nettles were and how rampant the brambles in summer, I might have hesitated. As it was, I decided then and there to buy and signed the papers the next day.

Back in Sharjah the quality of my working life was deteriorating by the day. It was not at all fun any more. Farid had installed an Iraqi buddy as an accountant and the man made everyone's life miserable. My trusted technician Mustaq looked totally depressed. When I asked what had happened he told me that from now on he had to give every burnt out lamp that he replaced to the accountant for him to keep count.

'He treats me as if I am a thief,' Mustaq complained.

I protested that measures like this should be discussed with me before they were applied, to no avail. The stone walling action was in full force. Unfortunately Farid had also managed to get himself appointed as vice-chairman of the Arabian Leopard Trust. The chairman was the top official of the Royal Court, a man who was so important and busy that he could never attend meetings and told Farid to deal with all matters. At first this seemed to work alright, but that soon changed.

Three months after I had bought my French house, I took a month's vacation to move in. I spent a busy month getting a septic tank dug, fitting a kitchen and furnishing the house. I maxed out all my credit cards, confident of future earnings to cover the debts.

After the wonderful weeks in my green paradise, the desert looked more barren than ever and, within minutes, the stressed atmosphere at work wiped out the peace of the French countryside. But I was ready to tackle anything, I was happy to be with my animals again and I even greeted my staff with enthusiasm.

Two days after my return, Farid called me to his office.

'How was your vacation?' he asked amiably.

'Very good,' I said, 'I worked hard in my new house and enjoyed it immensely.'

'In that case you will probably like this,' he said, handing me a letter. I unfolded the sheet of paper. After a preamble of empty words praising my dedication and input, it said that I was being dismissed because I was too expensive to maintain due to the need of cutting costs. I was given two weeks to clear out the office and the house and return the car. My very first thought was: 'Thank God, now I don't have to tolerate these daily struggles any more and I can escape!' But then it hit me. What was I going to do? It was obvious that Farid had been planning this for a long time. I knew better than to fly off the handle but I did point out politely that I had a six months' notice in my contract and that I intended to use the full six months to find another job.

The next few weeks were a nightmare. I was forbidden to continue working and even to enter any of the desert park premises. The accountant gave me a statement with the proposed settlement of my dues, and it was clear that they did not intend to honour the commitments of my contract. I wondered if the sheikh knew about this dismissal. He was abroad and for a while I could not reach him, but when he was back in his palace in Kent, I called him. I explained the situation. Just as I thought: he had not been involved in the decision. He told me: 'Don't worry, we are friends and we work together. When I come back, I will sort things out.'

I settled down to wait. It was not easy. I was not getting any salary, and although I stayed in my free house I had to feed the animals and myself, pay my houseboy and run the car. I borrowed whatever I could on the credit cards, and then had to turn to a friend for help.

The only relief in this misery came in the form of three small furry animals.

The Head of the Sharjah Municipality Technical Department called. I always associated him with sewers because that was one of his main jobs – installing sewers all over the emirate. However, for some reason he was also the man who supervised the animal collection at one of the city parks and the person that was contacted when animals were confiscated at the port or the airport.

'I have just confiscated three leopard cubs at the airport,' he told me, 'They are still very young, possibly too young to survive. Shall I bring them to you?'

'Yes, please, I wonder where they came from.'

Trevor arrived with a cardboard box from which three fuzzy faces peered at me. They were not leopards but cheetahs. And indeed, they could not be much older than four weeks and they must already have been in captivity for several days. Undoubtedly the mother had been killed when they were taken from the wild. I called some cheetah breeders that I knew in Holland and asked them for advice. They gave me a feeding schedule and advised me to takes the cubs' weights every day to see if they were growing properly. I took out the bottles, nipples and powdered cat formula and started feeding the trio. Fortunately they immediately liked the formula, and sucked well. They did not seem to have suffered too badly from the ordeal of losing their mother and travelling to another country.

As soon as I had set eyes on the cheetahs I knew what had happened. About two years earlier a German animal keeper who worked for one of the Al Ain sheikhs had persuaded his boss that it would be great fun to see cheetahs hunt gazelles in the desert. He said he could train the cheetahs if he got cubs of a very young age. Since the sheikh was willing to pay great amounts of money, animal dealers were easily found who would illegally get him what he wanted. The project turned out to be a success. Soon the sheikh was able to entertain his friends with this novel sport. And so every one of the sheikhs wanted to have their own cheetah stable. Baby cheetahs started to come into the Emirates by the dozen. The vets in Abu Dhabi and Dubai were swamped with sick little cats. In due time it caused an uproar and National Geographic magazine published a short notice about it that featured one of my cheetah pictures but, at my request, did not mention my name or involvement. I had enough problems already.

In a way I could understand why that German tried to get his dream realised. He loved cheetahs and wanted to see them out in the open, doing what they did best – hunt. But I would not have disliked the guy so much if he had bred his own cubs first. Breeding cheetahs in captivity is not an easy matter, so the man resorted to poaching cubs, insensitive to the fact that his experiment would cost the lives of many cheetahs – the mother and at least fifty per cent of the cubs.

Undoubtedly these three were meant for one of the sheikhs and I knew I would have to give them up soon. I did not have to wait long. Within a week I had frantic phone calls from secretaries, assistants and friends of the sheikh, who happened to be one of the Abu Dhabi royal family. I had to let the little cubs go – far too soon. Still, in one week of proper care they had doubled in size and weight, and had become a lively trio. Since I had plenty of time I spent hours playing with them and observed that they were much more timid than the baby leopards I had met in the past. Whereas leopard cubs explored far and wide, took risks and got into scrapes, these small cats acted like real babies, tottering about a bit and pushing their mates gently and then falling over with the effort. They even sat still on the scales when they were being weighed. Of course, they were still very young, but I did feel that there was a great difference in temperament between the two species of cats.

Sheikh Sultan came back in September but I was unable to get an appointment with him. Obviously Farid had reached him first and told him whatever lie was needed to justify his action. When in early September the new Wildlife Centre, beautifully designed by Gerard, was opened with much fanfare, I was not invited to attend. I wondered if the sheikh had noticed my absence.

One morning the phone rang. A lady with a British accent, whom I did not know, asked if I could help her with something that had to do with the museum. I told her that unfortunately I could not help since I was no longer in charge.

'Do you mean you have been fired?' she asked. When I said that that was indeed the case, she exclaimed:

'But they cannot do that to you, of all people!'

'Well, they can and they have and I am just waiting to get something sorted out with regards to my notice time and pay.'

'This is a scandal,' she said. 'I shall have to help you. I am Hannah, the widow of one of the Nahyan sheikhs and I'll sort this out for you. Can you meet me for lunch tomorrow?'

She named a very posh hotel in Dubai for the meeting. I agreed to go, hoping that she would foot the bill. I felt that since she was a member of the ruling family of the Emirates she could probably afford it better than I.

The next morning I drove to the city and waited in the hotel lobby. From our telephone conversation I had deduced that Hannah knew me, probably from newspaper articles or TV appearances, and would be able to recognise me. When she arrived a little while later, she turned out to be a lovely British woman in her forties, dressed like a local. Over lunch she told me she had been following my exploits in wildlife conservation for quite a while and was shocked to hear how I was being treated.

'But never mind,' she said, 'we can turn this into something good. If you could make a plan for the next five years, what would you like to do most?'

I did not have to think about it for long.

'What the country could really use is an institute for wildlife research. There are a number of good people here who could work together to record the flora and fauna of the Emirates, make a proper library and put together some good reference collections of various things like shells, fossils, insects and whatever turns up.'

'That sound like a wonderful plan,' she smiled, as she buttered a piece of toast. 'What were you earning at the museum?'

When I told her the figure she said: 'Far too little for a position like that! Let's double it. Now what I need from you is a plan and a budget. Let's meet again next week and then I will bring my children. I would like you to meet them.'

The second meeting with Hannah also took place in a hotel

restaurant. The kids turned out to be very nice: a sixteen-year-old girl, very poised and polished, and a twelve-year-old boy with sparkling eyes. I liked them immediately. Hannah explained that she would like our project to develop into something that her children could run when I retired. I did not tell her yet that I was prepared to deliver only four or five years of work. First things first – I wanted to get the project off the ground.

We had a few more lunch meetings and Hannah was on the phone practically daily. Strangely, though, I never found out where she lived, she only had a mobile phone and I never saw her arrive at any of our meetings. I did not give it a second thought at the time. I was pinching myself to make sure that I was not dreaming. It all seemed too good to be true, but in Arabia these things do happen.

Back in Sharjah I finally managed to see the sheikh. During the talk the sheikh said he wanted us to part without hard feelings. I answered that that would be easier if the contract was respected. He seemed not to know what had been happening. Immediately he called in the crown prince and told him to settle all my dues to the last cent. But he did not offer me another job, even when I told him I could not go back to medicine after a four-year gap.

When I left the building I ran into the Chief of Protocol of the Court, a man who had always been very nice to me. He stopped me and said: 'I am very sorry for what happened. I want you to know that it is nothing personal.'

I did not understand what he was getting at, and the only thought that came to me was: *It may not be personal but it certainly feels that way.*

When matters had finally been sorted out at the desert park I decided to move out before the end of the notice time, since I now had prospects of another job. Fortunately I still had the rented house in Dubai. Moaz was away in South Africa on a course and would have to find another place to live on his return, the drivers would have to make place for Nambi and the ALT office could remain in my guest room for the time being. Thiruppa was now working full-time for Gerard and was staying in the zoo staff quarters.

Sandy observed the packing of boxes and crates with great suspicion. When the large truck came to move my belongings back to Dubai, she jumped into my four-wheel drive and refused to budge till we all piled in that evening to drive back to the city. Sandy had been back to the old place several times when we had needed to visit the vet, but Bas had been away for three full years. When we turned off the main road into the old neighbourhood, Bas sat up and looked around with ears pricked up with excitement. When we rounded the corner into our old street, he started barking madly. As soon as I opened the car door he jumped out and ran to the gate. Then he proceeded to show Adrian all the nooks and crannies of the place where he had grown up. He was really happy to be home again.

Hannah promised that I would be on salary as of 1 February and we started to look for a villa to house the new "Centre for the Study of Arabian Flora and Fauna". This was to be a temporary housing, as Hannah said she wanted to build a specially designed centre in a few years' time. I also started to line up staff. Tuan, the driver who served the Leopard Trust so well for many years, had had to be fired because of changes within the ALT. He turned down a good job in order to stay with me. I talked to three unemployed natural historians to join the centre as research staff and found a well-qualified lady as office manager. She also turned down another job to wait for this one at the new centre. I went shopping for a car, and did some test drives with wonderful 4WD vehicles.

However, as time went on, there were many promises and plans, but nothing real ever materialised. It was embarrassing having to keep everyone on hold. I needed a new visa, as I was still on the sponsorship of the ruler of Sharjah and that had to be changed. Three or four times Hannah set a date to do this new visa, but on the day itself no call came where I should go with my papers, and later she always called with some plausible excuse as to why it hadn't happened, and a new appointment was made. It was hard to pin her down. Now I realised how little I knew about her. I started to get quite anxious. But whenever I wondered if I should worry, I thought of the fact that Hannah had involved her kids in this project, and I was sure: 'A mother would not mislead her children.'

Then one day I had a phone call. It was from the partner of one of the real-estate ladies I had been dealing with in my search for a villa for the office. She said: 'I only know you from the newspaper, but I feel I want to tell you a few things about this Hannah that you are involved with, just so she won't lead you up the garden path much longer.'

I went to see her. The news was not good. It seemed that Hannah was known to seek out people to "help", promising them the world, keeping them on a string for a long time and then dropping out of sight. I checked a lot of what she told me with the facts that I had gathered about her over the months – they all fitted. The children were being used as a smokescreen. The whole thing was very, very sick.

I never had a chance to talk this over with Hannah. We had one more telephone call during which I did not let on that I was on to her, but she must have noticed something. Suddenly my calls to her mobile were no longer picked up. Since I did not know where she lived, I did not know where to find her. I never met her again. I never was able to present her with the invoice for the month I worked for her.

The strange thing was that in spite of the incredible con job, I found I could not dislike Hannah. She seemed so genuine, and until this day I think she was genuine in her concern. She just was unable to keep any of her promises, because, as I found out later, she was under tight financial control of an uncle of her late husband.

From time to time I heard that Hannah continued to find new projects to play around with for a while until she was found out and did her disappearing act.

40

THE FINAL YEARS

Back in Dubai I tried to defragment my life. After I paid back all my debts from the settlement with the Sharjah government, I had little left to live on. In order to get a job in my profession I had to take the medical exam again to regain my licence. For six weeks I crammed, trying to bring my medical knowledge up to date, but my heart was not in it. I did not really want to do medicine any more. I need not have worried for I never did worse at an exam. Medicine was out and I needed to find another source of income.

Thanks to the fact that I was well-known in the Emirates and that there were many people who wanted to be helpful, I landed some well-paid assignments doing environment impact studies that were now becoming mandatory before any new development was allowed to be carried out. I also sold photographs and handicraft articles at fairs and markets, pictures for calendars and books, and in the end managed to get sponsorship to write the guide to the wildflowers of the UAE that I had aspired to for years. It was illustrated with the pictures I had taken since the early days in Al Ain, complemented by others taken by friends in places where I had never been – mostly in the higher mountains. The four years leading up to my retirement seemed short, and the solitary life of writing prepared me well for life in the French countryside.

My free-lance business developed so well, that I could have made a comfortable living and maybe even some serious money if I had stayed longer. But there were two things to consider that kept me to my 2003 departure schedule. One was that I knew that my Dubai house, in fact the whole neighbourhood, was listed for demolition in the near future. I would never be able to find a house as cheap as this one and therefore any future earnings would only disappear into the pocket of some local house-owner. The other consideration was Sandy's age. She was thirteen and aging rapidly. I did not think she would survive another year and I wanted her with me, even in death. I was quite apprehensive of moving her, knowing how she hated strange surroundings and separation from me, but there was no way around it. I would just have to keep my fingers crossed and hope that she would survive the long journey to France without problems.

Soon after I moved back to Dubai I had to go away on business for two weeks. Coming back home I smiled when I saw the two black noses and four brown eyes that were peering through the gap underneath the gate. Bas and Sandy had taken up their old habit of waiting for me. As I opened the gate, they went into a frenzy of joy, jumping all over me and howling with delight. Adrian stood to the side, looking at the wild scene without joining in. Finally I had a chance to sit down and at that point Adrian walked up to me, pressed the top of his head firmly against my chest and sighed deeply. He, too, was happy I was back.

On New Year's Eve Sandy and I went off camping with friends, as we always did. When I returned Nambi came running from his room, looking distraught.

'What is the matter, Nambi?'

'Madam, cat had accident. She not good.'

'What happened?'

'You go away five minutes, she came crying. Leg was bleeding. I call you but phone not working. I go to doctor, he not there. I put her in bathroom.'

That was quite a speech for taciturn Nambi.

I opened the bathroom door and saw Catastrophe lying on the floor. She did not raise her head. I knelt down beside her on the floor, feeling how cold it was there, but fortunately Nambi had placed her on a towel. Her left hind leg looked a mess.

I contacted the vet on call and made an emergency appointment. As I picked her up carefully and put her in the car, I wondered what had happened. It could have been a car accident, or maybe she was chased by dogs and had miscalculated a jump. The vet-around-the-corner that Nambi had gone to fetch had already gone off for his own New Year's Eve celebration. I felt miserable knowing that I had not been there when my faithful companion of eighteen years needed me.

The locum vet, a man I did not know, operated on Catastrophe and fixed her dislocated hip. He also closed the superficial wound lower down – a dreadful mistake that cost her her life. I did not realise what he had done, because when I picked her up the leg was bandaged. As a doctor I knew better than to close a wound that has been open for more than six hours. Infection set in and although our own vet gave her a drip with antibiotics it was not successful. A few mornings later I carried Catastrophe to my bed which was in full sunshine at that time of the day. She had become painfully thin and was unconscious most of the time. But as I put her down in the warm sunshine and stretched out beside her, talking to her as I stroked her, she looked at me and touched my cheek with her paw. I hoped this was a sign that she was getting better, but it was not to be. Soon she was unconscious again. In the afternoon when I checked on her, she turned her head and let out a plaintive meow. It was as if she wanted to say: 'Help me! I cannot get better and I cannot die!'

I called the vet and he came over to end her suffering. We buried her in the garden under the papaya tree that Nambi had grown from seed. Nambi was very sad.

'She still strong, Madam, maybe she live for two, three years more.'

Oh, it is hard to say good-bye to friends.

Some time later I was visiting the offices of a publisher who was buying some of my photographs for a book. In the hallway I came across Shelley, one of the girls working there, who was also an active member of Feline Friends, the cat charity. She was sitting on the floor of the corridor, bottle feeding two tiny kittens. She looked haggard. I asked her what was happening.

'I have too much on my plate right now – this full-time job, gigs every night (Shelley played the harp and was much in demand for parties and weddings) and then these two little orphans.'

'Well,' I said, 'I have relatively little to do, so I can take care of the kittens, if you want.'

'Oh, would you? That would really be a help.'

'Fine, as long as you find homes for them.'

I had decided not to have a new cat until I had moved to France.

So I got busy bottle feeding the pair of two-week old kittens. I kept them in the cat box, only taking them out for feeds. Right away, Basje showed great interest. He sat next to the cat box, staring at the kittens that wriggled in my lap, and drooling.

'I guess you consider them a nice bite for lunch, eh?' I laughed at him, 'But you are not getting them!'

At every feed Bas was right there and a few days later one of the kittens strayed away from my lap, without my noticing. I looked up and saw Bas with the kitten in his mouth. I cried out in alarm, but there was something about the way in which he held the kitten that reassured me. He leaned over and carefully placed the kitten back into my lap, licking it gently. Suddenly it dawned on me – Bas *liked* them. From then on he took an active part in raising the kittens, cleaning their behinds and retrieving them whenever they crawled too far away. His gentle tongue did a much better job of "making them go" than my moist Kleenex, so he was appointed official brown-noser. It did not change his passion for killing adult cats. He only liked kittens.

That October we lost Adrian. The dogs did not seem to mind. Possibly they had been a bit jealous of my affection for the newcomer. Bas, however, suddenly developed a panicky fear for gunshots and fireworks. Whenever there was some celebration in our neighbourhood firecrackers exploded everywhere, and Bas cowered under my desk or near my bed, trembling violently and panting with fear. When New Year's Eve came around again I did not go camping - with last year's disaster still fresh in my mind I did not feel like it. It was better for Bas anyway that I stayed home to comfort him. Later, after we had found out what had happened to Adrian, I realised that Bas' fear of gunshots dated from the time of Adrian's disappearance. Had he sensed what had happened to Adrian? Bas had never seen a gun or had any experience with guns and when Adrian was shot he was miles away. Still, I felt that there was a link.

It was again a chance meeting with a Feline Friends member that landed me with four two-day old kittens to raise. There were three tabbies and one white one with black patches that had been found in a dumpster. Once again I was busy, this time with feeds every three hours. These babies were very young. Whenever I bottle fed them I marvelled at their tiny perfect paws, with the minuscule nails, pumping away at my hand that held the small bottle. Bas helped from the beginning and it seemed he really enjoyed his task, lying next to the cat box even between feeds.

The black and white kitten had pus coming from between his still-closed eyelids. I took him to the vet-around-the-corner, who gently prised the eyelids open. To my horror the eyeball burst between his fingers, pus streaming everywhere. How the poor thing must have suffered with that infection! The vet cleaned the eye socket and instructed me to continue doing the same for another few days. The little kitten took the treatment in his stride. Of course he became known as Nelson from then on.

Once, after a feed, the kittens had settled down on top of me as I lay stretched on my bed. There were two around my neck, like a necklace, one was on top of my head and one on my belly button. All four were purring like mad, replete with warm milk and tingling from Basje's tongue bath.

Heaven must be like this! I thought.

A few weeks later, when the kittens had become roly-poly playful balls of fur, one of the tabbies suddenly developed a swollen leg. It did not seem to hurt, but I took it to the vet anyway. For a few weeks we battled an unknown disease that caused swellings to all the joints and eventually weakened the kitten so much that we had to put it down. The vet decided it must have been some rather virulent auto-immune disease.

The three remaining kittens grew up uneventfully, and the

267

tabbies were taken to new homes. Nelson stayed. I did not want to give the one-eyed cat to anyone who would not know how to take care of him should anything happen to his other eye. He had become beautiful. His black spots turned out to be grey and black, in a pattern just like that of clouded leopards. They seemed embossed on his pure white fur. He always kept his eyes half closed so few people ever noticed that there was one eye missing. His ears were huge, a characteristic of warm-climate cats. His nose and the cushions beneath his feet were so pink they seemed to be made of marzipan. And he had the sweetest character of any cat I have ever come across.

He used to come in from outside through the dog flap and cry loudly in a strident voice as he ran through the kitchen. If I then called: 'I am here, Nelson,' his voice would change to the sweetest of soft tones as he called to me in long meows. He lay for hours on top of my monitor, dangling a leg or tail in front of the text I was working on. As soon as he heard the tones of the fax machine he rushed over to "collect" my faxes. He thought jumping on the miraculously appearancing of rolls of whispering paper was the best of games – after unrolling toilet rolls, of course.

Bas and Nelson were close friends, roughhousing together endlessly. I have a picture of Nelson on top of Bas, with his head completely inside Bas's mouth. I call it the "do you still have your tonsils" picture. No one who sees it believes that the same dog had already twenty-two dead cats on his conscience by that time!

All this time I was still on the visa of the Sharjah government. I had talked over my problem with the new Dutch consul who had tried for a long time to get an appointment with the sheikh to present his papers. Finally he managed to get through the Chief of Protocol, the man who on my last visit to the court had said that there was nothing personal against me. It turned out that there had been a serious misunderstanding with the previous consul which had disturbed the Sharjah authorities so much that they had decided never to be helpful to Dutch citizens again. What I had thought to be a vendetta against me had its roots in a diplomatic failure.

The new consul managed to put things right and when he finally met the sheikh, he mentioned my residence permit problem. The next day I received a call from the Ruler's court that my visa would be renewed.

By that time it was too late for Nambi, who had also held a Sharjah government visa. His permit had run out a month earlier and I had had to send him home to India. As I said good-bye to him at the airport, I reflected that he had been the most constant man in my life – a good friend for fifteen years! Thiruppa, who had quit his job with Gerard, was now a driver for a Dubai hotel and remained my contact with the family in India. From him I heard a few months later that Nambi had had a stroke but had survived and did not have any severe after-effects. I knew he had it coming for he had consistently refused treatment for his high blood pressure and diabetes, but it was still sad.

Tuan, our ALT driver, who now worked in another job, and his lovely wife Jameela, came to live in Nambi's rooms. Jameela had a job somewhere but also helped cleaning my house, which she always did singing softly to herself. Sandy fell in love with Jameela, following her around and spending long evening lying in front of her open door watching her as she relaxed in the evening. It was then that I noticed that Sandy was growing deaf, for she did not react when I called and was startled when I approached and touched her.

Running the Arabian Leopard Trust was becoming increasingly difficult, because our honoured vice-president, who was the person who should provide us with an extension of our trade licence, kept promising to do so, but never did. Without the licence we could not operate legally and were liable to fines if we sold goods to raise funds or wanted to organise another fund raising event. At this time we had a local man, Ahmed, as treasurer. He was a real animal lover and hailed from Sharjah, so he was in a unique position to go to the *majlis* of the sheikh and report the matter. The fact that he never did goes to show how *wasta* works. Farid was related to the royal family and therefore higher up the ladder, even though Ahmed was older and a retired CID policeman.

Once, when the ALT was planning to organise a fund-raising event together with the Emirates Environmental Group, Farid called the EEG's chairwoman, not knowing that she was a friend of mine, and told her that we were working illegally and that he was never going to give us a trade licence again. Of course, my friend reported the telephone conversation to me. When I told Ahmed, he was furious about Farid's behaviour, but he did not take our problem to the sheikh. I could do nothing either, as any complaints against Farid would have been dismissed as "sour grapes" over the loss of my job.

Our hard-working ALT secretary retired to Europe, and with my departure approaching rapidly there was not much chance that the ALT would ever work properly any more. So I wrote to the sheikh, who was officially our patron, and asked what he wanted me to do. Several letters remained unanswered. It seemed an appropriate time to disband the ALT, because a few months earlier the World Wildlife Foundation had opened an office in the Emirates and was soliciting the same donors that had always supported us. We had a meeting with the WWF representatives at which we promised to let them have all the data about local wildlife that we had gathered, specifically concerning possible areas for future nature reserves. WWF would be in a much stronger position to persuade local authorities to create these reserves than the ALT ever could.

Eventually I wrote an official letter to the sheikh explaining the situation and announcing the demise of the ALT. It was never acknowledged. Together with a handful of loyal volunteers Tuan and I spent many hours selling the contents of the ALT offices and left-over promotional goods. Whatever we could not sell we gave to the animal charities K9 and Feline Friends for their fund-raising bazaars. The money we had left in our account was spent producing a field guide for mammals, put together from the animal fact sheets that we had handed out to schools and students during the past ten years. I gave the last three years of financial statements and accountant's reports to Ahmed and destroyed the correspondence and other papers of ten years of work.

That winter of winding up the work of ten years and losing Adrian and the loyal Nambi was very depressing and made me long to return to a world where I would feel more secure. If anything it was a good preparation for difficult good-byes that were ahead.

41

THE MOVE TO FRANCE

The date for my move was set at the end of April - when it would still be cool enough for packing the household and moving the animals. It involved a great deal of work. I had to squeeze it all in while finishing the flower guide, for which I was still supervising the production.

First the animals had to be prepared for their journey to Europe: France demanded rabies vaccinations and proof that the vaccination had had its desired effect. They had to have chips inserted and a bill of health had to be issued a few days before departure. It cost a lot of money. I started the process in January on the two dogs and Nelson, but I was not able to finish it in Nelson's case.

I woke one night at 5am with a pounding heart and with one thought: *Something has happened to Nelson*. He had been with me at ten the previous night but must have gone out later as he did most nights. I listened for any sounds of animals in distress, but the night was quiet and cool. I told myself not to be silly, Nelson was out so often, why should anything have happened? I went back to bed and tried to sleep. It was impossible. I quickly slipped on some clothes and went out in the pitch dark night. I spent the next hour criss-crossing the neighbourhood, looking for an injured cat and calling Nelson. I returned home empty-handed.

Nambi and I talked to all the neighbours – they all knew the pretty one-eyed cat. Everyone helped by looking in their yards to see if he had crawled away somewhere after being injured. A week or so afterwards Nambi came to tell me what he had heard on the neighbourhood grapevine. Two blocks away, on the other side of a larger road, where I had not searched, apparently a man had run amok that night. He had gone out into the street, shooting everything that moved. Several households had lost their cats and dogs. I assume he must have targeted Nelson also. Like Adrian, he was killed for no reason at all by a trigger-happy idiot. Both wonderful creatures were with me only one year and a half, but they will always be alive in my memory. They had great beauty and sweetness of character.

My old 4WD Nissan also fell prey to people with destructive tendencies. It failed to start one day at the end of the dog walk, and I had had to ask Tuan to come and rescue us in his little car. We left the car where it was, parked on the side of the path that ran through a large stretch of desert near the royal palace. The garage couldn't send a mechanic till the next day and when he arrived the car had been completely destroyed – the windows were broken, the tyres slashed, the paintwork scratched. That solved the problem of selling that car. But I still had another one: the Mitsubishi bus that had been the ALT's when we still had lots of goods to be transported to fairs and bazaars. Nambi told me that the owner of our neighbourhood laundry would like to buy it. I had used that laundry for many years and knew the short, friendly young man who ran the laundry. He came over to discuss the price. He stood looking at the bus with dreamy eyes, stroking the white paint with his small brown hand. He was obviously in love. We agreed on a price, and I asked him if I could keep it till the day of my departure, as I needed it to transport the two huge travel cages for the dogs. That was no problem, but we had to do the transfer well ahead of time.

I went to get the transfer papers from the traffic department and was referred to the ladies' section. There I was told by the *abaya*-covered girl behind the desk that I had a fine to pay.

'What is it for?' I asked.

'Registration finished!' she answered curtly.

'But I thought you are allowed to exceed the period by one month,' I protested.

'Only when renewing, not when cancelling,' was the illogical answer.

'OK, how much is it?'

'One hundred and fifty dirhams.'

As I pulled out my checkbook I muttered: 'You are robbing me blind!'

Suddenly the girl started yelling: 'I am not robbing! I am not thief! I am doing job!'

'Calm down,' I said, 'it's just a saying in English.' (I did not think "figure of speech" would be understood)

This made her even more furious. She stood there, spastic jerks agitating her black cloak, eyes ablaze.

'I understand, I speak *good* English, you no can fool me.'

Goodness gracious, I thought, *I am going to land in jail if I don't do something.*

I knew how dangerous it can be to be suspected of insulting someone. Hadn't I experienced how little is necessary to become a *persona non grata* when I had irritated the VIP lady at the Al Ain hospital so many years ago?

So I apologised profusely, told the girl her English was excellent, paid my fine and ran out as soon as I had my papers.

A completely different incident happened later that day when I went to the electricity office to pay my last bill and arrange for transfer to the new occupant of the house. The young man at the counter asked me why I was leaving the country.

'I am going to retire in France,' I said.

'But why? This is a nice country and we like you to stay.'

'Thank you very much, but I have been here twenty years and I want to go home to Europe,' I countered.

'Well, if you are so determined… but please, when you get to France, raise a glass of wine to me!'

This coming from a Muslim in a "dry" country amazed me so that I laughed out loud. We parted the best of friends! I had had some difficult times in the Emirates, but one thing is sure: there never was a dull moment!

The Mitsubishi bus was duly transferred to the laundryman. The new owner glowed with pride when he showed me the laundry's name painted on the side: "Al Shabaab Lundry." It pleased me to know that the small sums I had paid throughout the years to have my linens washed and dresses dry-cleaned had contributed to his pride and joy. I did not have the heart to point out the spelling mistake in his logo.

My friends from the Dubai Natural History Group and the ALT combined efforts to give me a party, a farewell present and a "memory-book" to which many contributed pictures, letters and poems. Seventy people came to the dinner at the Dubai Country Club. I was happy to see all the well-known faces and knew I was going to miss many of them. Some I would see again in Europe when they came to visit me but others I might never see again.

In my speech I mentioned some of the things I would not miss (the construction sites, the pollution and traffic jams of Dubai as well as "sand in my shoes") and some of the things I would miss: my many friends, the six dirham shoarma-and-falafel dinners from the corner shop, having my laundry done for next to nothing, the silence of the mountains and the beauty of the wadis after rains.

I held a garage sale of the many things I was leaving behind. A parade of Indian and Filipino housemaids, with their boyfriends and husbands came to look at the goods. They drove hard bargains, and of course, I did not want to make things expensive for them. In the end I gave practically everything away for free. The only thing that annoyed me was when I discovered that my small camera, with which I had recorded the events of the day, had also been taken "for free".

Our flight was scheduled for midnight. The movers came on the day of the departure. I was still running around trying to supervise the printing of the cover for the flower guide. A phone call came from an Arab driver of the Sharjah court. He had something to deliver to me but could not find my place. I gave him directions but he kept calling back from various points around the suburb, where he had gotten lost. Finally I arranged to meet

274

him in front of a well-known and easy-to-find shopping mall. Even so it took him ages to turn up. I stood there waiting, impatient and annoyed, and a little bit anxious at what this delivery was about. Finally the man came driving up. He handed me a folio sized envelop and drove off again. Inside the brown covering envelop was another, of hand-made white carton with embossed black letters and coloured crest. The letter inside was a farewell letter from the sheikh:

Thanking you for all your sincere efforts in Our country. We assure you that you will always get from Our side all the facilities and cooperation to make you achieve your appreciated goals in the fields of wild life conservation and studies of plants in the U.A.E.

It was nice to know, but they were only words. Four years earlier I could have used the offered help...

When I returned to the house, my stuff had all been packed and was being transferred to the container on the moving van. As I stood with the supervisor watching the loading, the man glanced at my parked little van and asked: 'And how is the lundry business these days?'

It was time to go. Friends were driving me and the dogs to the airport in the bus, so I said good-bye to Tuan and Jameela at the gate. We were all crying, realising that we would possibly never see each other again. Sandy whined, the first time I had ever heard her whine. She must have felt that this was no ordinary trip.

At the airport I coaxed the dogs into their boxes, and locked the padlocks. The keys, leashes and customs papers all went in zip-lock bags taped to the top of the boxes. Sandy was nervous, wide-eyed and panting. Bas took it all in his stride.

Going through customs I was asked to take the dogs out again, as the customs officer wanted to check the boxes – for smuggled goods?

In my anxiety I lashed out at the poor man who was only doing his job. Finally I had the dogs back into their crates again, which were then loaded on a trolley to be taken to the cargo area by a porter.

I checked in, paid the dogs' fare and shouldered the heavy bag with valuables that I was carrying by hand. As I still had some time before departure, I walked slowly through the shops of the huge duty-free area. Suddenly I felt someone tugging at my sleeve. I looked around and there was the Indian porter who had taken the dogs away.

'Madam,' he said, smiling, 'I just wanted you to know that Sandy is fine!'

I stared at him in amazement. Not only had the man observed my anxiety and remembered my dog's name, he had gone to the trouble of tracking me down in this enormous shopping mall, just to make me a little happier. I could have hugged him. Here was one of those people I was going to miss most – the unassuming, gentle, thoughtful and considerate working people who made this country unique.

42

COQUELICOT THE CANTANKEROUS CAT

I did not sleep a wink on the plane. I was so exhausted that I was beyond sleep. It felt as if the flight would never end. France was still in darkness when we landed. I retrieved the dogs, who seemed to be all right, and made my way to the rental car area. No one checked the health certificates that had been so difficult to get.

In the feeble light of dawn the two dogs and I set out on the six-hour journey to the southwest of France. It was a nightmare. It rained practically the whole time, and the patter of drops combined with the swishing of the windshield wipers to lull me to sleep. I had to stop several times to drink double espressos and finally parked in a recreation area to take a nap. The dogs were good as gold, enjoying their small walks around parking lots and catching up on sleep during the drive. Late in the afternoon we drove up the sweeping path to my house, our new home.

It took me three months to really get over the fatigue that had accumulated during the last stressful months in Dubai. It was a relief to be able to go back to bed whenever I felt tired, no matter the time of day. The dogs loved their new place. Of course the old smells were there, particularly after the container with goods from Dubai arrived. But they were also intrigued by the new smells of the French countryside. The desert has few smells, apart from that of small rodents and dead animals. Here there were exciting little animals to be chased, holes to be dug to find moles or mice, herbs were everywhere, and the perfume of spring blossoms pervaded the air.

One of the neighbours had a litter of kittens and I arranged to have one of them at two weeks of age, so I could hand rear it and thus prevent trouble with my cat-murdering Bas. I chose a calico kitten that had light triangles above her eyes. Her fur was black streaked with ginger and grey, the colour of rusting wrought iron, or as a friend said: 'It looks as if a painter has wiped all his brushes on her.'

Her nose and chin were pitch black on the left, exactly up to the midline and rusty brown on the right. Bas took his task as kitten minder seriously again and the kitten grew up considering herself to be a dog.

I named her Coquelicot, having just learned that this is the French word for poppy. (I always used the name "poppy", which is Dutch for "little doll" as a term of endearment for all my animals). Unfortunately, Coquelicot decided that she did not like her name. She only came if and when you called Basje and you could chase her away by just mentioning her French name.

In the winter she would come for a cuddle in my wool-covered arms, snuggling her nose into the soft textile and giving me rather painful acupuncture massages. Whenever I felt I had had enough and needed the use of my arms again, all I had to do was to whisper endearments interspersed with her name into her ears. At the second mention of Coquelicot her tail would start whipping back and forth, at the third mention a deep growl would rumble in her little throat and if you persisted, she'd jump up and leave in a huff.

She was the most cantankerous cat I have ever known. Even the vet who sterilised her, said afterwards: 'Oh la la, quel tempérament!'

She liked gardening best. Several times she gave me a near heart attack when she had hidden in a bush near where I was weeding. When I reached for a bit of grass suddenly something small and furry would jump out and hit my hand. Then the whole cat would come rolling out of the bush, attacking my gloved (thank God!) hands with her sharp claws before prancing off in sideways jumps with stiff legs and an arched back. She may not have been cuddly, but she did make me laugh!

Strangely Bas did not care for her much after she outgrew the kitten phase. It was Sandy that sought her company, gave her a warm embrace for naps and tolerated her games. Up till then I had thought that dogs either liked cats or didn't, but now it seemed that they liked certain cats and not just any cat.

Every morning Coquelicot would groom Sandy's face, as she lay watching me having breakfast. The little cat sat next to her long nose and licked every hair of it. If Sandy lifted her head during this process, the cat's paw would shoot out and hit her nose, pressing her snout back to the floor so she could finish her job.

Sandy seemed to have taken a new lease on life. She had many health problems by now but it did not prevent her from having a good time. She could no longer jump into or out of the car and as she was too heavy to lift, I constructed a ramp from a large plank with a coconut fibre mat nailed to the surface. Carrying the heavy plank from the boot to the door and back four to eight times a day kept me in good form. She participated in our half-hour walks with stiff arthritic legs, oblivious to traffic because of her deafness. I soon learned to find dead-end roads and forest paths. She had been incontinent for quite a while now and at retirement age I found myself shopping for Pampers for the first time in my life. From these I removed the elastic bits after which I taped the pampers to her mat, marvelling at the amazing ability of the material to absorb liquid. Whenever a Pamper showed swelling, I just removed it and taped on a replacement. It worked fine!

Bas' enjoyment of our paradise was rudely disturbed when the hunting season came around. In France the worst shooting occurs from October to December when hunters shoot migrating pigeons from elaborate hides in the forests. That first autumn I discovered that one of those hides was only 150 metres away from my house on the other side of the valley. On weekends it felt as if I was in war zone. Bas was terrified. His behaviour changed completely. He hid in the darkest corner of the house and only dared to go outside after nightfall. Although he still enjoyed car rides, he did not dare walk in front of the house to the garage. Fortunately the garage was in the barn that had a door to the guest room. If I opened the guest room door, the door to the barn and the car door, I could persuade Bas to make a run for it. However, he would no longer leave the car for countryside walks. If we walked around in a village he was okay. Apparently he had figured out that buildings provided cover. In itself this was remarkable, for I am sure he had no concept of bullets or that hiding behind something might prevent something dreadful. If he heard a gunshot somewhere in the open, he would seek cover between my legs.

Every year on 1 March the hunting season ends. During the early months of the year the shooting is usually much less and many days can pass without a single shot being heard. This made no difference to Bas. He still refused to come out of the car and stayed in the furthest corner of the backseat, shivering violently and yawning in fear if I tried to pull him out.

Every year on 1 March he jumped out of his own volition and enjoyed his walk as if he had never heard a gunshot in his life.

Even when he had become quite deaf, no longer reacting to gunshots or fireworks, he remained fearful during the hunting season, preferring town walks to walks in the wild. Thunderstorms still caused him to try and squeeze himself in the fifteen centimetre gap between my bed and the bedside table. It was probably the fall of atmospheric pressure that affected him. He became my infallible four-legged barometer, often predicting approaching storms long before there were any obvious signs, and often contrary to the weather forecast.

Coquelicot developed into a great hunter. Most of the wall lizards on the facade of my house became tail-less, many ending up dead in the hallway. Once the cat came in, yelling at the top of her voice. I rushed to the hallway to find out what had happened. There she sat, proudly looking at her catch – a metre long grass snake! At times she deposited her prey into the bath tub. Since this tub was chocolate brown and the bathroom was not brightly lit, I have stepped onto something large and cold which turned out to be a foot-long green lizard, or on something large and furry – a huge rat, probably caught in my neighbour's yard which is one of the messiest places I have ever seen. Mice and shrews were almost daily prey, the former being eaten completely, the latter never touched. For a while she hunted the horse-shoe nosed bats that lived in the roof of my house, but I scolded her strongly for doing that and since she was a smart cat, she gave up on that prey. I also scolded her when she brought in birds and often rescued ones that she was still trying to play with. I hated this endless play with her prey and was happy that Bas did not tolerate it either. Whenever he noticed it going on, he stepped in and killed the little victim with a quick bite.

Coquelicot never became a cosy cat. She remained a half-wild creature, using some of the comforts offered, but leading the independent life that cats enjoy.

43

ANOTHER NEW BEGINNING

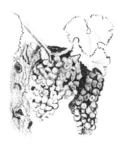

I am sitting on the grass next to one of the flowerbeds, weeding. The August sky arches dark blue above me, the sun caresses my back and crickets chirp in the tall grasses. Bas Chalas is busy digging for a mouse below the rosemary bush. Old Sandy lies nearby, dreaming in the hot sunshine. Coquelicot, the new kitten, jumps at my busy hands and then prances away, pretending to be scared.

Tomorrow is my sixtieth birthday – quite a milestone, but I have not mentioned it to anybody. I have a dinner invitation for tonight, but that is quite accidental I'm sure. Still, it'll be nice to go out and enjoy company.

A car slowly crunches up the driveway. Basje darts towards it in happy anticipation while Sandy gets up stiffly and gives her pleasant "hello there" bark. I scramble up to see who it is, trying to remember whether I was expecting a delivery of some kind. Then I recognise the face in the window – my brother! My jaw drops and unexpected emotion rises inside, moistening my eyes.

'I could not let a day like tomorrow pass without seeing you.' He smiles broadly, as he unfolds his long legs from the small car. It's a rental from the airport. We hug and laugh. What a wonderful surprise. Peter has been here before, but he has not yet seen the changes I have wrought since my arrival here four months earlier. I show him to his room and go to the kitchen to fetch a few cold beers. The terrace at the top of the garden is cool with the slight breeze that rattles the leaves of the palm tree. Peter sweeps an admiring glance over the garden that is a lot tidier than last time he was here. We have barely settled down when another car appears. I walk across the grass to meet whoever this is and now my surprise is even greater: Heidi and Anneke, two friends from Dubai.

'What the hell are *you* doing here?' It does not sound welcoming, but the ladies laugh, understanding my bewilderment.

'We thought that your birthday was a good excuse for a French visit.'

'How wonderful, how crazy! Did you drive all the way from Holland?'

'Yes, but in slow stages.'

Suddenly I remember my dinner invitation.

'This is so unexpected,' I say. 'Unfortunately I have a dinner invitation for tonight, and it is now too short notice to cancel that.'

Heidi smiles broadly: 'The dinner invitation is with us! We arranged for John and Pam to invite you, so that we would be sure that you'd be home and would have no other plans. We are staying with them in their B&B. They even made a reservation for us at "La Camelia". So relax and bring out more beer.'

I introduce them to my brother, who takes an immediate liking to extrovert Heidi and quieter Anneke. Heidi used to be on the Arabian Leopard Trust committee with me and her friend Anneke has a spectacle shop in Dubai. I am wearing the pair of glasses she made for me.

As we sit on the terrace looking out over the sloping garden to the forests in the distance, Anneke asks: 'Are you happy here?'

I don't need to ponder that. 'Yes, I am. Very happy. It took several months before I got rid of the stress and paranoia of Dubai, and now it feels like heaven here.'

'You look good,' says Peter, 'much better than when we visited you in May.'

'Well yes, you came when I had been here for less than a week. At that time I was still stressed and tired from the trip down here.'

'Your face has changed,' Heidi states. 'Apart from having lost weight, you seem very relaxed.'

'Who wouldn't be, surrounded by nature, in blissful silence, the only sounds I hear are birdsong and the clanging of some agricultural equipment of old Joseph next door. I thoroughly enjoy the lack of responsibility and all the free time – it is wonderful.'

'But what do you do all day?'

'There is plenty to do. I start the day slowly reading the French newspaper over breakfast. Every day I learn a few new words. I only had my school French of forty years ago to fall back on and the paper is a good way to learn modern French. I walk the dogs, work on the house, do the gardening and have French conversation lessons in the nearby town. I am getting to know some people here and in the summer there are many special events: concerts, markets, fairs, all interesting.'

Basje has heard the mention of walks and sidles up to me with expectant eyes. A strong rosemary smell clings to his thick woolly coat.

'You smell good enough to be barbecued,' I tell him.

He wags his tail happily. Anything for a little attention. Sandy has her head on Heidi's lap, expecting her share of the cheese cookies.

I scratch Basje's ears as he leans his soft body against my knees.

'People here grow very old, I have noticed. It must be the lack of stress and the sense of security – no crime, good medical care, active communities where people still know and care about each other. It will give me what I needed: a peaceful life that will be perfect for writing – which, after all, is why I came here!'

We have become a little quiet as the day makes the subtle change into a summer evening. I enjoy it when a friendship is good enough to allow for silences.

Life in France is good. Retirement is proving so busy that I cannot imagine ever having had time to work. With no servants to help me to take care of the house and the huge garden I am becoming much stronger and healthier. I am still fat, but not only do I know that fat legs don't matter, they even have a purpose now – to give cover to Bas when the hunt is on!

****

That day lies almost seven years back as I write this. In the mean time much has changed.

Sandy and Bas Chalas sleep their eternal sleep under the rose-bush and a new dog has taken their place. Nambi has died of a second stroke, a few years ago, in India. CC died just last year. I never saw him again, although I kept up contact by telephone. The ALT no longer exists and Arnold, our first leopard, died at the grand old age of sixteen. The little desert foxes joined Bas and Sandy in canine heaven. Even the house in Dubai has disap-peared, razed to the ground to make room for bigger villas that have not been built as yet, due to the economic crisis.

I had said I never wanted to go back to the Emirates, but then out of the blue came an invitation to attend the tenth anniversary celebration of the Wildlife Centre in Sharjah. I had not been invited to the opening, so somebody must have had a change of heart... and I did too. I accepted the invitation with gratitude and finally found closure to that period of my life that was tumultuous and difficult but never boring

GLOSSARY

abayah	black cloak worn by women
arta	woody shrub of the sandy desert
badgeer	wind tower
barasti	palm frond woven into wall or roof sections
barchan	sickle-shaped dune
bedu	desert dweller, often migratory
bulbul	local bird of the *Pycnonotidae* family, with blackbird-like song
burqa	face mask
dhow	fishing or trading boat, formerly with sails, nowadays with an engine
dhub	spiny-tailed agama or *Uromastyx acanthinurus*
dirham	currency of the UAE
farash	servant , coffeeboy
ghaf	indigenous tree in the UAE
godown	large storage building
hamour	fish of the *Epinephelus* family, cod-like
harm	saltbush
hummus	dip made of chick peas
jibali	mountain dwellers

kibbe	torpedo-shaped fried croquette stuffed with minced beef or lamb
majlis	meeting of the sheikh and his subjects, also reception room in house
mesquite	non-indigenous common tree, *Prosopis juliflora*
mezzeh	first course of a Lebanese meal, consisting of a number of varied dishes
moutabal	dip made of roasted aubergine
qahwa	coffee, often also a drink based on cardamom
sabkha	salt flat, both along the coast and between inland dunes
saluki	desert hunting dog, similar to but smaller than a greyhound
samosa	pastries with savory filling
suq	market
yella	an exhortation meaning 'come on' or 'move'
wadi	riverbed, mostly dry
wasta	influence, power linked to status, often called 'vitamin W'

Ingram Content Group UK Ltd.
Milton Keynes UK
UKHW042207080523
421401UK00001B/228

9 781906 852146